The
Second
Coming of
Steve
Jobs

Alan Deutschman

BROADWAY BOOKS   NEW YORK

The Second Coming of Steve Jobs

BROADWAY

Broadway Books titles may be purchased for business or promotional use or for special sales. For information, please write to: Special Markets Department, Random House, Inc., 1540 Broadway, New York, NY 10036.

BROADWAY BOOKS and its logo, a letter B bisected on the diagonal, are trademarks of Broadway Books, a division of Random House, Inc.

Visit our website at www.broadwaybooks.com

Library of Congress Cataloging-in-Publication Data

Deutschman, Alan, 1965–
The second coming of Steve Jobs / Alan Deutschman.
p. cm.
Includes index.
1. Apple Computer, Inc., 2. Jobs, Steven, 1955–   3. Computer industry—United States. 4. Corporate culture—United States. I. Title.

HD9696.2.A454 D48 2000
338.7'6100416'092—dc21
[B]
                                                          00-035796

FIRST EDITION

Designed by Lee Fukui

ISBN 0-7679-0432-X

00   01   02   03   04   10   9   8   7   6   5   4   3   2   1

To my parents and Katharine
And very special thanks to Suzanne Oaks and Suzanne Gluck

Contents

The
Second
Coming of
Steve
Jobs

Preface

It was all going to hell.

His followers were abandoning him. His friends no longer believed in him. The press, which had adored him for so long, now excoriated him. His money was running out. An awesome fortune—nearly squandered. He had made a hundred million in a handful of years, and now he was blowing it just as quickly on his failing startups. Within a few months, it could all be gone. Super rich and world famous in his twenties, and now, in his thirties, he was . . . what? A has-been? A guy who got lucky once but couldn't do it again? A fallen hero, the victim of his own hubris?

He had vowed to show that his precocious success at Apple wasn't a fluke, that the board had been wrong to kick him out, that he could launch another great company and once again change the world with a revolutionary machine. But after seven years of intense struggle, his new venture, Next, was one of the most conspicuous flops in American business. Apple sold more computers in a single day than Next sold in a full year. Next was bleeding money, *hemorrhaging* money, and seemingly *everyone* was walking away: his sales honcho, his hotshot marketing chief, even four of his five cofounders.

Steve himself was very close to quitting. He told a friend that he contemplated giving up entirely, abandoning his career. He was right at the edge—emotionally, psychologically, financially. He felt trapped. He dreaded the shame of walking away from a great public failure, the embarrassment of conceding that he *couldn't* do it again, that he couldn't go it alone, that maybe it *had* all been a fluke.

In a meeting at Next's headquarters on the shore of San Francisco Bay, he looked around at the besieged refugees of his thinned-out executive team and he told them, in a tone of bitterness and envy: "Everyone here can leave—except me."

■   ■   ■

ON FEBRUARY 10, 1993, Next announced that it was shutting its factory, killing its computer, and laying off most of its peo-

The
Second
Coming
of
Steve
Jobs

ple. The following day, a newspaper reporter went to Next's headquarters for a conversation with Steve. She asked him point-blank: "Does this mean that Next is a failure?"

Steve sunk his head into his folded arms on the table.

He rubbed his fingers into his temples.

"I don't want to do this interview," he said softly. "I don't want to do this interview." He seemed fragile, depressed, and withdrawn.

He got up and walked away.

For months he was emotionally distraught. He *had* failed, and it was devastating to him. Gut-wrenching. Humbling, even.

On May 25, 1993, Steve was scheduled to deliver the keynote address at the annual Next convention at San Francisco's Moscone Center. He was going to talk about his plans for resuscitating the company. That morning *The Wall Street Journal* ran a front-page story about him—a brutal put-down. It said that Steve had taken "a steep fall from a very lofty perch" and that he was "fighting to show that he still matters in the computer industry."

His public relations handler saw him as he prepared to go onstage in front of a thousand people.

He had read the article.

"It could have been worse," she said, trying to lighten the mood.

"Yeah," he shot back morosely. "If you were me."

■ ■ ■

THE NEXT LAYOFFS PROCEEDED BITTERLY. Three hundred people cleared out of headquarters. The place seemed like a wasteland. A bunch of salvagers and used-furniture dealers went to the Next factory for an auction of what was still left. They bid on hundreds of lots that were laid out on the barren cement floor. They bought everything on the cheap— the chairs, the trash cans, the paper shredders, all the surplus Next computers and laser printers and oversized monitors. It was weirdly reminiscent of the famous scene from *Citizen Kane* when the many possessions of the vanquished mogul are carted up and then either shipped away or burned in a great fire.

Steve's dream was being liquidated. He was at the nadir.

■   ■   ■

By the end of 1993, he had virtually disappeared from the public's consciousness. And then, only two years later, something happened that was sublimely bizarre. He suddenly reemerged in the spotlight: triumphant, vindicated, and far richer than ever before. His stunning redemption came from an unexpected source: it turned out that he owned *another* company, Pixar, which had struggled quietly for a decade. In November 1995, Pixar released the first full-length computer-animated feature film, *Toy Story*. The following week, Steve took Pixar public, and investors clamored to buy the shares. His 70 percent stake was suddenly worth more than a billion dollars. And then, only a year later, he returned to Apple, which during his long absence had suffered a desperate decline and began spiraling toward its demise. In the summer of 1997 he took the title of interim chief executive officer and became the company's unexpected savior. He propelled Apple's stock price from $13 a share to $118 a share in late 1999, raising the market valuation from less than $2 billion to almost $20 billion. It was an extraordinary resurgence.

On January 5, 2000, he stood at San Francisco's Moscone Center, where only a few years earlier he had agonized over the premature postmortem in *The Wall Street Journal*. This time, though, he was facing the crowd as a conquering hero.

He stalked the stage for a very long time—two hours and thirteen minutes. Who else, besides Fidel Castro, could command the attention of his troops for such a long oration? No one in American business was so hypnotic. No one was so charismatic. And so they sat there patiently, four thousand people waiting for the news. By now, they knew exactly what to expect from one of Steve's grand speeches. He always saved his biggest revelation for the very end. He created an unbearable sense of anticipation. And when he finally got around to it, he always dropped the bomb in the most casual way, as though it were an afterthought, as if he were oblivious to all the excitement.

"One last thing," he said nonchalantly. After two and a half years of hesitation and indecision, he was finally accepting the title of chief executive officer of Apple Computer.

The thousands rose and rejoiced. Wave after wave of applause resonated through the vast hall. They chanted his name like a mantra: "STEVE! STEVE! STEVE! STEVE!"

His attempt at stoical coolness finally gave way to a half-smile that betrayed his pride and then to a look of bashfulness at the unbridled commotion he had caused.

"Thank you, thank you," he said, and within seconds an eerie quiet was restored, as the faithful waited for more words from their leader.

"You guys are making me feel funny now," he said sheepishly, "because I . . ."

He was so emotional that he had to stop for a moment and regain his composure.

". . . because I get to come to work every day and work with the most talented people on the planet," he said. "It's the best job in the world."

■   ■   ■

AS THE YEAR 2000 BEGAN, Steve Jobs was adulated by a press corps that only a few years earlier had delighted in lambasting him. The old rap claimed that he was some kind of mystical visionary but he couldn't run a company—he wasn't a "manager." But now his photo appeared on the cover of the January 10th issue of *Business Week* for its story "The Top 25 Managers of the Year." The following week *Fortune*, which had once called him a "snake-oil salesman," put his smiling face on its cover with a headline exclaiming "Stevie Wonder!"

As he turned forty-five in February 2000, he was as legendary and celebrated as when he first became a pop-culture icon during the glory years of his twenties—maybe even more so. Still, for all the press coverage, it was hard to find a profile of Steve Jobs that went beyond the sycophantic and the smoothly superficial. His public image had become a cliché: the ex-hippie vegetarian, barefoot, in faded blue jeans and black mock turtleneck shirt, raging in his relentless and fiery passion for great technology and cool design. The legend was well entrenched, but it represented little more than a crude sketch. The man himself remained largely a mystery, and he liked it that way.

For nearly two decades he had refused the requests of writers who wanted to discuss his personal life in any sort of detail. In the late 1990s he exerted fierce control over the media coverage of his companies, Apple and Pixar, often walking out of interviews abruptly or refusing to cooperate with publications that hadn't proven their willingness to stick to his official version of his story. He met only sporadically with tough-minded journalists from newspapers like the *New York Times*, and he limited them to fleeting fifteen-minute sessions during which he would only talk about the latest product or service that he was promoting. He had the temerity to stand up a *Times* reporter. He stood up an entire PBS film crew. He walked out on *The Wall Street Journal* after its reporter asked him a single question. When he wanted to kill a *Wired* cover story about him, he called the executives of *Wired*'s owner, the Condé Nast publishing company, with the implicit threat of withdrawing Apple's advertisements from its many magazines. And still the press treated him with awe.

He succeeded in becoming the Jackie Kennedy Onassis of business and technology—a figure who was ubiquitous as a symbol of his times but little known as a human being.

When I set out on interviews for this book, I was looking for Steve Jobs the person rather than Steve Jobs the icon. He is an exceptional person, to be sure, but I wanted to get at what made him exceptional as well as what made him real. I set out to discover the deep sources of his character and motivation. I strived to find where he got his unusual ideas about leadership, management, and the creative process. I tried to trace how he had been changed by his years of wealth and celebrity and by his years of struggle and failure.

Between February 1999 and February 2000, I talked with nearly one hundred people who have known and worked with Steve Jobs, including many of his closest colleagues and friends from the various stages of his life. Drawing primarily on their recollections, anecdotes, and insights, I have focused this narrative on Steve's long comeback, his so-called second coming. The story begins in the summer of 1985, when he was exiled from Apple, and goes through early 2000, when he officially became Apple's chief executive.

Since Steve Jobs is the head of a movie studio, it seems oddly appropriate that his real-life scenario fits so neatly into the "three-act" structure of a classic Hollywood screenplay. In Act One, the protagonist sets forth on his quest, in this case a bid for vindication after an embarrassing fall. Act Two brings the dramatic complications: our hero struggles, he fails, he comes perilously close to the edge. In Act Three, he overcomes the formidable forces aligned against him and achieves his goal, though in a way that he could never have anticipated when the story began. . . .

—Alan Deutschman
San Francisco
February 2000

Andrea "Andy" Cunningham was so tired when she got home from work that she went to sleep without checking her answering machine. The following morning, around eight-thirty, she played the tape. The message was short and cryptic: Andy should show up at Steve's house at 10 A.M. for a press conference about his new company, Next.

The idea troubled her. Andy was a public relations consultant, one of the shrewdest and most insightful in the technology business. She wasn't summoned to press conferences as a last-minute thought. She was supposed to be the one who orchestrated the events following weeks of careful preparation, reflection, brainstorming, and strategizing, after thoroughly thinking through the message and exactly how it would be conveyed.

She didn't even know where Steve lived. And besides, he wasn't even her client.

She called around to get the address, then drove the five minutes from Palo Alto to the village of Woodside, which lay in the foothills of the Santa Cruz Mountains. It was just beyond the Stanford campus. Woodside was not far from the banal concrete sprawl of Silicon Valley but at least it *felt* isolated and remote, with narrow winding country roads and dozens of bridle paths but no street lamps or sidewalks. Traditionally favored by hillbillies and folksingers, it had more recently become home to a few centimillionaires, who made their money by promoting futuristic visions but, ironically, preferred to live in a semirural hamlet that evoked the romance of a lost era.

A few minutes before ten, Andy pulled through the wrought-iron gate to Steve's house. The gravel driveway was crowded with parked cars. She beheld a sprawling, dilapidated robber baron mansion in the Spanish mission style, that numbingly ubiquitous cliché of California architecture, with the de rigueur stucco walls and the sloping red adobe roofs, like tens of thousands of little anonymous tract houses throughout the valley's brutally cramped suburbs. The difference was that this crumbling monstrosity was large enough to be a real eighteenth-century Spanish mission. It had enough space for an entire order of monks to go about their daily routines.

She passed through the grand arched entrance loggia and

came to a huge cavernous living room. Standing around, idle, restless, gossiping among themselves, were twenty reporters Andy knew well. The *Business Week* correspondent. The *Newsweek* writer. The reporter from *USA Today*. They were shifting uncomfortably from foot to foot because there was simply nowhere to sit other than the cold wooden floorboards. The living room was devoid of furniture, barren, austere, un-welcoming, a hollow decaying shell like the rest of the whole empty spooky house, the maze of echo chambers where Steve lived as a solitary bachelor. The closest thing to furnishings was a clear plastic case with an architect's carefully crafted and scaled topographical model of the property—just the lush pure mountainside land, not the presumptuous robber baron manse that Steve had never gotten around to demolishing.

Andy made her way into the kitchen. Still no furniture at all, no tables or chairs, just a few computers strewn across the floor and another bunch of people huddled together. Andy recognized them as refugees from Apple. They had worked with her on the launch of the Macintosh the previous year, in January 1984. Now they were the cofounders of Steve's new company, which was going to do . . . who knew what it would do?

Steve was on his feet, talking about what he was going to tell the reporters.

Screw John Sculley, he was going to say. *Screw him!*

Screw the Apple board!

We are going to change the world!

Andy was appalled. There was no *news* for the putative news conference. There was only Steve's impulse to express his anger, his rage, his raw hurt, his need for vindication and heal-ing and honor. He wanted to flail out against the injustices and betrayals he had suffered. It was understandable. It was *human*. But this wasn't the way to do it, not the time or the place. You don't summon the cynical elite of the West Coast press corps, with their notebooks open and their cassette tapes rolling, to participate in some kind of group therapy session. This wasn't an encounter group or primal scream or gestalt or est, it wasn't some kind of 1970s Californian human-potential seminar; this was *business*.

At first Andy didn't recognize the man sitting on the floor right beside Steve, though she quickly surmised that this was Steve's new lawyer. He was visibly starstruck, comically awed, his mouth agape, his eyes glazed by the proximity to celebrity. He clearly wasn't in the proper state of mind to offer cautious advice. No one was telling Steve what should have been obvious, a matter of the simplest common sense. No one would confront the legendary figure and play the necessary role of tough naysayer.

Well, Andy thought, I have nothing to lose. I haven't even signed the account.

"I don't think this is a good idea," she told them flatly. Apple was suing Steve and his apostates, accusing them of stealing secrets. And they had no legal strategy for defending themselves. It wasn't going to help win public opinion if Steve treated the reporters to an impassioned tirade against Apple.

She looked at Steve with seeming disbelief at his rashness and thoughtlessness.

"Why did you let all these journalists know where you live?" she wondered aloud.

■　　■　　■

IN THE SUMMER OF 1985, when Steve Jobs was stripped of power at the company he cofounded, when his office was moved to a vacant building he called Siberia, he didn't know what to do. He was thirty years old, and he owned more than

$100 million worth of Apple stock. He didn't have to work, not for the money, at least, and not for the fame. He had appeared on the cover of *Time* and had accepted the National Technology Award at the White House. His niche in economic history was already secure as the preeminent popularizer of the personal computer. His mention in American cultural history was certain as well. In an era when commerce was equated with conformity, when industry was seen as the staid and soulless province of balding older men, he was an unprecedented phenom. He was a businessman posing as an idealistic revolutionary, striving for social change. He was a capitalist who appropriated the rhetoric of the commune where he had lived. He was a barefooted chairman of the board who took his girlfriend to Grateful Dead concerts and quoted an entire verse of Bob Dylan lyrics at a shareholders meeting. He was a "young industrialist," as he preferred to call himself, an epithet that sounded delightfully unlikely. He was a pop-culture icon, a media hero, a role model, a sex symbol, and teen heartthrob.

Born at the midpoint of the postwar baby boom, Steve Jobs was one of the most enduring symbols of his generation, reflecting all of its virtues and failings and self-delusions. He was the figure who turned business leaders into rock stars, objects of public fascination. And like so many actual rock stars, he could have quit, or faded, after a brief, spectacular career.

Steve told his closest friends that he was thinking of cultivating his garden. He wasn't alluding to Voltaire's famous line. He didn't mean it in the metaphorical sense of exploring his own mind and spirit rather than trying to change the world. He had *already* explored his mind and spirit in a whirlwind of eclectic experimentation in his late teens and early twenties, when he dabbled in bizarre diets and Eastern mystics and rural communes and primal screams and hallucinogenic drugs. For that matter, he had *already* changed the world. No, he was thinking of cultivating his garden in the *literal* sense: he would devote his extraordinary intelligence and his frighteningly intense energy and his unremitting aesthetic perfectionism to planting flowers on his eight-acre plot. Rather than the finale of *Candide*, his scenario was more like a chapter from *Atlas Shrugged*, in which the world's most brilliant industrialists drop out of a society that scorns their genius; as a weird act of protest, they apply their heroic talents to conspicuously trivial endeavors. Perhaps a select few friends would eventually have the privilege of visiting his private garden, and they would think: What artistry! What unique creativity! If only those damn fools had let him keep on making truly useful things for the good of millions upon millions of people!

At times he would lay around the house, abject, depressed. One of his closest colleagues, Mike Murray, feared that Steve would kill himself. When Steve emerged from his funk, he pondered all kinds of escapist notions. He thought of asking NASA if he could fly on one of the space shuttles, maybe as soon as the following year on the *Challenger*. He visited Moscow, where he suspected that the television repairman who came to his hotel room unsolicited, for no apparent reason, was actually some kind of spy. Nonetheless, he considered living in Cold War Russia and promoting computers in the Soviet schools for Mikhail Gorbachev. He talked with shadowy behind-the-scenes political consultants about making a bid for a Senate seat in California. He approached the architect I. M. Pei with the idea of building a perfect new house on the Woodside property once he tore down the robber baron embarrassment. They got as far as making the scale model of the land. Impulsively he ran away to Europe, bicycled through Tuscany. He telephoned one of his loyalists at Apple, Susan Barnes, and said that he had to cancel their dinner plans for that evening because he wasn't in California, he was in the south of France, and he was thinking about staying and living there as an expatriate, assuming the pose of an alienated artist. Barnes listened and cried.

He suffered his midlife crisis at thirty and compressed it into three months, an overachiever even at personal trauma. He spent the summer flirting with romanticized notions of self-imposed exile, but ultimately he wasn't able to resist the siren of public life. For all his accomplishments and fame, he still hadn't fully proven himself, not to his own satisfaction and not to the world.

17
Next

No one denied that Apple's rise was aided immeasurably by his astonishing energy and persuasiveness and charisma and *chutzpah* (a word that he loved). And it was *his* personality that created the company's culture and mystique. *He* was the media sensation. But from the early days Apple was actually run by older and more experienced businessmen, who were put in place first by the financial backers and later by the board of directors. Steve was allowed to head a renegade division, not the whole company. He never had the authority to approve expenditures of more than $250,000. He could buy a Bösendorfer grand piano for his team of engineers or fill up the office refrigerators with freshly squeezed fruit juices, but he couldn't build a new factory or create a new computer without arduously lobbying for approval from other men. When he had wanted to try something spectacular, like risking $20 million in an effort to build a radically flat computer screen, the Apple board lacked confidence in him and rejected his plans.

By 1985 he hadn't proven that he could thrive as the chief executive officer of an important corporation. Nor had he proven that he could repeat his initial success and show the skeptics that it wasn't just a lucky accident of time and place, a once-in-a-lifetime historical fluke. His latest creation, the Macintosh, was greatly admired by the technocracy and attracted a small cultlike following on college campuses, but it seemed doomed to remain a commercial flop. Apple had optimistically projected sales of fifty thousand Macintoshes a month in 1985. The actual sales fell to five thousand a month, a pitifully low figure, an *embarrassment*. Wall Street blamed Steve for the financial failure of the ballyhooed machine; when he was ousted, the stock price rose. To the outside world it looked as though he had been fired by John Sculley, the executive he had recruited to run Apple. Their falling-out was incredibly painful, a "divorce," as Steve told his friends. Before the split he had never felt so close to another person as he had felt to John, he said, but now he understood what divorce must feel like.

The rift with Apple's board member Mike Markkula was also wrenching. Markkula had been something of a father figure to him. When Apple was still in Steve's garage, Markkula had invested his own money in the company and helped write the business plan. Now, Steve told his friends, Markkula was bullying him, trying to scare him off, threatening to put him in prison for leaving Apple and supposedly stealing its technology.

Steve needed vindication. He openly ached to show that his vision of the future of computing was correct, that Apple's board was wrong for pushing him aside, that he could change the world *again*. He left Apple with his cool hundred million, his "fuck-you money," an expression he loved. And now, in September 1985, with the press assembled in his living room, he had the uncensored raw urge to say "fuck you" to Apple.

Andy Cunningham entered his kitchen and talked him out of it.

For her good advice, she received the most dubious of rewards: *she* was the one who had to go out there and try to tell the impatient reporters that the speech was off.

■ ■ ■

APPLE COMPUTER BEGAN in a tract house; Next Computer was founded in a mansion a few miles away. In the early days of Apple, Steve would play Bob Dylan tunes on his guitar in the backyard while his mother, Clara, washed his baby nephew in the kitchen sink. They had the luxury of beginning in obscurity. During the early days of Next, in September 1985, his co-founders lounged on the lawn behind the mansion, reading about themselves in *Newsweek*. They were on the cover of the Asian edition, which they'd had specially delivered to the house. They had been slated for the American cover, too, but they were knocked off by the devastating 8.1-magnitude earthquake in Mexico.

On the early autumn days they would get some sun and then go back inside and dial away at their Rolodexes. During the daytime they would venture out without Steve to look at office spaces. This way the landlords wouldn't recognize their fabulously wealthy proprietor and raise the lease rates. They had to sneak Steve in at night to see the buildings. They considered making a deal with the Catholic archdiocese to take over an abandoned monastery not far from the Apple campus. The building, with its gracefully proportioned bell tower rising above a straw-colored pasture, looked like it belonged in Tuscany. Working there would have been a nicely ironic twist in Steve's personal history, since he had thought of entering a monastery (albeit a Zen Buddhist one in Japan) instead of starting Apple. Finally they rented a small structure of concrete and glass on Deer Park Road, a secluded stretch of the voluptuous Stanford hills. They would be surrounded by the scenic undeveloped open land where Steve loved to walk, where he had spent hour after hour walking with Sculley. In the divorce Sculley kept Apple, but Steve was claiming possession of the Stanford hills.

One day Steve was driving in his black Porsche with his finance executive, Susan Barnes, the only woman among the six cofounders. She had a master's of business administration from Wharton, the top school for finance. She was in her late twenties, smart and even-tempered and quietly self-confident, which were all advantages in dealing with such a fierce-willed, emotional boss.

What bank should we use? Steve asked. They didn't need money, because Steve was putting in $7 million, but they had to set up a payroll account and print their checks.

Let's call Citicorp, she said. That's a big, solid, fancy bank.

So she lifted Steve's cellular phone and dialed the number for Citicorp. The call was patched through to a random bank officer, one of hundreds. Steve took the phone.

"This is Steve Jobs."

The banker was utterly incredulous. Steve Jobs! Coincidentally, at that moment he had his newspaper open to an article about Steve Jobs leaving Apple and starting a new computer company. And now some guy was on the phone saying *he* was Steve Jobs. It had to be a practical joke. It had to be one of his buddies trying to get an easy laugh.

The banker decided to have some harmless fun toying with the obvious prankster.

Sorry, Mr. Jobs, but we don't handle startups, he said dismissively. Call us back when you're a real company, when you've got at least $50 million in annual revenues.

The phone went dead.

Steve told Susan that he knew what to do. He called the headquarters of Bank of America and asked for an appointment with the *president*. Steve always believed in starting at the top. And with his extraordinary fame, he *could* start at the top. The head of the nation's largest bank was happy to see him, even ostensibly for the most comically trivial of matters,

something they could have easily handled at any local suburban branch office.

Steve's fame opened nearly all doors for him, and he wasn't
at all reluctant to take advantage of it. At Apple, he had liked to
personally deliver Macintoshes to other celebrities he had long
admired. That was his calling card for meeting the likes of
Mick Jagger and Yoko Ono and Andy Warhol. Apple had a
philanthropic program, called The Kids Can't Wait, that donated computers to public schools, but the inside joke was that
Steve ran a rival program, "The Stars Can't Wait." He paid
millions for the top two floors of one of the towers of Manhattan's San Remo, the great art deco apartment house on Central
Park West, and he made periodic pilgrimages to New York to
go out with accomplished actresses, artists, and writers. On his
Gotham excursions he dated Maya Lin, the designer of the
Vietnam Veterans Memorial in Washington, D.C., and saw
Lisa Birnbaum, the best-selling author of *The Preppy Handbook*.
At one point a friend wanted to set him up on a blind date with
a downstairs neighbor from the San Remo, a woman named
Diane, so Steve called her, not even knowing her surname.
They chatted amiably for a while, then Steve suggested a time
and place for their rendezvous.

"Okey dokey," she said.

The way she said it, so cheerful and flippant and charm-
ingly goofy, was oddly familiar. It sounded a lot like . . . Annie
Hall, the character from the Woody Allen movie.

"Diane, what's your last name?" he asked.

"Keaton."

Fame facilitated his social life but it often complicated his
work. He had a love-hate relationship with his own celebrity.
When he started Next, he wanted to put together a team of
people who were comfortable with him, people who weren't
awed or intimidated by his presence, people who didn't believe

his mythology, people who wouldn't treat him as an icon. When Susan Barnes invited partners from major law firms and accounting firms to visit Next and pitch for its business, Steve subjected them to a cruel, quick, calculated test. He would show up wearing a suit, as though he were a respectable businessman, sit across the conference table, and ask good-naturedly to see their client list. When they handed it over, he would hardly glance at the printout before he crudely insulted them.

"This is a lousy client list," he would say.

In almost every case, the sycophantic pitchmen would acquiesce immediately, confessing sheepishly that Steve was right, their client list was lousy. But one accounting partner from Peat Marwick was so incensed by the arrogant, cavalier, cursory treatment that he reacted furiously, looking as though he would throw a knockout punch at Steve. That's what Steve deserved for his impertinent behavior. And that's exactly what he was hoping for. That was the kind of outside counsel he wanted to hire.

Susan Barnes and Dan'l Lewin, Next's marketing executive, had worked with him at Apple. He knew from experience that they had the self-assurance to stand up to him when necessary. But even they had trouble accepting his happy conceit that he was really one of them, a peer.

For Dan'l, a telling moment came one morning soon after they moved to Deer Park Road. He arrived at the office around six, wearing blue jeans, since they all preferred casual dress for the days when they didn't have to represent the company in outside meetings. A few hours later Steve showed up in one of his elegant Brioni suits from Wilkes Bashford, the most expensive and highly regarded men's clothing store in San Francisco.

"Hey, we're going to the bank today," Steve said enthusiastically, as if he were a schoolchild opening his very first savings account. They had to drive up to the city to meet with the head of Bank of America in the hulking dark tower that dominated the skyline.

"I'll go home and put on a suit," Dan'l said.

"Go to my house and get one of my suits," Steve insisted.

Dan'l knew that Steve's clothes wouldn't fit him. Dan'l had been a swimming star at Princeton, and he had a swimmer's physique that required custom tailoring. He was six two and weighed 200 pounds with a broad 46-inch chest but a disproportionately slender 32-inch waist. He needed unusually large arm holes in his jackets to accommodate his big shoulders. Steve was shorter and smaller, around six feet and 160 pounds. They simply couldn't swap a suit. And besides, Dan'l's house wasn't far from the office. But then Dan'l had an insight. He grasped the unconscious subtext of Steve's friendly offhand gesture. Steve was looking at him and thinking: I'm just like you; I'm one of the guys. Steve was treating him like a brother, implying: We're the same.

But they weren't the same, Dan'l knew. Steve was the kid with all the marbles.

Steve would often talk about "the other Steve," the character portrayed by the press, as if it were a purely fictional creation. He would say that he only kept from going insane by thinking of his media image as someone else entirely, another person. He sometimes yearned for his lost anonymity. Once, as he walked through Palo Alto, he rushed to help a woman who had fallen on the street. As he reached out his hand, she recognized him and exclaimed: "Oh my God, it's Steve Jobs!" The episode made him deeply upset. He hated calling attention to himself. He disliked it when the travel agency would send aides in conspicuous yellow jackets to meet him at the airport gate, blatantly signaling that he was some kind of very important person. He began to enjoy walking through the streets of New

York City for the surprising anonymity they conferred, if only for an hour or two at a time.

Steve could be charmed and amused when people failed to recognize him. Once at the video rental store in Woodside, the clerk had a newspaper open to a story about Steve Jobs. When the real-life Steve stepped up to pay for a video, he pointed out the article.

"Yeah, he's a customer here," the clerk said nonchalantly.

Then he added: "You sort of look like him, but he's *much* better looking."

■   ■   ■

IF THE FAME WAS BOTH a blessing and a curse, so was the money.

In the earliest days of Apple, Steve was the ideal person for the challenge of starting a business with hardly any money or experience and few connections. It was a struggle that would reward his scrappy ingenuity and his shocking brazenness. But at Next, the situation was entirely different. Now he had seemingly limitless amounts of his own money to invest. He quickly sold $70 million of his Apple stock, and Susan Barnes put it into short-term Treasury bonds, safe and liquid, ready for him whenever he needed capital. And he had as much time as he wanted to take. His legend ensured that he could recruit people who were exceptionally talented and motivated. His access to the media was unrivaled by any other entrepreneur. This time he had every possible advantage. Paradoxically, that was the hardest obstacle. His personality thrived on scarcity and adversity but struggled with abundance and ease. Obsessive perfectionists are in constant need of severe constraints and hard deadlines. They need strict budgets. They need limits that force them to choose, commit, and move on. Otherwise they can be paralyzed by their powers of self-criticism or, alternately, overwhelmed by the excess of promising ideas that they can envision.

At Apple, his background had prepared him perfectly for running a garage startup deprived of resources. He initially discovered his talent for making money out of nothing when he was growing up in a family that wasn't poor but never had very much. They didn't own a color television. His mother, Clara, had to baby-sit other people's children to pay for Steve's swimming lessons when he was five years old. Later she worked part-time as a payroll clerk. His father, Paul, was an earnest journeyman, a high school dropout who worked at various times as a machinist, a used-car salesman, a repo man, a real estate broker. Paul Jobs moonlighted by buying old cars and fixing them up. He always had incisive judgment about finding value and getting good deals. He'd muck around junkyards looking for parts he could purchase cheaply. But when it came to selling, Paul had a quaint sense of honor and fairness that bespoke his Midwestern background. He was a good person but not necessarily a very good business person. He didn't ask for more than he thought his work had been worth. That high-minded ethic was not assimilated by his adopted son. Steve had his father's sense for shrewd buying but combined it with a more opportunistic approach to selling. Even as a teenager Steve had the soul and the skill of a dealmaker. If his father was a self-consciously fair trader, Steve was more in the image of a Persian-rug merchant. His father had a cynical, dour outlook, but Steve was an optimist. He would go to a yard sale, buy a stereo receiver, fix the headphone jack, and then hawk it for a substantial profit. His closest friend in high school, Bill Fernandez, lusted for the great TEAC reel-to-reel tape deck that Steve acquired through his artful trading. Bill realized even then that Steve could become a good business-man. Steve knew it too. In tenth grade he told his girlfriend Chris-Ann that he was going to be a millionaire.

Steve even talked his way into going to college for free. His parents couldn't afford to send him to an expensive private school, but he went ahead nonetheless and enrolled in one, willful and defiant and unafraid to improvise his way through an impossible situation. Dan Kottke, who became Steve's best friend at Reed College, recalls that Steve's adventure in higher education was something of a scam, a boondoggle. By the time Dan met Steve in October of their freshman year, only a month into their first semester on campus, Steve had already dropped out. More accurately, he had never really *dropped in*. He enrolled in courses and moved into the dorms but he never paid for tuition, room, and board. When the bill for thousands of dollars was thirty days overdue, the money wasn't there. Steve's parents weren't paying. Steve didn't have the funds. So the college couldn't recognize him officially as an undergradu-ate. But Steve had already established an easy rapport with the dean of students, Jack Dudman. He convinced the dean to let him audit classes and live in the dorms for *free*. There were plenty of empty dorm rooms. Many students dropped out of Reed during their first year because of the academic rigor. Other prestigious colleges had responded to the loose permis-siveness of the sixties by easing their standards, but Reed re-mained uncompromisingly intellectual. It wasn't surprising when freshman transferred to other schools with shorter read-ing lists and lower expectations. Steve wasn't dropping out to escape the college and its intellectual life. He was finding a cre-ative way to be part of it.

He freeloaded and scrounged out of necessity but he learned that he was good at it. He found free sources of vege-tarian food at the local Hare Krishna temple and the All-One

Farm commune. For an impromptu getaway he and Dan hitchhiked to the Oregon coast and spent the night sleeping on the beach. The teenage bohemians didn't figure on the shifting of the tides. In the morning they woke up drenched in cold salty seawater. At least the vacation was free. When Steve wanted to go to Mexico, he hung out for a while at the Portland airport and talked his way onto a private plane that got him as far as San Diego.

He could talk his way into almost anything.

Steve knew how to get along without money, but then the money came and he didn't know what to do with it. The money came so suddenly. He went from impoverished freeloader to instant millionaire in a frighteningly short time. At twenty-one he was a boomerang kid living rent-free in his old bedroom in his parents' house. When Apple was incorporated in January 1977, the month before he turned twenty-two he had almost nothing. Then the Apple II began selling. "When I was twenty-three, I had a net worth of one million dollars," Steve later told a reporter. "At twenty-four it was over ten million dollars, and at twenty-five it was over a hundred million dollars." The figures were accurate. But he remained ambivalent about his windfall, uncomfortable with it, uncertain and self-conscious and insecure about how to spend it. His conflicted attitude toward money was confusing to his friends. When he had traveled to India with Dan Kottke, they often talked about their shared belief in renouncing materialism. Later Dan was astonished when Steve's high school girlfriend Chris-Ann mentioned Steve's teenage aspirations of becoming a millionaire. Dan realized that Steve was a complex personality who kept aspects of himself hidden even from the few people who knew him well.

As the millions accumulated, as his wealth increased exponentially each year, his official residence was a cheap comical

crash pad of a house that he shared with Dan and Chris-Ann.
Dan named the property Rancho Suburbio as an ironic appreciation of its consummate shag-carpeted tract-house tackiness.
He filled the spare bedroom with foam packing material and
invited the neighborhood kids to jump around in it as though it
were an amusement park attraction. They had picked the location because it was a short walk from Apple's office. (Curiously,
it was down the street from Steve's alma mater, Homestead
High School, where he had been something of a loner.) Steve
moved in with his meditation cushion but he was rarely there.
For two years he really lived in a rickety little wooden shack in
the Santa Cruz Mountains with his new girlfriend, Barbara
Jasinski, an astonishingly attractive Eurasian who worked for
Apple's public relations firm. He didn't even own the shack; it
belonged to her. It had the Zen virtues of simplicity and mod-
esty. Steve would occasionally drop by Rancho Suburbio to
pick up a change of clothing. On his way out he would glance
around and pause to remark good-naturedly: "What a dump!"

Dan had grown up in a well-off family in New York's
Westchester County, and he could enjoy the campiness of the
Rancho, but Steve had grown up poorer, and he reacted
against the down-market banality of the suburbs. Following
the example of his role models, the older hippies, he romanticized the purity of the country, the lush damp redwood forests
in the hills, but at the same time he aspired, instinctively but
vaguely, to the sophisticated, refined tastes of the urban elite.
His money was new but his mindset was never nouveau riche.
He rejected wastefulness and ostentation. From the early days
at Apple he had a fascination with design and an innate sense
of the importance of aesthetics. He had wanted Apple's computers to come in cases made from koa, a beautiful blond
wood. He possessed a few koa boxes and loved their appearance. But the wood proved far too costly, and the Apple I was

sold without a case. For the Apple II he was forced to settle on plastic cases but he insisted that the edges be rounded and sleek, and the computer's appealing look was an important factor in its unprecedented commercial success.

In 1977 Apple's headquarters was in the same building in Cupertino as the regional sales office for Sony, a company that was known for good design. The Sony suite was where Steve met Dan'l Lewin, who had recently graduated from Princeton and was working as a field salesman. Steve would come over and look with great interest at Sony's marketing materials, its letterheads and logos and graphics, the paraphernalia of its corporate identity. He would *feel* the paper stock to get a sense of its weight and quality. He had an obsession with the visual and the physical, but his judgment was not yet highly developed. He had the impulse for aesthetic perfectionism, but not the unshakable self-confidence that he needed to achieve it. He had the money and the desire but not the knowledge or the skill.

He relied on ad hoc gurus for aesthetic guidance. One of his closest friends from college, Elizabeth Holmes, had minored in art history, and she had showed him a book about the artist Maxfield Parrish, whose work she admired. He decided to purchase a Parrish. It turned out that a well-known collector lived not far away in northern California, in Atherton, an exclusive old-money enclave. Gary Atherton was the scion of the family that had given its name to the town. He owned about twenty Parrish canvases, though he hadn't expected that a twenty-four-year-old kid would come trying to buy one. Where was he going to put it? Steve had just bought a house in Los Gatos, a prosperous village not far from Barbara's shabby hill shack. He needed to remodel. Could Gary suggest someone?

Gary sent over a man named Jamis MacNiven, a somewhat

older hippie who was as inexperienced as a building contractor and interior designer as Steve was at being a millionaire and tycoon. MacNiven had bluffed his way into contracting, relying on his offbeat charm to distinguish himself from others who had real credentials. He was a gleeful jokester, irreverent and gregarious, which helped conceal the inconvenient fact that he didn't know very much about his craft. Gary Atherton's estate in Atherton had been his first job and so far his only job. "I went to fix a doorknob and stayed for three years," he recalls.

Jamis went to call on Steve at the address in Los Gatos. He drove through a hillside development to find an old plain stucco house without architectural distinction. The yard was half dead. It was a kind of nothing house, he thought. It certainly wasn't a showplace.

There was no furniture. Steve and Barbara had moved in with just a mattress flopped in the bedroom. Jamis saw an Apple II on the floor. Steve showed him a VisiCalc spreadsheet, demonstrating the software with great enthusiasm. So what? Jamis thought.

"How many people do you have?" Jamis asked.

"Five or six hundred."

Jamis took the job and quickly discovered that Steve was very vulnerable emotionally. He was forced to grow up while in the public eye, like a teenage pop star. Steve found it excruciatingly hard to make decisions about spending his money and committing to statements about his personal style. He drove a Mercedes 240D, the kind of Mercedes that nobody wanted, one of the German manufacturer's rare flops, but he kept driving it because he couldn't pick another car. He never had a couch in the Los Gatos house. The only pieces of furniture in the living room were two enormous seventeenth-century highboy chairs. He never had a bed. He looked at many beds, but nothing ever pleased him, so he slept on a mattress. Jamis thought: He's a *millionaire* and he's still sleeping on the floor. It wasn't that Steve didn't try hard enough. He lavished time on decorating and remodeling, and he was willing to spend whatever was necessary to ensure the highest possible quality. Jamis took him on many expeditions to antiques stores and furniture showrooms, but the contractor constantly felt frustrated: they saw so much good stuff, but Steve just couldn't choose. "He was a victim of over-choice," Jamis recalls. Steve wasn't prepared to commit to a fixed conception of his taste, his persona, his image of himself. He couldn't articulate his aesthetic vision, which was half-formed but nonetheless uncompromising and burdensome. Unless he could have the best, most perfect things, he would have nothing. The problem was that he wasn't sure what constituted the best.

31
Next

He already had an appreciation for austere minimalism, but at times he would show a more playful side. At an antiques store he saw an authentic medieval suit of armor priced at $40,000. Steve was intrigued. He told Jamis that the people at Disney wanted to give him a set of "animatronics," the robotics that controlled the mechanical characters in the attractions at Disneyland. Steve asked: What if we stuffed some animatronics into this suit of armor, so it could walk around the living room as if it had magically come to life?

"Great idea," said Jamis. At last, progress! But Steve soon abandoned the notion. He suppressed his momentary lapse of gleeful exuberance for what his wealth could bring.

Steve treated his hired contractor as an equal, a personal friend and confidant. They would meet at MacNiven's house way up beyond the ridge, on the Pacific side of the mountains, near where the Hell's Angels congregated and where Ken Kesey and the Merry Pranksters had lived in the heyday of psychedelic drugs. They'd hike through the redwoods on the trails near Skyline Drive and then put salmon steaks on the barbecue. Steve was essentially a vegetarian but sometimes he ate fish. He consumed healthy foods but limited himself to very small quantities. One Sunday afternoon, Jamis took Steve and Barbara on a hike to visit a modern house by a prominent architect. As they explored the structure, the owner was so absorbed with work at his desk that he ignored them.

Weeks later, Jamis mentioned to the owner that the mysterious visitor had been Steve Jobs.

"That was Steve Jobs? The one person in the world I've wanted to meet!"

As the remodeling began, Steve and Barbara moved back into the rickety cabin. Steve's friendship with Jamis devolved into an acrimonious working relationship. Steve demanded a level of extraordinary craftsmanship and obsessive attention to detail that Jamis couldn't deliver or even grasp the rationale for. There was a panel in the basement for telephone wires. Steve insisted that the wires must be laid out with meticulous neatness and the wood cabinetry built with fine detail. Jamis balked. Who was going to see a wiring box?

"I want the very best I can get!" Steve insisted.

"This house isn't worth it," Jamis argued. "It's not economic."

As the work progressed, the two men would yell at each other. They managed to put in beautiful hardwood floors and a Bösendorfer piano, but the remodeling was never done. "It was hairy," recalls Jamis. "He had demands I just couldn't fulfill. He really wanted an I. M. Pei but at that point he didn't know who I. M. Pei was. So he got me."

■   ■   ■

HIS OBSESSIVENESS was one of the reasons for his success, but it carried the potential for his self-destruction as well. His impulse for perfectionism was there even as a teenager. While they were at Reed College together, Elizabeth Holmes was deeply concerned that Steve suffered from eating disorders. "His attitude was, What I eat has to be perfect, who I am has to be perfect," she recalls. Steve's diets were extreme. He fasted for long periods. When he did eat, he consumed shockingly few calories. He would go through phases of eating only fruit—a "fruitarian" diet—and then only grain for a while. He would subsist on Roman Meal, the kind of grainy bread that the Romans supposedly ate, which was very popular in the 1970s counterculture. To Elizabeth, he always seemed "starving." There was abundant food at the All-One Farm, some forty miles southwest of Portland, where their group of friends would go for weekends, holidays, and summers: Chris-Ann, Elizabeth, Dan, Steve, and his classmate Robert Friedland, an LSD proselytizer who dressed in flowing Indian robes. It was Robert's rich Swiss uncle who owned the 220-acre farm. Elizabeth had studied with an organic gardening pioneer, so she helped to lay out the commune's garden. The volcanic soil was spectacularly rich. They grew their own wheat, blowing on conch shells to chase away the deer that strayed near the fields. But even amidst this bounty of natural foods, Steve was intent on self-denial. Robert's wife, Abha, the mother figure at the commune, would prepare magnificent feasts, which they called *subji*, the Hindi term for vegetarian dinners. They shared the great meals with an eclectic array of visiting mystics: Tibetan monks, Buddhists, swamis, healers, meditation gurus. "The meals were a big pull for the hungry Steve," Elizabeth recalls. Steve would gorge himself on the delicious food but then induce himself to vomit it all up, acting as though he were bulimic. Abha was appalled. She thought that Steve's actions were extremely disrespectful. Food was *sacred*, she believed. Moreover, she put so much hard effort into the cooking.

Such was the degree of his perfectionism. In his youth it

was tempered and turned inward. His friends from his high school and college years knew him as an easygoing guy, highly intelligent but not maniacally driven. But at twenty-one when he cofounded Apple and envisioned the potential of the personal computer to change society, he was transformed by his revelation. He became motivated by a missionary zeal, a sense of his own destiny.

At thirty that destiny seemed uncertain for the first time. As he flirted with ideas of becoming an expatriate or an astronaut or a gardener, he also saw the impatience of his followers. His loyalists who remained at Apple were restless and unhappy there. The people he trusted were beginning to disperse, to move on. If he wanted them, he had to act.

■   ■   ■

THE FIRST PERSON he approached was Dan'l Lewin. In September 1985, on the Tuesday after Labor Day, at nine in the morning, he telephoned Dan'l. He said that he wanted to start a new company that would make great computers specifically geared for students at colleges and universities.

Higher education was Dan'l's forte. At Apple he had put together a consortium of twenty-four elite universities, including all the Ivy League schools, which committed to buy Macintoshes and resell them to students, usually at a substantial discount from the prohibitively high list price. The program was a terrific success, helping to turn the Macintosh into a campus cult. So far it was the *only* conspicuous success for the machine.

Dan'l was interested. The team came together quickly: Susan for finance, Bud Tribble for software, George Crow and Rich Page for hardware. The following week, on the evening of Friday the thirteenth, the five recruits all came to Woodside. The iron gate was open. The front door was unlocked, as it always was. Even as a centimillionaire, Steve had no security at his house, where there was very little that anyone could possibly steal. An hour later Steve arrived, dressed in a suit. He had just told the Apple board about their new venture.

Apple sued him. The company filed legal papers alleging that Steve was the mastermind of a "nefarious plot" to steal its technology and undermine its business.

Steve hired a law firm from San Francisco. One of its attorneys drove to the house to talk with Steve's five cofounders and gather facts for the defense. There were few facts to assemble. The Next colleagues had only the vaguest notion of what they were going to do.

"Do you have a business plan?" the lawyer asked.

No, they didn't.

"What about equity? Are you getting stock in the new company?"

No. They hadn't really talked about it.

"Do you know where you're going to work?"

No. They were camped out on the floor of the unfurnished run-down house.

Dan'l Lewin thought he grasped what the lawyer was politely trying to tell them.

"You mean that we have a great case against Apple but we're *stupid*?" he said.

■   ■   ■

THEY WEREN'T STUPID, but their decision to join the new company was undeniably an act of blind faith. They were committing to a risky new venture based on little more than their belief in the leadership of Steve Jobs, his creativity and his drive and his will.

The five of them had much in common. They were smart

and idealistic, with softer-edged, lower-key personalities than Steve. They were young, mostly in their early thirties, roughly the same age as their leader. They had impressive academic credentials. Bud Tribble, the software guy, had a combined M.D.-Ph.D., a "mud phud," as the degree was known. He had worked on the creation of the Macintosh during a three-year break from medical school. Susan Barnes had an MBA from Wharton, the business school known for its preeminence in finance, which was her role at the new company. The fancy academic credentials were important to Steve, even though he was the most celebrated college dropout in American business, a compelling argument against credentialism. His colleagues understood his psychology: they thought of him as a "brand-name shopper," someone who demanded the highest quality but was insecure in his own judgment. Prestigious pedigrees offered a sense of comfort, safety, and reassurance. All he had to do was to tell people that Bud had an M.D.-Ph.D. and they would know that Bud was exceptionally smart.

Of the five disciples, Dan'l Lewin was the closest to Steve, a brother figure. They *looked* as though they could be brothers, both slender and tall with straight dark hair. Dan'l projected more of the chiseled handsomeness of a sports hero or matinee idol, while Steve's features hinted vaguely at the Middle Eastern heritage of his birth father. There was a visible sense of mutual admiration between the two men. As a child Steve didn't take part in team sports, but he did try to compete in swimming, with its emphasis on individual performance. Dan'l was a swimming star in college. They also shared an interest in the music and life of Bob Dylan. For his senior-year thesis for the politics department at Princeton in 1976, Dan'l asked his faculty adviser if he could apply academic theories of charismatic leadership to Dylan's exploits in the 1960s. (To his astonishment, the adviser not only encouraged the idea and agreed to sponsor it, but said that Dan'l could also study David Bowie if he liked.) That same year, Steve was playing Dylan tunes on his guitar in the backyard while he took breaks from assembling Apple I's in the garage. Since Steve was a teenager he had idolized Dylan. For hours and hours he would listen to bootlegged Dylan recordings on his reel-to-reel tape player. Elizabeth Holmes believed that Steve became the lover of Joan Baez in large measure because Baez had been the lover of Dylan.

■   ■   ■

THE NAME OF THE COMPANY, NEXT, was intentionally vague. Steve had a notion of creating computers for students, but they had little idea of what exactly that meant. It would be foolish to commit to specific plans until they resolved the Apple lawsuit and knew where and how they would be free to compete with their old employer. While their product had to remain undefined. Steve turned his energy and his obsessiveness to the *process* of creating the perfect company.

With his seemingly unlimited money and the luxury of time, he could devote extraordinary attention to the most minute details. He paid $100,000 to Paul Rand, a septuagenarian Yale art professor and design guru, to create the Next logo. The price was astonishingly high, especially for a startup company with few employees and no products or revenues. Rand came up with the image of a black cube, tilted at an oblique twenty-eight-degree angle, with brightly colored letters in orange, yellow, green, and purple spelling "NeXT." He presented his design to Steve along with a pamphlet explaining that the conspicuous lowercase *e* could stand for "education, excellence, expertise, exceptional, excitement, $e=mc^2$." It said that the logo "brims with the informality, friendliness, and spontaneity of a Christmas seal and the authority of a rubber stamp." Steve read the explanation and was so enthused that he rushed to embrace the professor. News of the design was covered prominently in the national media. Such was the public fascination with Steve and the intense curiosity about his next move.

The office on Deer Park Road was costly and attractive to begin with, but he gutted it anyway and spent lavishly on the remodeling. How could they create truly great products unless first they created an ideal place where they could think and work? They needed *inspiration*! If they were going to design objects of the highest quality, they needed to be *surrounded* by objects of the highest quality! Steve put in a circular staircase in the lobby and beautiful hardwood floors throughout the two levels. He purchased large black-and-white Ansel Adams photographs to adorn the walls. He had couches and chairs made from the most supple and elegant black leather. There were walls of glass. Even the kitchen counters were made from fine granite. He achieved an environment of austere elegance, though it was subverted a bit when his colleagues set up a sunbathing deck on the roof, complete with a campy little inflatable children's pool, and called it Silicon Beach.

The business press was anxious to learn what Steve was plotting. Never before had a technology startup incited such attention or anticipation. The national publications hardly noticed when Intel was created in 1968, even though its cofounder, Bob Noyce, was the inventor of the silicon chip, which was already a revolutionary product. Through the 1970s *The Wall Street Journal* didn't bother to cover entrepreneurial ventures like Intel. The newspaper's editors rationed their ink for real companies that were already large and well established and had public stocks that were traded on the New York Stock Exchange. But Steve was the first businessman as rock star, and the media craved a look inside his new company the way that teenage groupies fantasized about sneaking into a recording studio.

In early 1986 Dan'l Lewin called the *Business Week* technology correspondent, Katie Hafner, and invited her to come to Deer Creek Road and meet with Steve. It was a shrewd choice. Katie was the perfect reporter to cultivate a relationship with: she was very new on the beat and still in awe of the Silicon Valley scene. She had just taken over the assignment from Deborah Wise, who had written a sycophantic article about Apple while the company was foundering. *Business Week* had run the story on its cover under the bold headline "Apple's Dynamic Duo," with a photograph of Steve Jobs and John Sculley together, smiling, framed by a sunset. Her story implied they were still a harmonious team, even though by that time they were fierce rivals. The piece was an embarrassment, especially when John ousted Steve a few months later.

It's easy to understand why reporters fell for Steve Jobs. He was *seductive*, that was the most accurate word for it. When he was trying to woo a person—a reporter new on the beat, an executive he wanted to hire for a job, a potential customer, a strategic partner looking to make a deal—he could be extraordinarily charming. He had the kind of rare hypnotic eyes that are perhaps the most essential quality of a Hollywood star. If you were meeting him for the first time, he would look at you eye-to-eye with a searching, unyielding, laserlike stare. He would say your first name, say it often, insert it casually at the beginning or end of a sentence. You would be flattered by the personal attention and recognition that you were receiving from such a vaunted pop-culture icon. One-on-one he was better than anyone in the valley. No one was nearly as good at explaining the technology, making it seem understandable to people who weren't engineers or executives, and conveying a sense of excitement about it.

Even more important than the substance of what Steve said was the compelling way that he said it. His enthusiasm was carried by the rhythms and tones of his speech. It was the kind of verbal gift that belonged to the most persuasive politicians and evangelists. JFK had it. So did Billy Graham. It was so powerful and infectious. You met him and listened to him and then you just wanted to be around him as much as you possibly could. It affected men as well as women. And there was something undeniably sexual about him. "He flirted outrageously, in a pleasant way," recalls one prominent reporter who often interviewed him when she was single and in her twenties. "He always invaded my space a little."

Katie Hafner was new on the technology beat for *Business Week*, and she too was attractive, single, and in her twenties. When she met Steve at Deer Creek Road, he was extremely gracious to her. He suggested that they go out to lunch. As they walked through the Next parking lot, they saw a Porsche. It was one of the lower-priced models.

"That's the kind of Porsche that dentists drive," Steve said dismissively.

Moments later they were standing in front of Steve's car, which was . . . a Porsche.

"I assume this is the kind of Porsche that dentists don't drive," Katie shot back.

They drove to the center of the Stanford campus and enjoyed a pleasant lunch at the student cafeteria. Katie was impressed by Steve, who seemed exceptionally smart and charming. As they were leaving, she mentioned that she had recently met with John Sculley and she had talked with John about his ideas for creating innovative new products at Apple.

As he listened, Steve's gracious charm quickly gave way to blatant anger. "Are you kidding?" he said. "John Sculley wouldn't know a new product if it hit him on the head."

AT THIRTY, Steve had a sleek black Porsche and he couldn't help but show it off, like a teenager with a new hot rod. But in the unwritten code of Old Silicon Valley, an expensive car signaled a character flaw. One of his former mentors, Arthur Rock, wouldn't have approved of the Porsche. Art was the highly prestigious San Francisco venture capitalist who invested in Apple in the early days. He was a legend in his field. He was the brilliant financier who four decades earlier had helped to form Fairchild Semiconductor, the company that made the first microchips and turned the Santa Clara Valley, a thinly populated expanse of orchards, into what became known as Silicon Valley.

41
Next

Like Steve Jobs, Art Rock had also appeared solo on the cover of *Time*. And Art had a rule about the entrepreneurs he was willing to invest in, the ones who seem destined to succeed. If the founder of a startup was driving a fancy, expensive car, the deal was off. Art wanted to entrust his money to guys like Bob Noyce, the cofounder of Fairchild and later the cofounder of Intel. Bob's colleagues joked about how he drove "the oldest car in the world," a 1940s Ford that was falling apart. The car was such an embarrassment that they asked him to hide it in the back of the parking lot so it wouldn't scare off customers who visited. That was the kind of entrepreneur Art Rock idealized: a guy who *hated* spending money unnecessarily, even once he was already wealthy.

When Steve started Apple, he had the same frugal scrounging mentality. But his mindset was changing. It was most apparent when his five cofounders traveled with him to Austin, Texas, for Educom, a national convention about computers in higher education. Susan Barnes insisted that they economize and all fly together in coach. Steve agreed. But when they were on the plane, he was so frustrated by the experience that he repeatedly complained to the hapless flight attendants, as if *they* were responsible for the airline.

"Aren't you embarrassed to serve such shitty food?" he said.

Later, as Dan'l Lewin walked through the cabin, one of the beleaguered crewmates accosted him and said: "We've heard that Steve Jobs is on the plane. Who is he?"

Dan'l pointed to the handsome but obnoxious passenger.

The flight attendant was visibly disappointed. "That's what we were afraid of."

■   ■   ■

STEVE JOBS WAS TRANSFORMING HIMSELF from frugal operator into free-spending aesthete. Was it time for Silicon Valley to change, too? It was no longer a business of engineers making tiny electrical components that they sold to other engineers, an insular technocratic priesthood. Now it was a business of making lifestyle products for millions of ordinary people. It was about design and image as well as efficiency and performance. If he wanted to create the Porsche of computers, a machine that was superior in aesthetics as well as engineering, why shouldn't he spend a few minutes every day in the Porsche of automobiles? Why couldn't that be a source of inspiration? He wondered why most personal computers were aggressively ugly with their beige boxes and their disdain for styling. Why couldn't computers look like pieces of stereo equipment, which were black and sleek and beautiful *and* functional. It couldn't be a simple matter of cost, because even a cheap $100 stereo looked so much nicer than a $2,000 personal computer.

Steve wanted to inspire his Next cofounders with his passion for aesthetics, and took them on a junket in the fall of 1985, when they all flew to Pittsburgh to spend a few days at Carnegie Mellon University, one of the most distinguished research centers for computer science. The main purpose of the trip was to meet with professors, recruit the best graduate students, and collect ideas that they could use for the new computer they were conceiving. But then, at the end of the visit, Steve took them on an unusual day trip. He had arranged for them to drive two hours into the Pennsylvania countryside and spend an entire day on a special private tour of Fallingwater, the architectural masterpiece by Frank Lloyd Wright, the landmark modernistic house of concrete, glass, and steel, cantilevered above a waterfall. He wanted them to understand the nature of good design by studying a creation that was both beautiful and functional.

"Ever since I've known Steve, he had a very strong affinity for thinking of things involving aesthetics and style," recalls Bud Tribble. "He approached it by seeking out and gathering around him people who could teach him about it. He's kind of a name-brand shopper in the world of aesthetics." When Next needed a logo, Steve asked around to find who was considered the *best* person in the world at logos. He found Paul Rand. When he took an interest in architecture, he asked many intelligent, cultivated people about who they thought was the *best* architect. Frank Lloyd Wright was the winner of the informal poll.

Tribble thought of Steve's method as "the Delphi approach"; this was how Steve overcame his insecurities about determining his own style. He relied on what was most popular among the people he admired; this method would ensure that his tastes were safe and respectable, and it wouldn't result in a quirky iconoclastic choice. Conducting a survey in the middle of the 1980s would give you a perennial pop favorite like Frank

Lloyd Wright, a dead genius enshrined in every college textbook, not a controversial figure like Frank Gehry, a living radical whose work wouldn't be fully appreciated for another decade. If you asked around about the greatest composer and the best piece of music, you'd probably get Beethoven and the Ninth Symphony. No one could fault you for liking Beethoven. The Ninth Symphony may well be the most wonderful piece of music in Western culture, but an independent thinker would probably try to distinguish himself by advocating the subtler virtues of a composer whose work hadn't been so thoroughly assimilated by the masses.

Steve wasn't that kind of boldly independent thinker about art and aesthetics. Although he had good instincts, he lacked the self-assurance that came from real mastery. He hadn't studied art, architecture, or design, at least not formally; he couldn't draw on a deep reserve of training or knowledge. But once the Delphi method produced a winner, Steve was a remarkably quick and thorough learner. When the survey came up with Frank Lloyd Wright, Steve devoured books about the great man. "He soaks up information," recalls Bud Tribble. "The guy's a sponge once he zeroes in."

■   ■   ■

IN JANUARY 1986, four months after Steve Jobs revealed that he was starting the new company, Apple dropped its lawsuit against Next. Once the tensions had dissipated somewhat, the Apple executives realized that suing their legendary founder wasn't a good public relations ploy. When your company has a wonderful Genesis mythology, you don't impugn Adam. Besides, the lawsuit had a number of unintended effects. It kept Next in the news and made the startup seem like a serious threat to Apple's business. And for the band of five Next co-founders and their leader, being sued and demonized by their ex-employer was an intense "bonding experience," as Bud Tribble recalls. It solidified their resolve to make Next work. With the lawsuit ended, now they could really begin to build a company.

Steve was *fanatical* about hiring the best people. He said that they would interview one hundred people for every one whom they finally chose. And he would fill positions with people who were massively overqualified. The example that everyone talked about was a reputedly brilliant guy named Alex, a young hipster who had made it to the middle ranks at Apple. He had an undergraduate degree from Harvard. He was an art collector. His colleagues found him fascinating. He came to Next. Maybe he would become a marketing executive? A project manager? Steve made him the *receptionist*. The offer was something of an insult, but he took the job just to get in the door. "They were in the habit of hiring extremely experienced people to do fairly menial jobs," recalls David Wertheimer, himself an early hire. "Because of Steve's legend, he was able to recruit great people to be receptionists. The attitude was that we can get very senior-level people to take low-level jobs."

Wertheimer had to interview with thirty different employees there before he was hired. "You basically had to meet everyone in the entire company and they all had to give you the thumbs-up. It really felt like a fraternity. Everyone had to love you. So the feeling you got was that anyone who got through had to be 'the best of the best'—that was the phrase they used. In the early days they had the ability to hire *anybody*. There was one after another phenomenally talented person. People wanted to be around Steve and be a part of this." And if the receptionists needed Harvard degrees, the engineers had to be *geniuses*.

Steve could recruit prodigies seemingly at will. The hires were young and driven by a sense of idealism. Who wouldn't want to be part of a small group that was trying to change the world, with a leader who had already proved that he *could* change the world? His pitch was enticing: They were making computers for education, they were trying to give great tools to *students*, they were taking a powerful lever and placing it right on the fulcrum that had the greatest possible influence on the future of society. Steve liked to say that they were making a radically new machine that might enable some obscure kid to simulate a multimillion-dollar microbiology laboratory on his screen and then . . . find a cure for *cancer!* "We signed up with Steve because we were going to revolutionize education," recalls Allison Thomas, who was a consultant to the company. She had gotten to know Steve Jobs in the early 1980s when they worked together on California governor Jerry Brown's commission on industrial competitiveness. "In the early days at Next, there was a sense of mission and crusade. It was like how he inspired the original Macintosh."

Dan'l Lewin was Next's marketing honcho, and he needed to recruit a vice president of sales. Through the circles of Princeton alumni in the Bay Area, he had developed a friendship with Todd Rulon-Miller, who was a star salesman at IBM. Todd was an Australian who had studied Russian history and played football at Princeton.

Dan'l called, speaking in tones that were crisper and more formal than usual.

"Come work for Steve," he said.

Todd hesitated. "I hear he's tough to work with."

"No way. It's Sculley who's the asshole."

Todd agreed to meet Steve. He was curious, lured by the chance to meet a legend.

The salesman came to Deer Park Road and sat in a conference room, waiting for his interview. In the center of the table, he saw a block-shaped object covered by an opaque drape. It had to be the Next computer! Todd was charged with a sense of anticipation and drama. He was going to see it! It was October 1986. For the past year, all of Silicon Valley had been speculating about what the hell Steve Jobs was doing. Next sustained an aura of mystery. Steve insisted on strict secrecy. Hardly any details had leaked out. Near his desk Steve had hung a vintage poster from the World War II era: "Loose Lips Sink Ships."

And now, Todd thought, I'm going to see what's under the veil!

Steve made his big entrance, bounding into the room, dressed in old blue jeans with conspicuous holes. Immediately he launched into an energetic half-hour speech about his vision for the company. "He was the most ingratiating, personable guy I've ever met in my life," recalls Todd. Throughout the monologue, Todd kept glancing at the draped object.

Finally, with the timing of a master dramatist, Steve said:

"Are you ready to see what's beneath the drape?"

Steve pulled off the cloth. He revealed . . . a cinderblock, not a state-of-the-art computer. A cinderblock that was roughly the same size and shape as a computer monitor.

Isn't it *cool*? Steve asked.

Todd was baffled. He was looking at a cinderblock propped up on a stand.

Isn't this a cool new *monitor stand*? Steve said. It tilts! It's patented! Isn't it *cool*?

After a year of work, Next didn't have a computer. It didn't even have a monitor. What it had was a monitor *stand*. But Steve was maniacally focused on every detail. It was important to him that they have the *best* monitor stand, a *breakthrough* in monitor stands. As a practical test, they had found a cinderblock that was the same weight as a monitor.

Todd knew he was expected to show enthusiasm and say: "Oh, wow."

But he was really thinking: *Oh, my God!* What am I getting myself into?

Still, Steve Jobs was just so incredibly compelling. He took the job.

For Todd Rulon-Miller and all of the first two hundred employees, joining Next was an act of faith. New recruits weren't allowed to know any specific details of the company's plans beyond the vague notion of creating a computer for higher education. It was only once you had actually gone to work there that you began to get the details. You had to commit based solely on your conviction in *Steve* and his charismatic leadership, not based on even a cursory appraisal of the company's technology or strategy. The secrecy persisted even into the summer of 1988, *three years* into the life of the company. That's when Steve interviewed a marketing guy named Paul Vais. They sat for forty-five minutes at a picnic table in a patch of dirt behind the offices on Deer Creek Road. Vais was physically uncomfortable. It was late afternoon and the California sun was "hot as hell," he recalls, and ants were crawling through the dirt all around. Steve wanted him to hire a bunch of people and put together a dramatic public event for the introduction of the Next computer. But Vais couldn't see the computer or know anything about it, not until he took the job.

"It was a real leap of faith," he recalls.

But Steve was so extraordinarily compelling. He made the leap.

■   ■   ■

THREE YEARS AFTER ITS FOUNDING, Next was burning through money, bleeding money, *hemorrhaging* money, without ever having released a single product under its own name. "All we've shipped is a T-shirt," went the joke at Deer Creek Road.

The faithful still believed in Steve: after all, hadn't the creation of Macintosh taken so much longer than planned? But now Apple was earning hundreds of millions of dollars a year thanks to the Mac's delayed success. Anyone who doubted Steve's vision could find reassurance by looking at the contrast between the interfaces of the Microsoft-Intel PC and the Mac. In 1988, almost everyone with a PC was still staring at a single font of clunky fluorescent text against a black screen. Mac users enjoyed the intuitive ease-of-use of pointing and clicking with the mouse and icons and windows, while PC people were still forced to struggle with arcane keyboard commands—Alt-Shift-F5!—to perform simple tasks. Microsoft's programmers had tried to imitate the look and feel of the Mac, but their Windows was still so buggy, unreliable, and artless that it was considered something of a joke, and it had attracted few users. It would take Bill Gates's crew a long struggle to catch up—another four years until the 1992 release of Windows 3.1, the first version of Windows that worked passably well, and then another three years after that until the debut of Windows 95, which was remarkably like the Mac.

49
Next

But during the years when Steve's technological achievement was still far ahead and his legend was far greater, Bill was beginning to eclipse him in wealth. In 1980, when Apple Computer had its initial public offering, Steve was a folk hero with stock worth $240 million, and Bill was still an obscure figure. But Bill catalyzed his career by making the deal to provide software for the IBM personal computer. In 1986, when Microsoft went public, Bill's stock was worth $375 million, and his face was on the cover of *Fortune* as the computer industry's rising young star. Meanwhile, Steve's wealth had diminished to around $100 million.

During the early days at Next, Steve discovered that one of his business associates, a young software entrepreneur named Heidi Roizen, was a good friend of Bill's. He told her that he'd like to know more about the Microsoft centimillionaire.

"I think it's odd," she said, "that Bill lives right next door to Gary Larson but has no idea who he is."

"Who is he?" Steve asked guilelessly.

Larson was the famous creator of *The Far Side*, a humorous cartoon with a dark, twisted sensibility. It was one of the most popular features on the comic-strip pages of daily newspapers. It was the source of best-selling books and desk calendars. Larson's work was part of the zeitgeist. It was easily recognized by much of the American population, but not by the two moguls, who remained oddly aloof from mass culture. It was even stranger for Steve not to know than for Bill, since Steve was famous for his instincts about the tastes of the masses.

Heidi, who was single and had a crush on Steve, realized that she could exploit his fascination with Bill as a way of drawing Steve into accompanying her on social occasions. At the time, Bill was in a long-distance romance with one of Heidi's closest friends, Ann Winblad, a brilliant self-made software entrepreneur who had sold her startup company for $15 million and moved from her native Minneapolis to an Edwardian mansion in San Francisco's fashionable Pacific Heights district. When Bill was in town, the foursome—Bill and Ann, Steve and Heidi—would meet in the city and go out for what Ann thought of as "double dates."

Their first outing was inauspicious. It was January 1987. *Macworld* magazine was holding a ceremony: the first annual Eddy Awards for excellence in Macintosh software. Heidi was accepting the award for the best Mac word processor, WriteNow. Bill was the winner for best spreadsheet, with Microsoft Excel. Ann was planning to accompany them to the black-tie event at the Four Seasons Clift Hotel near San Francisco's Union Square. Heidi invited Steve to meet them at the Redwood Room, the elegant art deco bar next to the hotel's lobby, scheduling the rendezvous for around the time the awards presentation was supposed to end. But she purposely didn't mention that they were coming to the city to take part in an Apple event; otherwise, he surely wouldn't have shown up. It was eighteen months since his ouster from the company, but he was still deeply embittered.

51
Next

When Steve arrived at the bar, the others weren't there yet. He looked around, appalled. The hotel was filled with Apple people in town for the Macworld Expo. *Crawling* with them! This wasn't where he wanted to be. He was annoyed at Heidi for inviting him.

The awards presentation was running late. Bill and Heidi had to stay to the end, so Ann Winblad rushed down to the bar to talk with Steve and keep him from walking out. She introduced herself, expecting to engage in a few minutes of small talk or conversational icebreakers. But then, abruptly and apropos of nothing in particular, Steve said:

"I would have married Joan Baez but she was too old to have my children."

Ann was taken aback. Why did he feel compelled to tell this to her?

She wasn't susceptible to his famous charisma. When they sat next to each other at dinner, she felt that he was trying to assert some kind of moral superiority by flaunting his vegetarianism.

"What do you recommend here?" asked Ann, since Steve had picked the restaurant.

"I assume that you eat meat," he said casually but a bit condescendingly.

"I haven't eaten meat for fifteen years," she shot back.

Bill was upset with Heidi for plotting to arrange the date. Bill and Ann were always trying to set her up, but Bill had trouble understanding why she had a crush on Steve Jobs.

"What do you see in him?" he asked.

■   ■   ■

A FEW MONTHS LATER, Bill and Ann and Heidi were together at Bill's house in the suburbs of Seattle. It was two in the morning. They were drunk. They were having a merry time. In a fit of inebriated exuberance, they joked that it would be fun to make a few prank phone calls. How about calling . . . *Steve Jobs!* Heidi knew Steve's home phone number. She had gotten it initially because they were partners in the software business, but she had memorized it because she had that persistent crush on him. She took the phone and dialed Steve's number. The answering machine came on. Bill seized the phone and began recording a message in a comically thick Gallic accent. He was pretending to be Philippe Kahn, the bombastic Frenchman who was one of the biggest players in the software industry. As the tape rolled, he exulted in a hyperbolic rant about the flaws of Steve's cherished creations.

"Zeez eeez Feee-LEEEP Kahn!" he exclaimed. "Zeee Macintosh *sucks!*"

He hung up the receiver and they laughed hysterically.

Then Heidi dialed Steve's number again. This time, Bill pretended to be a disgruntled Next engineer who had finally summoned the nerve to tell his boss to fuck off.

Inspired by the alcohol and the camaraderie, they all broke into hysterics again.

The next day, when they were finally sober, Bill asked Heidi: "Who were we really calling last night?"

"Steve Jobs!" she said.

Shit! They really had called Steve Jobs!

Bill didn't know that he was *really* leaving a message on Steve's answering machine. He thought it was all a pretense!

Heidi had to play the diplomat. She made an appointment to see Steve, who kept her waiting in the Next lobby at Deer Park Road for an hour and forty-five minutes. An eternity. When Steve finally emerged, she calmly explained the embarrassing situation.

"That was dumb," Steve said.

Still, he didn't fully grasp what had happened.

"What was Philippe Kahn doing at Bill's house?" he wondered aloud.

Time passed, and eventually Steve and Bill were slated to appear together on a panel discussion at an industry conference. As they saw each other on the dais, Steve reached into his pocket and pulled out a tape—the kind that's found in answering machines.

"This is the tape," he said mischievously, as if he intended to play it for the crowd.

53
Next

■   ■   ■

THE ANTICS BETWEEN Bill Gates and Steve Jobs hinted at a rivalry that would become one of the most enduring and fascinating in American business. It was more than a competition for money and media attention. Each man quietly envied the other's image. The media portrayed Steve as the visionary and Bill as the businessman. But Bill believed that he, too, was a seer of the technologic future. While only a trivial percentage of the population owned personal computers, he predicted that there would be a computer on every desk and in every home (all running *his* software). The media recognized Bill for his tough dealmaking skills, the way that he had gotten the better of IBM in the deal of the century, but Steve was just as fierce and unyielding a negotiator. Bill envied Steve's movie-star charisma, his ability to captivate an audience of a thousand people, and Steve watched along with the rest of the world as Bill became the richest person on earth. But each man saw himself as the complete mogul rather than his typecast character in the press.

But they did represent opposite approaches to business and technology. Bill was the ultimate pragmatist. He put out bad software, buggy and flawed, but he got it out to the market, and then he fixed some of the problems in the next version, and then the next and the next. He persisted and he struggled and *eventually* he wound up with a good piece of software. He was poor Sisyphus pushing the rock up the hill, but he kept pushing. It was a messy process, it was infuriatingly incremental, it was full of angst, but it worked. He had a bias for action. He took pride in the fact that his company *shipped products*.

Steve, in contrast, was the ultimate perfectionist. When he came out with a new computer, it had to be revolutionary, astonishing. In his own words, it had to be "insanely great." He wanted a huge leap forward, not an incremental push. He wanted something that people would love, not tolerate grudgingly because they had no other viable alternatives. He conceived of his engineers as artists and even had them sign their names on the inside of the Macintosh. He had exhorted them with the mantra "Great artists ship." Picasso and Matisse didn't hold on to their canvases for years; they finished them and sold them off.

But Steve had trouble shipping. The Macintosh was a creative triumph but it took years longer than he had anticipated. He had planned for Next to release its first computer by spring

1987, within eighteen months of the company's founding. But as 1987 began, they weren't even close to completion. Steve's ambitions were constantly aggrandizing. It wasn't enough for the new machine to be distinguished by one particular break-through. *Everything* about it had to be a breakthrough. For the software, he was taking an entirely new approach, starting from scratch, trying to create the most elegant lines of software code ever written. The industrial design had to be like no computer ever created. It had to be as gorgeous and sleek as Steve's black Porsche. Even the *factory* had to be beautiful, and it had to be as fully automated as any factory in the world. At first, the Next founders thought that they would hire a larger company to make the machines for them. But Steve had created a highly automated factory to build the Macintosh, and he had to do even better this time. The Next computer was going to be in the image of the Macintosh, but much, much better. Steve would take his earlier creation, with all of its flaws and compromises, and now, with the benefit of money and time, he would make it absolutely *perfect*. Unlike his years at Apple, this time there was no one else to answer to, not even a board of directors to provide oversight or serve as a voice for restraint. Steve was in complete control.

But time was passing, and the money, the $7 million that Steve had invested, was nearly gone. Seven million . . . in a little more than a year! The company was *bleeding* money. Steve still had a fortune left. He could easily put in more. But Next needed independent investors who would give it more credibility in the industry. At this point it had to look like a real business, not just the expensive frivolous hobby of some rich guy. Steve had thought that he could finance the company entirely on his own, which would let him keep total control. But now he realized that it was a good idea to bring in some "smart money." He began talking with venture capitalists, the professional investors who specialize in risky technology start-ups. He was willing to sell a 10 percent ownership stake in Next for $3 million, but the investors thought that was too high a price for a company that still wasn't close to actually shipping a product and beginning to bring in revenues.

Then Next received an unsolicited call from one of the most famous names in the computer business, H. Ross Perot, the legendary founder of Electronic Data Systems.

"You'd never guess who just called," Steve told a colleague. "This is incredible."

The irascible Texas mogul had seen video clips of Steve on a television documentary, *The Innovators*, and he was mightily impressed. Steve seemed like a brilliant iconoclastic entrepreneur, a visionary. He was sort of . . . a reincarnation of Ross himself! An image of Ross in his own youth! Only much taller and much better looking.

"If you ever need an investor, call me," Ross said.

Steve badly needed an investor, especially one with that kind of prestige.

In January 1987 Ross's limousine pulled up to the Next factory building in the working-class eastern side of San Francisco Bay, in a town called Fremont, not far from the state-of-the-art Macintosh factory Steve had created. The Next structure was still an empty shell. There was nothing to see, but they could *imagine* what would rise here with the help of Ross's millions: the smooth hum of smart machines making other smart machines. In the center of the cold bare floor there was a long conference table with folding chairs and an over-head projector. A screen was attached to one of the narrow steel support columns. They were going to have lunch and then Steve would make his big presentation. But before they could sit down, Steve saw that *something* wasn't exactly the way he wanted it.

Suddenly he began screaming at one of the Next employees, berating him, subjecting him to a brutal verbal assault while Ross and other Next executives looked on.

Was Steve losing his mind?

Why risk blowing the deal with Perot?

Ross seemed oddly unfazed as Steve humiliated one of his own people. Ross turned to the man next to him and said: "I used to be like that when I was his age, but then I learned you catch more flies with honey. Steve, leave him alone and let's get to work."

■   ■   ■

IN FEBRUARY 1987 they did the deal. Perot paid $20 million for 16 percent of the company, or $1.25 million per percentage point. Steve had snookered him. Days earlier Steve had been offering stock to the Silicon Valley venture capitalists at *one-fourth* that price, only $300,000 per point, and they had rejected the offer as far too expensive. But Steve shrewdly grasped how excited Ross was. The older guy didn't even flinch when Steve lost control and revealed his dark side. So Steve asked for an outrageously high price, and Ross paid up without hesitation.

Ross craved a piece of the future and he didn't want to blow his chance over a few lousy million dollars. In 1979 he had talked with Bill Gates about buying Microsoft but he had balked at the asking price, which was less than $60 million. In 1986, after Microsoft went public, its stock had a value of well over $1 billion. Ross had passed up the opportunity to make more than sixteen times his money, a billion-dollar profit in only seven years. The easiest billion dollars . . . ever! He had blown it with Bill Gates! He wasn't going to blow his second chance now with Steve.

So he visited the empty factory, he toured the Next headquarters at Deer Park Road, he met the staffers. They were wary of his media image as a jingoistic curmudgeon—Susan Barnes's mother in Dallas had a bumper sticker that said "Honk if you hate Ross Perot"—but Steve asked them to decide for themselves. When they actually met Ross, they were charmed by him.

Weeks later, on his second visit to Deer Park, he bounded out of his limousine, entered the building, and greeted the receptionist by name. Then he went on to greet *everyone* by their first names. He amiably chatted up every employee who passed him randomly as he went through the hallways, no matter whether their positions were lofty or lowly. He would talk with them all as if they were old buddies. His approach to human relations was straight from Dale Carnegie's *How to Win Friends and Influence People*. He was an old-school salesman, a master of a dying art.

He did the deal, and he expected a lot of attention for it. When Ross talked about holding a press conference, he said: "Steve, you know we'll get a lot of people to come, because you're a white monkey and I'm a white monkey. Put the two of us in a cage and it's a real circus."

It *was* a circus. Louise Kehoe, a correspondent for London's *Financial Times*, was astonished by how the aging billionaire was so visibly awed by the younger entrepreneur, how Ross Perot was exhibiting such fawning admiration. "He was acting like a starstruck teenager," she recalls. "He was just totally blown away by Steve."

■　　■　　■

IN THEIR BRIEF COURTSHIP Ross Perot saw the captivating side of Steve Jobs, though that day in the factory he also had a glimpse of Steve's darker side, his penchant for turning on colleagues with a wicked tongue. Ross was wrong in his quick appraisal that as Steve got a little older he too would learn that "you catch more flies with honey." Steve *already* knew how to catch flies with honey. He could be all sweetness and seduction, especially when he was wooing prospective employees or business partners. But when it came to realizing his vision, he used every possible strategy to get people to strive for perfection as he saw it. He would praise them and inspire them, often in very creative ways, but he would also resort to intimidating, goading, berating, belittling, and even humiliating them. He could be Good Steve or he could be Bad Steve. When he was Bad Steve, he didn't seem to care about the severe damage he caused to egos or emotions so long as he pushed for greatness.

From his years at Apple his reputation was known throughout the valley. People had heard about the Steve Jobs "reality distortion field," how his persuasiveness was so powerful that it could be blinding. Some of them even heard about the "hero-shithead roller coaster," how Steve would go to such extraordinary efforts to hire brilliant people, his heroes, and brag to everyone about their exceptional talents, and then, suddenly and unexpectedly, he would look at something they were working on and say that it "sucked," it was "shit." Susan Barnes labeled this practice the "seduce and abandon" technique. People became entranced by Steve's approval and acceptance; then, when he abruptly withheld it, they would struggle mightily to regain it, if only for a fleeting time. "The charm is all the more valuable if it is withheld, especially with the people who see him every day," says Heidi Roizen.

No one was really sure where Steve got his ideas about managing people, whether he was motivated by a consciously held philosophy or if he was just acting on his instincts, if that was simply what he was like as a person. Somehow, though, it *worked*. He got his people to push themselves extremely hard, to strive maniacally, and often to achieve personal goals or improve the technology far beyond what they had thought was possible.

The perplexing fact was that Bad Steve seemed as integral to his success as Good Steve. And somehow they were two faces of the same man. At other companies, the good cops and the bad cops were different people. At Intel, Chairman Bob Noyce had been the wonderfully charming guy who got people to do things because they loved him. His No. 2, Andy Grove, was the harsh taskmaster who got people to do things because they feared him. Bob flashed the irresistible smile, Andy wielded the whip. Steve was a casual friend of Bob Noyce, and greatly admired Bob, but he had a lot of Andy Grove in him, too.

Steve was willing to be loved *or* feared, whatever worked. "Steve was the master of knowing which buttons to push with different people," recalls Susan Barnes.

"He applied charm or public humiliation in a way that in most cases proved to be pretty effective," says Bud Tribble. "I think he continued to do it because he got positive reinforcement from the world that this was a way to get things to happen."

Bud believes that Steve's occasional outbursts of fierce criticism helped to create an expectation of unremitting quality that was assimilated by the engineers at Next. Most of the time Steve left them alone. Ninety-nine percent of the time, in Bud's estimation, Steve wasn't looking over their shoulders. But that other one percent "he would just come down like a hammer," and his verbal assaults could be terrifying. Engineers would be so disturbed by the episodes that the rest of the time they would *feel* as though Steve were looking over their shoulders with his uncompromising eye, even though he wasn't. He was the corporate superego, the surrogate parent they all wanted so much to please.

Bud believed that Steve operated this way intentionally. Receiving criticism from Steve "wasn't a pleasant experience," he says, "but it let the engineers know that it wasn't OK to be sloppy in anything they did, even the ninety-nine percent that Steve would never look at. It's almost like a training mechanism, and it's effective." It was Steve's way of infusing his perfectionism into the work of hundreds of people, his way of making them internalize his own striving. A classic example came when Steve tormented his people by scrutinizing countless look-alike paint samples before he decided on the precise pigment of black for the casing of the Next computer. "He was incredibly picky," Bud says, "but it set the tone for thousands of other decisions that Steve was not involved in at all."

Other people were shocked by the fierce behavior of Bad Steve, but Bud wasn't. As a graduate of medical school, Bud was used to that kind of treatment from his brilliant teachers. When he was an intern, the chief surgeon would come down like a hammer and berate the pupils over seemingly trivial matters. That was how the great surgeons demonstrated the discipline and carefulness that their trainees would need to acquire. The interns might have cursed the chiefs, but later they would appreciate the crucial experience.

Bud believes that Steve reinforced his perfectionism by using his charm and creativity just as much as by applying criticism and intimidation. He was the master of inspiration through example, like that time he took his cofounders on the tour of Fallingwater. When he held an "off-site" meeting for the entire staff at the Garden Court, a small luxury hotel in Palo Alto, Steve brought in aikido masters to conduct an hourlong demonstration and explanation of their art. The Next employees realized that this martial-arts class was supposed to be a metaphor for their relationship to the rest of the industry. Like an aikido master, Steve wanted them to deflect the hostility and negative energy of the outside world and turn it into their own positive force or energy. He never explicitly made the connection; that would have been too heavy-handed. But the Next people understood the subtle message, and it impressed them so much that they would remember it for many years. What other business executive would think of something so creative and original?

He was Good Steve at least as often as he was Bad Steve, and probably more often, but the Bad Steve episodes began to color his reputation. Even a single anecdote of humiliation would be passed along like a virus through gossip and storytelling and would add a negative strand to his evolving image. He was no longer just the admirable wunderkind; by now, he was also known as an enfant terrible.

■   ■   ■

SOMETIMES THE BAD STEVE persona was simply a theatrical mask that he could put on at will whenever he thought it would get results. Once, when they were still at Apple, Susan Barnes walked over to ask Steve to sign some papers. As she stood at the side of his cubicle, she saw that he was screaming into the phone, shouting a stream of derogatory and obscene epithets while hyperventilating as if he were about to be overcome by a heart attack. Then he hung up, the tension instantly disappeared, and he began laughing, obviously pleased with his dramatic performance.

"Well, we'll see if that method works!" he said optimistically.

Most of the time, though, when Steve seemed angry or upset, he wasn't acting. His passion and his perfectionism would plague him with intense aggravation when his people couldn't grasp his grand visions or figure out how to fulfill them. "His frustration level would build up when he thought that he was the only one who got it," Susan recalls.

Steve's people reacted to his foul temper and his foul language in a variety of ways. Sometimes they simply tried to ignore him. Susan once asked Bud Tribble: "When he's screaming at you because the software isn't done, does that upset you?"

"No," Bud said. "Steve can scream at the sun but that's not going to get the sun to set any sooner."

Bud could be preternaturally even-tempered, a quiet, thoughtful guy with the self-confidence that comes from great mastery of a craft. A few other Next executives were also able to listen calmly to Steve's outbursts. They believed that Steve was simply a passionate soul given to hyperbole, so his fiery words needed to be discounted from their face value, translated to find their real message. "When Steve says you're an idiot, that doesn't mean he thinks you're an idiot," says David Wertheimer. "It means he disagrees with you."

Some members of Steve's inner circle had a harder time controlling their own emotions when they got into confrontations with their leader. "He told me: 'Susan, when you're upset, you're not articulate,'" recalls Susan Barnes. "The same is true of Steve. But when he's upset, it's for a reason. Steve had brutal delivery mechanisms, but if you listened through his yelling, Steve had good ideas. And Steve is a rare person because even if he's really mad at you, you *can* hang up and later he'll call you and talk more calmly."

Another trick to working well with Steve was understanding that while he was a smart, ruthless editor of other people's ideas, he desperately needed other people to be smart, ruthless editors of his own constant onslaught of brainstorms. "Steve's great strength is throwing out a hundred ideas and ninety-nine are stupid but one is great," says Susan Barnes. If she thought his latest idea was stupid, she would just ignore it. "That's what I like about you," he once said. "If I tell you to do something, you either do it or not."

■　■　■

STEVE WAS PRONE to speaking with radical honesty, raw and uncensored and undiplomatic. He often seemed like a child who hadn't learned that he wasn't supposed to say out loud exactly what he was thinking. When French president François Mitterrand held a formal dinner during a visit to California, Steve didn't want to partake in the refined French cuisine. He asked Mitterrand whether he could have some pasta instead, since he had recently been to Tuscany and enjoyed such great pasta there. Imagine, the outrageousness! Asking the French leader for Italian food!

Once he abruptly interrupted his business partner Heidi Roizen in the middle of a negotiation and asked her whether she was really a blonde.

"Do you color your hair?" he asked. "Why do you color your hair? What color is it naturally?"

Another time they bumped into each other and Steve said: "Have you gained weight?" And when Heidi introduced Steve to her mother, he blurted out: "So, *you're* Heidi's mother? What drugs were you on when you conceived her?"

Whether with a head of state or a corporate colleague or a personal friend, he was astonishingly uninhibited, but his wide-eyed questions often seemed more innocent than insolent, and his unconventional behavior almost always passed without repercussions.

Steve's colleagues learned to accept and even to appreciate

his bizarre frankness, his disarming directness, his aura of what-you-see-is-what-you-get. "Working with him you never felt that you were getting false praise or that he was being gracious to you when he was really mad at you," says Susan Barnes. While the Next insiders came to understand Steve's personality, they were always fearful that his childlike antics would embarrass them in front of outsiders and jeopardize their most important business relationships. Before Susan took Steve for meetings with investment bankers on Wall Street, she gave him a warning speech during the flight to New York, as if she were a mother imploring a rambunctious five-year-old to be on his best behavior in the presence of adults.

"You're going to be good," she instructed. "You're not going to tell them that their suits are lousy or their food is lousy."

It worked. He behaved.

The odd thing was that Steve wasn't the stereotypically introverted nerd who lacked social skills and simply didn't know how to comport himself. He *knew*. When he wanted to charm, no one was more charming. Susan thinks that Steve persisted with his innocent-insolent routine because ninety-nine times out of a hundred he got away with it. He wasn't entirely innocent. He used the rude-child persona to disarm other powerful people, to make them slightly uncomfortable and thus give himself a subtle advantage.

■   ■   ■

STEVE ACTED WITH extraordinary chutzpah—a posture of nerve and brazenness reinforced by a presumptuous sense of entitlement—and the people who worked with him either had to respond in kind or acquiesce to his dominating will. The result was that his inner circle sometimes seemed like the archetypal Jewish family that was bound by unspoken love but thrived on acrimonious confrontation. One of the young superstars of Next's software team was Avie Tevanian, a brilliant Ph.D. from Carnegie Mellon. Avie's persona was gentle, quiet, and a bit shy, but when Steve tested him Avie could defend himself unyieldingly.

"Steve, you're just wrong!" he'd say.

"Avie, you're missing the entire point."

"No, you're just wrong."

Avie could wrangle acrimoniously with his leader because Steve had so much respect for his talents. Similarly, Steve had great admiration for a Next employee named Susan Kare, a young artist and graphic designer who had created the friendly "icons" for the Macintosh. Susan's colleagues marveled at how confidently she could hold her positions against Steve. Though her personality was usually sweet and huggy, she wasn't afraid to speak out with brutal sarcasm or to say, "Steve, you're full of shit," in front of the whole crew. But the confrontations were so emotionally draining that sometimes she would call friends in the industry and confess that she had spent the morning crying in the bathroom.

For Andy Cunningham, Next's public relations consultant, working with Steve was like a master class in self-assertiveness and spine. One day Steve called Andy into the conference room at Deer Creek Road for a meeting with him and Susan Barnes.

"We called you here because we're not happy with your work and we're going to fire you," Steve said.

Fire her? For a smallish startup company that still hadn't shipped a product or revealed more than the vaguest conception of what it was doing, Next had received a surfeit of publicity. It was the subject of big articles in all the major magazines: *Newsweek, Time, Fortune, Business Week*. And still, Steve wasn't satisfied? He was *firing* her?

Andy looked at Susan Barnes, who nodded but remained silent.

"What about my bills?" Andy asked. Next owed her $25,000, which was a lot of money for her. She was in her twenties and hadn't been working for herself for very long.

Steve said coolly: We're not going to pay because we're unhappy with your work.

Andy was nearly in tears as she left the building and drove home. That night, she asked her husband what she should do.

"Talk to Regis," he said.

Regis was her old mentor, Regis McKenna, a shrewd, polished Silicon Valley veteran who had been Steve's marketing guru in the early days at Apple. Andy had learned her profession at Regis's large p.r. agency before deciding to open her own small firm.

Andy approached Regis.

He said: "You've got to think of what *you* have over Steve Jobs."

I don't have anything over Steve Jobs, she thought. I'm just a kid starting out on my own. He's a powerful person, a legend in the industry.

"If you know something he doesn't know, you're in great shape," Regis advised.

Then Andy finally grasped what she had.

She went back for another meeting with Steve.

She summoned her bravado and said: "I talk to members of the business press fifteen times a day, and they're always asking me: 'What is Steve Jobs really like?'"

Steve went for his checkbook and paid her the $25,000 right away.

It wouldn't be long before he would try to hire her back.

■   ■   ■

CONFRONTATION was a basic requirement for Steve's colleagues. So was commitment. Steve's life was overwhelmed by
his work, and he expected the same of his people. At times it
seemed that he didn't realize how hard he was pushing them,
or how hard they were pushing themselves. In the autumn of
1986, he assembled the several dozen Next staffers and exhorted them to work nights and weekends until Christmas,
when they could take a week off. Someone said: "Steve, we already *are* working nights and weekends." Steve would schedule
meetings for Saturdays, seemingly unaware that Dan'l Lewin
had a wife and young children to be with then. Dan'l would
bravely say, "I'm unavailable."

■　　　■　　　■

FOR THE FULL DECADE of his life since college, Steve's obsession with his work had put extraordinary stress on his
friendships and romances. At twenty-two, when he moved into
the Rancho Suburbio house-share with Dan Kottke, his best
male friend, and Chris-Ann, the only serious girlfriend he had
ever had, Chris-Ann was still in love with him. But by then
Steve had been transformed by his newfound sense of destiny.
"From the time Apple started, Steve was never interested in
Chris-Ann," recalls Dan. "It was clear to me that he was never
emotionally involved with her. He was emotionally involved in
his company."

While he felt wedded to his work, his libido remained
healthy. On a visit to the offices of the Regis McKenna agency,
Steve met a public relations consultant named Barbara
Jasinski. She was half Eastern European, half Southeast Asian,
with striking dark hair and high cheekbones, a model-like
beauty in comparison to Chris-Ann's hippie-chick variation on

the girl-next-door. "She made a big impression on him the first day he met her," recalls Dan.

Steve and Barbara began a romantic relationship, and Steve essentially lived in Barbara's shack in the mountains. Sometime during that period, Chris-Ann became pregnant and insisted that the child was Steve's. When he didn't seem to care, she reacted with violent outbursts. She threw plates at him, scrawled angry words in charcoal on the walls of the bedroom where he hardly ever slept. Steve denied his parentage and refused his support, even though some of his most trusted friends—including Dan Kottke and Elizabeth Holmes—believed that he was the father. They couldn't understand how the Steve they knew, who had struggled emotionally for so many years with the knowledge of his own abandonment and adoption, could make an orphan of his own child. They had trouble thinking that the Steve they knew— honest, generous, sharing, empathetic, spiritual, searching— would deny his role and refuse his responsibility. It was bad karma.

Chris-Ann went off to the commune in Oregon, the All-One Farm, where she gave birth to Lisa in 1978. But soon the mother and daughter were back in northern California, living on welfare. The county sued Steve for child support and subjected him to a blood test at UCLA, which determined a 94.4 percent probability that he was the father. Still, he doggedly denied his parentage and refused to provide financial support. Chris-Ann asked for a settlement of $20,000, a sliver of Steve's paper wealth. His colleagues on the Apple board implored him to settle. They worried about the potential for adverse publicity, especially since the company was preparing to go public. Just before Apple's initial public offering in 1980, Steve finally agreed to pay $385 a month in child support.

The Chris-Ann story remained quiet, but as Steve's

celebrity grew, it was inevitable that it would be revealed. In 1982, *Time*'s San Francisco correspondent, an affable Oxford graduate named Michael Moritz, interviewed Steve for a story on American entrepreneurs. Steve's portrait ran on the magazine's cover. Soon after, Steve agreed to give him unhindered access to write a behind-the-scenes book about Apple. Michael interviewed Dan Kottke, who talked about the episodes with Chris-Ann and Lisa. Dan didn't think that he was revealing anything that wasn't public knowledge: he thought the story had run in the local newspapers, and surely it was openly discussed by all the other Apple insiders.

As 1982 came to a close, Steve knew that *Time* was planning to make him its "Man of the Year" for his role in the computer revolution. Then Moritz informed his editors about the darker side of Steve's personality. So the issue was published with "the computer" as "Machine of the Year." The cover story was followed by a shorter three-page piece on Steve, an accurate, well-balanced portrait that described his accomplishments as well as his autocratic bent. It also revealed his prolonged refusal to support his out-of-wedlock child.

Steve was enraged. He gathered together the entire Macintosh team and accused Dan Kottke of betrayal. The two men had been the closest of friends in college. They had dropped acid together and traveled to India together. They had worked side by side in the now-legendary garage. But from that day onward, Steve would no longer talk to Dan.

■　　■　　■

WHILE HIS EX-GIRLFRIEND Chris-Ann had shared his interest in the counterculture, Barbara was part of the realm of business and technology, where Steve was now immersed. He could take Barbara along with him on social outings with techno-geniuses like his buddy Bob Metcalfe, an MIT Ph.D. who had done breakthrough work in computer science. Steve and Bob were neighbors in Woodside and they liked to double-date together, driving up to San Francisco and staying over at Bob's crash pad there. Once, on the way home, they pulled onto the shoulder and struggled trying to replace a flat. There they were, the father of the personal computer and the father of computer networking, and neither of them was any good at changing a tire.

71
Next

Bob invited Steve and Barbara to his wedding in 1980, but Steve didn't RSVP either way. Bob and his fiancée, Robyn, had no idea whether Steve was going to show up. He knew that Steve was always oddly noncommittal about coming to public events.

As Steve and Barbara made their unexpected entrance at the little white church in Woodside, the crowd was instantly captivated by the celebrity among them and his companion. "When Steve showed up with such a really gorgeous woman, devastatingly attractive, it was almost like Robyn and I were irrelevant," Bob would recall two decades later. "To this day, people say, 'Yeah, I remember your wedding. Steve Jobs was there!'"

■　　■　　■

STEVE AND BARBARA were a brilliant couple, but their romance was frustrated by Steve's nearly messianic sense of mission. Their contractor, Jamis MacNiven, recalls the couple's interaction as "stormy." Steve would call his confidant Elizabeth Holmes, one of his closest friends from Reed College, and talk about the relationship. "Barbara was first of all beautiful, physically striking, very intelligent," Elizabeth recalls. "She had this steel spine. You could push her so far and no further. I think she was a bit bewildered by Steve. She was genuinely in love with Steve, and she liked the life, but Steve was so driven in those years. He was just focused on what he was doing, and he had a sense of destiny."

Elizabeth herself was in the mold of Steve's girlfriends, a bright, creative woman, fascinated by the counterculture, who had a striking appearance (five ten and slender, with beautiful blond hair). They were never involved romantically: she was Dan Kottke's girlfriend in college and for a while after. But Steve had a kind of brotherly affection for her, and they often talked about life. Over the years, one of Steve's favorite topics of conversation was the importance of finding the right woman. Elizabeth wasn't convinced that he was ready for the "wear and tear" of an intense relationship. She suspected that it would be easier for Steve to fall for women who were in awe of his renown. Instead, it turned out that Steve was the one who was in awe of other celebrities.

In the early 1980s, Steve and Barbara went together to a Joan Baez concert on a lawn of the Stanford campus, where they picnicked with Dan Kottke and Elizabeth Holmes. Before long, Steve would abruptly end his relationship with Barbara and begin an affair with the charismatic singer-activist. Then came Steve's period of courting New York women. In late 1984 he told *Business Week* that he liked "young, superintelligent, artistic women." He added: "I think they're in New York rather than Silicon Valley."

But soon afterward he did meet a Silicon Valley woman and began a relationship that would last, on and off, tempestuously, for five years. Christina Redse was a graphic designer who had worked for computer makers such as Osborne and Hewlett-Packard. People often said that she looked like a young Daryl Hannah, a Hollywood starlet of the day, but they added that Tina was even *prettier*. She was strangely beautiful in an utterly unpretentious, earthy way. She didn't wear makeup and she almost always dressed in blue jeans and a simple black T-shirt that contrasted starkly with her fair skin and her extremely blond hair. Her friends remember the one time she wore a dress, for a company dinner, and how awkward she looked that night, as if her natural beauty was somehow diminished or corrupted by the formality. She dressed almost like a twin to Steve, who had taken to the bohemian artists' uniform of Levi's and turtlenecks. And the sexual chemistry between the two of them was intense and palpable. Many years later, Next veterans would still recall the couple's passionate "make-out sessions" in the Deer Creek lobby. At what other company would the chief executive be seen acting that way?

Like Barbara before her, Tina had the strong and fiery will that Steve needed from the people around him, whether they were his lovers or his business colleagues. Tina was unimpressed by his wealth and uninterested in his financial help. She was determined to live on her own modest means. When Steve bought her a new car, Tina was so mad at him that as she rushed to drive away from the Deer Creek parking lot, she shifted into reverse instead of drive and crashed against the building, totaling the vehicle.

Tina would try living with Steve for a while in the nearly barren Woodside mansion but she wasn't happy there. When she told Heidi Roizen that she had moved out once again, Heidi asked why.

"Because I'm tired of living in a house with no furniture," Tina said. She had lived there for a year without even a living-room couch, but Steve wouldn't let her buy furniture.

Tina was young and artistic and intelligent, if not

"superintelligent," but she didn't share Steve's ambitiousness. "Tina wasn't hard-driving at all," recalls Heidi Roizen. "She was smart, but it wasn't connected in a directed way. Tina would work capably on things but she didn't have a CEO mentality." She was lax enough that she was surprised when Pacific Bell disconnected her phone because she hadn't paid the bill. She was also a gentle idealistic soul. While Steve worked on Next, she volunteered to help people with mental disabilities. She was a hippie chick, like Chris-Ann, *and* an industry insider, like Barbara.

■   ■   ■

WHILE HE WAS PURSUING his romance with Tina, he was also getting to know two other women who would become vitally important to his life: his sister and his daughter.

In the early 1980s, Steve finally discovered his biological family, whose identity had always been a mystery to him. He found that his mother, Joanne Simpson, had been a speech therapist in Green Bay, Wisconsin. His father was a political science professor of Middle Eastern heritage. Steve was born out of wedlock in 1955, and they immediately put him up for adoption. Within two and a half years, though, they had married and Joanne had given birth to a daughter, Mona Simpson, whom she kept and raised.

When Steve met his sister in the early 1980s, she was living in Manhattan and beginning a career as a novelist. She studied fiction writing in the prestigious Masters of Fine Arts program at Columbia University and worked as an editorial assistant for *The Paris Review* while she completed her first novel, *Anywhere But Here*. It was the story of the relationship between a quirky, egotistical mother and her teenage daughter as they move to

Los Angeles and build a new life without the father. The novel was funny, emotional, acutely observed, gracefully written, and transparently autobiographical.

"My sister's a writer!" Steve exclaimed to Elizabeth Holmes with the utmost delight, as if he had found genetic confirmation for his own innate artistry and specialness. He was thrilled that Mona was in so many ways a reflection of himself: extraordinarily intelligent, driven, creative, and intense. They even looked very much alike, both lean and angular and dark-haired. It was a little like a feature that ran every month in *Spy* magazine, called "Separated At Birth," that matched photos of two celebrities to reveal an unexpected resemblance. The difference was that Steve and Mona really were separated at birth.

Steve had never gotten along that well or felt particularly close to his younger sister Patti, who was also adopted. Paul and Clara Jobs had wanted children so much that they adopted two of them, and as parents they were unfailingly loving, supportive, and self-sacrificing. They even let their college-dropout son take over their small house for his screwy idea of starting a company. They were good people, earnest and hardworking, but they weren't intellectuals or artists (and neither was Patti). Steve returned their love and accepted them as his "real" parents, but he had always been deeply troubled by the fact of his adoption, the mystery of why he was abandoned. Discovering Mona was a way of more fully understanding himself, perhaps even envisioning what his life could have been like if he had been born in the home of a professor rather than that of a blue-collar worker.

In 1987, the editor of *The Paris Review*, George Plimpton, threw a party at his Manhattan townhouse to celebrate the publication of *Anywhere But Here*. Mona made her entrance along with the two people to whom the book was dedicated:

her mother, Joanne, and the man she introduced as her brother, Steve Jobs. *The* Steve Jobs. His identity was a revelation even to the well-informed elite of Manhattan's media circles. Mona's famous literary agent, Amanda "Binky" Urban, later told the *New York Times:* "I had known Mona for quite a while. She had said she had a brother who worked in the computer industry. But that party was the first time I learned that her brother was Steve Jobs."

Anywhere But Here was a publishing rarity, a finely crafted "literary" novel that was both a critical success and a strong seller. It established Mona as one of the most promising novelists of her generation. Steve was so proud of his sister's work that he filled one of his office's bookshelves with copies and gave them out freely to his colleagues. Mona began composing her prose on a Macintosh.

Mona became very close to Steve and to the other women in his life. Mona spent time in northern California and got to know his adoptive mother, Clara, before she succumbed to cancer in 1986 after a prolonged illness. Her death had a profound and enduring effect on Steve. Some years later, when he heard that his friend Heidi Roizen's father had died, he would rush to her house and sit with her for hours, listening to her with the concern and empathy of someone who deeply understood her loss and her need for catharsis.

Mona developed a friendship with Tina. She also spent time with Chris-Ann and Lisa, who turned nine in 1987. Steve had finally overcome his denial and accepted the sweet precocious little girl as his daughter. He brought her to the Next offices. As Steve's colleagues walked by, she sprang cartwheels through the hallways, gleefully shouting "Look at me!" in her high-pitched voice. He was trying to get more involved in her life. It was happening slowly, fitfully, and a bit awkwardly, but it was happening.

Steve himself was growing up.

Steve was intensely private about his family and especially protective about the women who loved him. One of his public relations consultants from that period recalls: "We knew Tina but we were admonished severely never to talk about her or about Mona." They were off-limits to reporters, and details about their relationships with Steve never appeared in the media. But there was one thing that Steve couldn't possibly control:

Mona drew on her closest personal relationships for her autobiographical fiction. And Mona was remembering *everything*.

■   ■   ■

IN 1987, as Steve began resolving the conflicts in his personal life, he was still driven by the intense need for vindication in his career. His passionate work and his accomplishments at Next remained shrouded by self-imposed secrecy; meanwhile, no one in the industry could ignore the stunning comeback that Apple was making in his conspicuous absence. When Steve left the company, Apple's stock was trading below $10. He dumped his seven million shares quietly, in staggered sales over several months, always at prices under $15. By early 1986, he had disposed of all but one share, which he held on to as a symbolic gesture. As a financial maneuver his timing was remarkably bad. The stock began climbing. Before the start of 1987 it surpassed $20 a share. Within months it rocketed to a high of nearly $60 before settling in the mid-$40s for most of 1988. With Steve out of his way, Sculley had doubled Apple's sales, tripled its profits, quadrupled its stock price, and restored the faith of

Wall Street, and he did it all in the brief period of only three years.

But Steve's earlier struggles were at least partly responsible for Apple's renewed success: his cherished creation, the Macintosh, was enjoying an impressive resurgence. Steve was looking on: he talked about Apple "like a proud father," recalls Bud Tribble. There were hints that he quietly yearned to be asked to come back to Apple now that the swift course of history had proved him right, a latter-day Napoleon returning from Elba.

In 1987, a high-ranking Apple executive named Larry Tesler called Steve, albeit accidentally. Larry wanted to offer a consulting contract to a Macintosh software developer named Steve Jasik. He looked through his phone directory, and his eyes fixed not on the correct number but on the very *next* number in the alphabetical listing. Unknowingly he dialed the digits for Steve *Jobs*, not Steve *Jasik*. He heard an answering machine tape:

"This is Steve. Leave a message."

"Steve, I want to talk to you about a job."

A while later, when Larry was out, there was a response from Steve Jobs.

"Larry, I got your message, and I have one question. Are you talking about *you* coming to Next or *me* going to Apple?"

In reality, Apple didn't want him back. Many people argued that the Mac's triumph came about because of the *undoing* of Steve's worst decision. The Mac was saved by the phenomenon of "desktop publishing," as artists and designers used the machine to print homemade newsletters and magazines and brochures with stylish graphics. And desktop publishing was only practical if you could open up the casing of your Macintosh and load in all kinds of extra memory cards and graphic boards and such. Steve had demanded that the Mac's case be bolted closed. He viewed the Mac as his finished product, an artistic creation that shouldn't be tampered with. Sculley turned it into the equivalent of a hot rod with an engine that could be souped up for better performance by kids who liked to tinker under the hood. That's what proved to be the salvation of the computer and the company.

Steve's bitterness toward John Sculley remained intense. Bob Metcalfe, a friend and neighbor of the two men, invited them to his big Christmas party at his mansion in Woodside. Steve and John both showed up, but they were so unhappy to be in each other's presence that they spent the evening on opposite sides of the house. The tension between them was only exacerbated when Sculley published his book, *Odyssey*, a detailed account of their friendship, their falling out, and his own subsequent success.

With Sculley redeemed and Apple resurgent, the pressure intensified for Steve to unveil something great. His people felt the worsening stress. When Steve took them to a resort for another "off-site" retreat, he put a transparency on the overhead projector. It was a list of the problems they faced. At the top Steve had written: "Deep Shit." That wasn't all. He removed the transparency and replaced it with another one: "Ankle Deep Shit."

His perfectionism raged. He was obsessed with minute details that no one else in the computer business was even slightly concerned about. Even the hidden electronic guts of the Next computer—the "motherboard"—had to have a clever, visually appealing design.

"Who's ever going to see the inside?" one of the Next designers asked.

"I will," Steve said.

Sometimes his quest for creativity had comical results, like when he searched for the most innovative designers of the day to create the shape and look of his new machine. He noticed a London firm that won a contest for its styling of a flashlight, and he hired the firm to build a prototype for the Next computer. When the work was completed, Steve and Bud Tribble flew to London. They sat in a conference room looking at a shrouded form on the table. These guys had the same sense of drama as Steve did! The British designers talked at length about the thinking that informed their approach. Then, finally, they pulled off the shroud and revealed . . . a computer in the shape of a human head! Steve was shocked, appalled. He had flown thirteen hours from San Francisco to London for . . . this?

Finally Steve ended his search for new talent and wound up rehiring the industrial designer of the Macintosh, Hartmut Esslinger of the German firm frogdesign. But his new creation couldn't look at all like the Mac. It had to be radically different, radically *better*.

■   ■   ■

IN THE SUMMER OF 1988, Steve's on-and-off artistic muse, Susan Kare, had a ridiculously large bulge under her coat as she walked through Sausalito to the apartment of one of her favorite photographers. Steve had insisted on secrecy. No one from the outside was allowed to see the Next computer. But Susan needed to have some publicity stills taken so they'd be ready for the unveiling in September. So she covered the prototype with her coat, which made her look as though she were in an advanced stage of pregnancy. With twins.

Safely inside the apartment, she pulled away the garment to reveal an oddly beautiful box of the sleekest blackest magnesium. It was a perfect cube, exactly twelve inches long and wide and deep. It looked like abstract minimalist sculpture, but it housed the complex circuitry of the computer. The monitor was also black and starkly elegant. Steve had wanted the black Porsche of computers, and that's what he finally got.

Susan didn't like it. She thought it was too much. As the photographer planned the lighting and the camera angles, she treated him to a sarcastic critique of the design. It was the *Terminator* look, the clichéd boys-and-their-toys aesthetic. She despised how it shouted ne plus ultra, like a gadget from the Sharper Image catalog. It didn't have any of the virtues of the Macintosh, which seemed so accessible, friendly, even cuddly and lovable. The Next machine was very elegant, yes, but it also looked intimidating, even forbidding. It was the Death Star of computers.

As the photographer readied to shoot, Susan took out a bunch of children's toys, playful little dinosaurs in bright colors. She arranged the figurines on top of the austere black box. It was a whimsical gesture, her own subversive way of restoring the softer human element that she loved.

The camera clicked and clicked.

■   ■   ■

THAT SUMMER, Steve would drive through the mountains to San Francisco and camp out at Susan Kare's old Victorian house. They worked together preparing the graphics that he would show during his speech onstage for the Next unveiling. Susan's husband, Jay, would work the espresso machine and bring them café lattes as Steve sat there, obsessed with finding the perfect shade of green for the background color of his slides. He looked at twenty-seven subtly different hues before determining the color that would be precisely right.

He put equal care into composing his text. "Every slide was written like a piece of poetry," recalls Paul Vais, a Next executive who worked closely with Steve on the event. "We spent hours on what most people would consider low-level detail. Steve would labor over the presentation. We'd try to orchestrate and choreograph everything and make it more alive than it really is." Steve wanted to achieve a powerful visual impact. So they paid $60,000 for the video projectors used at rock concerts. Steve wanted to show off the Next computer's ability to play stereo-quality music, an astonishing capability at a time when most personal computers couldn't honk out more than a few crude beeps. He wanted a setting with superb acoustics, so he rented the Davies Symphony Hall in San Francisco. He even hired the symphony's principal violinist to play a Bach duet with the computer.

As the launch approached, Steve was plagued by nervousness, and his scrutiny of fine details remained relentless and obsessive. He read all the copy for every advertisement that would go out for the computer. He approved the invitation list, vetting everyone who would get a coveted ticket for one of the three thousand seats. He even edited the menu for lunch.

The night before the event, he assembled his two hundred employees for a kind of locker-room inspirational speech. He began by closing his palms together in front of him, as if he were praying in church. They knew that gesture well. It was Steve's signal that he was plotting something, that he was scheming about his next move, that he was up to something slyly conspiratorial and they were about to be let in on the whispered secret.

Tomorrow he would talk publicly of his lofty vision of a computer that could revolutionize higher education, a noble goal, and no one would doubt his sincerity. Tonight, though, he spoke of his own dark personal vendetta, which was equally honest.

He locked his praying hands and he spoke bitterly about Apple.

"We're going to get our revenge," he told them.

"We're going to kick their ass."

83
Next

W hile Steve Jobs was maniacally focused on Next, he also owned a second company that received very little of his time or attention. Ironically, this other entrepreneurial venture, which the Next executives referred to condescendingly as "the hobby," would consume far more of Steve's money. And ultimately it would prove far more important and enduring. It would be the source of his resurgence and his salvation.

It was called Pixar.

Like Next, it was a child of divorce. While Next was founded out of the painful separation of Steve Jobs and John Sculley, Pixar was an orphan of a company, put up for adoption as part of the marital split between the legendary movie director George Lucas and his brilliant editor, Marcia Lucas. Steve Jobs became Pixar's new parent and benefactor.

George and Marcia had met in Los Angeles in the late 1960s, soon after he completed film school at the University of Southern California. They were working together on a documentary, huddled in the editing room for many nights before George summoned the courage to ask her out. From the start they were a very odd couple. George was painfully quiet, inward, aloof, brooding, perpetually burdened by worry. Marcia was personable, outspoken, and uninhibited, a funny, sharptongued dynamo. On their first date, she told him to "lighten up." Through fourteen years of marriage, he never really did.

In the 1970s, Marcia became known as one of the most talented film editors in Hollywood. She was especially admired for her editing of *Alice Doesn't Live Here Anymore* and *Taxi Driver* for the director Martin Scorsese. When she collaborated with George, their opposite personalities worked magic in the creative process. She cut George's *American Graffiti*, turning reels of raw footage of improvised scenes into a coherent and surprisingly compelling narrative, and she won an Oscar for her work on the first *Star Wars* movie. As George's business partner and close adviser, she was instrumental in his success, but the intensity and stress of working together on the *Star Wars* trilogy was devastating to their marriage. Before the release of *Return of the Jedi*, George told a writer from *Rolling Stone*: "It's been very hard on Marcia, living with somebody who is constantly in agony, uptight, and worried, off in never-never land."

A week before the theatrical debut of *Jedi*, George called together his staff. As George and Marcia held hands and cried, they said that they were seeking a divorce.

According to California law, they had to split their marital property fifty-fifty. George wanted to keep ownership and control of their burgeoning empire, the alternative Hollywood that they had labored together to create in the celluloid hinterlands of northern California: the movie studio, Lucasfilm, and the special-effects house, Industrial Light and Magic (ILM), and the state-of-the-art postproduction facilities at Skywalker Ranch.

While George wanted the companies, Marcia wanted the money. Her half of the assets were worth an estimated $25 million to $50 million.

Now, he had his precious companies, but George desperately needed a way to come up with some cash. Was there some part of the business that wasn't essential, something that he could spin off into a separate enterprise and sell for really good money?

Maybe. Lucasfilm had a small band of computer graphics geniuses who weren't making profits. They were visionary types who dreamed of reinventing the animated movie. Instead of hundreds of animators slaving away with their pencils and ink and paper, they envisioned a new breed of artists using computers to control and maneuver their fictional characters and to achieve astonishing "three-dimensional" effects with lighting and form. So far it was only a far-off vision. It was a grand ambition that could take many years and cost tens, maybe even hundreds of millions of dollars before it would be realized.

In 1985, while he was still at Apple, Steve Jobs heard that George Lucas was trying to sell this computer operation. Steve was interested. He drove north over the Golden Gate Bridge and another fifteen miles to the offices of Lucasfilm in San Rafael. The company was in a crummy part of town, a warehouse district on the fringe of the Little Mexico ghetto. Clusters of illegal immigrants stood on the sidewalks, hoping that someone would drive up in a van or pickup truck and take them to construction sites to work for the day. As the last batches of unhired hands still loitered there, the Lucasfilm employees took to the pavements to buy cheap tacos and rice-and-bean burritos from the "roach coaches." Lucasfilm and ILM were housed in nondescript, unmarked buildings. They had tried putting up a sign during the *Star Wars* years but the crazy science-fiction fans would come by, snooping for the tiniest clues about what was going to be in the next movie. Now there was no sign and no indication that movie wizardry took place in the unglamorous locale. George Lucas himself and a few of his colleagues worked miles away in the baronial splendor of Skywalker Ranch, a neo-Victorian mansion with a wood-paneled library and stained-glass skylights, removed from the suburban banality of San Rafael, secluded on hundreds of acres of the unspoiled scenic majesty of the tall redwoods and the rolling foothills. It was an almost feudal arrangement: the lord in his manor, his serfs in the squalid town.

■   ■   ■

WHEN STEVE JOBS VISITED LUCASFILM, he had a revelation.

He was astonished by the beautiful high-resolution images he saw on the computer screens. He later told his Next colleagues that he had the same kind of "holy shit" reaction seeing the graphics at Lucasfilm as when he first saw the laser printer in the laboratories at Xerox's Palo Alto Research Center. He knew that it was going to be *hot*. Xerox had lacked the foresight or the will to commercialize its breakthroughs, so Steve had seized them for Apple. Now he was in a remarkably similar situation, another chance to capitalize on many years of brilliant research that had been supported by others at great expense.

It was déjà vu! It was history repeating itself!

George Lucas had lured the greatest minds in computer graphics but he couldn't afford to pay for the realization of their vision. Steve could come in for the slam dunk!

Steve wanted it.

George was asking $30 million.

Steve said: Let me know if the price drops.

Months passed. Lucas recruited another buyer, a consortium of General Motors and the Philips electronics company, but the deal fell through. And he needed the money *now*.

Steve shrewdly negotiated the price down to a desperation offer of $10 million.

In February 1986 he bought the business and incorporated it as "Pixar."

■ ■ ■

PIXAR WAS A TIGHTLY KNIT GROUP of some four-dozen people, mostly refugees from academia. Many of them had been working together since the 1970s, a nomadic tribe of high-tech gypsies moving from one multimillionaire's think tank to another's. They were like Molière's troupe or some other merry band of theatrical performers in the Renaissance, who would find a duke or count to be their patron, then put on their comedies and tragedies and improvisations for his amusement for a few years until he tired of their style of acting and they had to go calling at the château in the next province. After six years with Count Lucas, they were switching their allegiance to the noble and generous Baron Jobs.

The merry band had two leaders, whose experiences, personalities, and ambitions would play a vitally important role in Steve Jobs's future.

One was Alvy Ray Smith, a big, tall, bearded bear of a man who spent his childhood in the impoverished badlands near the border of New Mexico and Texas. Despite these inauspicious origins, his brilliance and charisma were irrepressible, and he achieved a precocious success. In 1971 an illustration from his Ph.D. thesis on game theory was featured on the cover of *Scientific American*. Alvy became an associate professor at New York University, but he chafed at the dull conformity of academia. After a skiing accident in New England, he was forced to spend three months lying on his back in a full-body cast, which gave him time to meditate about his life. He saw himself as an artist and a "wild-ass hippie." He was brilliant at math and computer theory, but he also enjoyed more iconoclastic pursuits like parapsychology and astrology. Being a respectable professor was "a yawn," he thought. His intuition told him to drop out and go to the bohemias of California.

Alvy moved to Berkeley and spent a year hanging out as a hippie. When he finally ran out of money, he scrounged for cash by teaching a course at the university. He also agreed to write the introduction to a new edition of a book by the great computer science theorist John von Neumann.

The Berkeley library didn't have some of the reference sources he needed, but the Stanford library did. It was only an hour's drive, but it was a trip that changed his life.

After spending the day in Palo Alto, Alvy had dinner with the family of a computer scientist he knew there, Dick Shalp, and he stayed the night at their house. Dick worked at Xerox's

Palo Alto Research Center (PARC) in the hills just beyond the Stanford campus.

In the morning, Dick said to Alvy: Come over and see what I'm doing.

Alvy was uninterested but he felt an obligation to his kind host, so he went.

Twelve hours later, he stumbled out of the PARC building.

He had experienced his own "holy shit" revelation.

My God, this is what I came to California to do! he thought, as if the hidden hand of destiny had finally explained why it had mysteriously attracted him to this place.

Dick had shown him a software program called SuperPaint and a powerful computer that was designed for storing images. With these two electronic tools, they simulated drawing and painting on the computer screen, creating lines, shapes, objects, patterns. And colors! Hardly anyone had seen colors coming out of a computer before.

Alvy was astonished, addicted. This was the perfect combination of his two great interests: art and computing. He had to find a way to hang around and play with this stuff.

There weren't any job openings at PARC, so Dick and his colleagues hired Alvy with a purchase order, as if they were paying for an office lamp or a water cooler. "I didn't care about titles or money," Alvy recalls. "I just wanted to make art on their machine."

For a while Alvy had the freedom to experiment and create. Sometimes he jammed on the machines along with one of his bearded hippie-artist friends, a motorcycle freak named David de Francesco. They wrote a grant application and submitted it to the National Endowment for the Arts. But before their grant could be approved, the bureaucrats at PARC canceled the purchase order and ended Alvy's stay as a technological squatter.

The hippies were stranded. PARC was the only civilian institution that had the graphics computer they needed, a hugely expensive machine called a frame buffer. They needed to find another one. They heard that the University of Utah was buying one of these whiz-bang contraptions from a startup that had been founded by a couple of its professors.

To Utah!

Alvy and David were so charged up that they drove Alvy's Ford Torino through the Sierra Nevada mountains in a treacherous snowstorm in their haste to get to Salt Lake City.

When they got there, the computer researchers said that they were too late. They had just missed the crazy rich guy from Long Island, who had come to town and quickly spent millions of dollars buying up every type of graphics computer that the professors' company was trying to sell. The only other customers for the new machines were from the military-industrial complex, and they wanted to make computer flight-simulators and other practical things. But this crazy rich guy wanted to make animated *movies* with the computers! He was interested in *art*! He wanted to be the Walt Disney of the computer era.

One of the older Utah researchers went over to Alvy and David and told them:

"Boys, if I were you, I'd get on the next plane to New York."

They did. Alvy spent the last of his savings on the ticket.

They flew east and stayed over with David's father in northern New Jersey. Then they borrowed a car and drove through a snowstorm—another snowstorm!—to Long Island.

They went to the moneyed enclave of the North Shore, Gatsby territory, and they entered the crazy millionaire's think tank, the New York Institute of Technology. The name made it sound like a real university, with dormitories and dining halls, but it was actually a row of gorgeous old Gatsbyesque mansions that had been enclosed into a compound. The computer laboratory was housed in the cavernous four-car garage of one of the big houses.

Alvy entered the garage and met the man who would become his intellectual partner and close friend for two decades: Edwin Catmull.

As a teenager Ed had dreamed of becoming a movie animator. In college he had the unhappy realization that he couldn't draw well enough. He switched to physics and earned a Ph.D. at the University of Utah. But he never relinquished his ambition of making movies; instead, he became impassioned about using technology to reinvent the process. In 1972 he created the first computer-animated film. The subject was his own left hand. He covered the hand with plaster of paris to make a mold, realizing too late that he should have shaved off the hairs. Then he covered the mold with a layer of latex and he drew hundreds of little shapes (or polygons) over small areas of the surface. He measured the distances between the shapes and fed the data into a computer, creating a 3-D digital model of his hand that he could view on the computer screen. By writing some software, he could rotate the virtual hand. He could portray the effects of lighting from different angles. He could simulate the view of a camera peering inside the hollowed-out hand. In his short film, called *Futureworld*, the hand looked more plastic than realistic, but it was nonetheless an astonishing work of art, simple but hypnotic, the start of a revolution.

After the eccentric millionaire went to Utah and bought up all the hardware, he hired Ed to come to Long Island and create the technology for a feature-length computer-animated film. Ed had a chance to realize his dream. And now he had Alvy as a brilliant partner.

Alvy and Ed seemed in many ways like opposite personalities. Alvy was a long-haired bearded wild-ass hippie, a subversive renegade, talkative and gregarious, and he could be fiery if provoked. He was single and unfettered and kept weird hours. He believed his natural clock called for "twenty-six-hour days." Ed was quiet and straitlaced and shy, a clean-cut Mormon who worked from nine to five so he could spend time at home with his wife and his small children. But both men had a sincerity and a certain gentleness, and they had great respect for each other's intelligence and commitment. They became close friends.

The eccentric multimillionaire they worked for was a figure of Gatsbyesque intrigue. His name was Alexander Schure, and he possessed great wealth, though no one seemed to know where his money came from. There was only myth and speculation. The most popular story went like this: Alex's father (or perhaps his grandfather) made a fortune in the fur trade. Then Alex multiplied the wealth by exploiting his family's close friendship with Major Alexander de Seversky, whom he knew familiarly as "Sasha." When World War II ended, Alex gained access to a large amount of surplus military electronics equipment, apparently thanks to the friendly major. When the GI Bill was passed and returning servicemen began enrolling in colleges, Alex started a correspondence school to teach electronics to the former soldiers. He took out hokey advertisements with a terrific gimmick: he promised to send all kinds of electronics equipment to his students—for *free*!

Such were the weird origins of Alex Schure's New York Institute of Technology, or so went the story. Eventually "New York Tech" began offering courses in classrooms—Alex bought a building near Manhattan's Lincoln Center—and granting undergraduate degrees. But Alex's operations always seemed somewhat suspicious.

Although New York Tech is now an accredited school, its early days were unusual. "New York Tech was a diploma mill," recalled Alvy Ray Smith. "The bookstore sold auto parts. We heard that it was subsidized by a land development deal in Florida."

Alex Schure exuded mystique. He was a trim, handsome man with dark hair and thick eyebrows. He dressed with excellent taste, but as soon as he began to talk, he revealed his eccentricity and weirdness. He spewed forth words like an incomprehensible rapper. Alvy thought of Alex's patois as "word salad" or "Casey Stengel speak." Alex's internal clock was out of sync with the rest of society's. He would come into the office to begin work at entirely unpredictable hours: he could start his day at 5 A.M. or 5 P.M.

Despite his unusual persona, Alex was an ideal patron for the band of computer wizards that Ed and Alvy attracted. They were completely independent of the dubious diploma-mill school in Manhattan. They could spend millions of dollars and hire people almost at will. They were never constrained by budgets or deadlines or even specific goals. They were entirely freewheeling. It was an extraordinary environment, a researcher's dream. Money! Time! Talent! Freedom!

After Alvy was there for only two weeks, he talked with Ed about Alex Schure's astonishingly laissez-faire attitude and his tenuous grasp of the technology.

"This guy doesn't have the foggiest!" Alvy exclaimed.

"I know," Ed said contentedly.

The bucolic setting only added to the pinch-me fairy-tale unreality of it all. When Alvy Ray Smith and David de Francesco went looking for a place to live near the research center, they saw a vintage British Vincent motorcycle parked in front of one of the neighboring estates. David had a passion for esoteric motorbikes, so they stopped to look. After chatting

97
Pixar

with the owners, they found themselves installed in the carriage house, living rent-free in a spacious three-bedroom apartment above the garage. It was the old chauffeur's quarters from an era when chauffeurs lived surprisingly well. Their landlord, Justine McGrath Cutting, was a sister-in-law of David Rockefeller. Though in her sixties she wore bikinis around the estate and referred to her bearded brainy tenants as "my physicists."

They lived on an estate, they worked on an estate, they did whatever they wanted. Although Ed would go home to his family at five o'clock, the rest of the bunch were young and single and stayed up late working and cavorting. Alvy was the joyous ringleader. In May 1977, the day that *Star Wars* opened, he drove his colleagues to Manhattan to see the movie. They were so captivated that they went back to the cinema to see another showing later that day. *Star Wars* was spectacular, but none of the special effects were created with a computer. George Lucas didn't have the technology they were developing in the garage. No one did.

■   ■   ■

COMPUTER GRAPHICS GURUS were almost ready to make very brief special effects for movies, but the idea of creating a feature-length film with computers was still way off. Part of the problem was that computer power was very expensive, and their art required overwhelming amounts of it. Here's why: The basic trick was to simulate the complex effects of the rays of light as they ricocheted off all the tiny crevices and curves and corners of every finely detailed object in a picture. That's essentially how the Old Master painters achieved their stunning illusions of realism back in the eighteenth century, and it was still the key to making a two-dimensional composition take on a breathtakingly three-dimensional look.

It was hard enough for a Rembrandt or a Vermeer to paint *one* picture with that level of realism—and a movie required twenty-four pictures (or "frames") per second multiplied by sixty seconds in a minute and then multiplied by around ninety minutes in a feature film. That was nearly 130,000 pictures, an effort far beyond the most Herculean efforts of even the best team of hundreds of masterful artists.

So that was where automation could come in. The computer, by making a mathematical calculation, could figure out how light careened off the angles and folds in every object in the scene. The computer could, essentially, pretend that it was shining a sliver of light onto a tiny region on the surface of the object (which the animators called a polygon). The more times you repeated this process, the greater the number of polygons, then the more finely detailed the picture. If the object had simple geometries and flat surfaces—a cube, for instance—you might need only a few dozen polygons to portray it. But if the figure was highly variegated and complex—a human face, say—it could take light rays reflecting off gazillions of polygons to look real.

While the basic idea behind computer animation was relatively easy to grasp, the execution was notoriously hard. You could write a software program to figure out the minute effects of lighting, but when you actually ran the program, it required an awesome number of mathematical calculations. It consumed computer power and time with a staggering appetite. You would have to buy roomfuls of hugely expensive state-of-the-art hardware to constantly crunch all the data. It took what computer scientists like to call "brute force."

In the late 1970s Alvy and Ed did a crude "back-of-the-envelope" calculation and determined that it would cost more than $1 billion to make a feature film with computers. At the time, most movies were shot for under $20 million. So their dream was still about fifty times too expensive.

Before long, that would change. The cost of computer hardware was falling dramatically, fulfilling the astonishing prediction made by Intel's cofounder Gordon Moore. His famous prophecy, known as Moore's Law, said that because of the rapid and relentless improvements in silicon chip technology, computer power became half as expensive every eighteen to twenty-four months. So Ed and Alvy could easily do the math: $1 billion worth of computers today would cost only $500 million when the next models came on the market. And a couple of years later, they would cost $250 million, then $120 million, then $60 million, then $30 million, and then $15 million, which was much more like it. And that meant that once the price had been slashed in half a total of six times—which could take nine years, maybe twelve years—then a Hollywood studio could afford to make the first full-length and fully computer-animated feature. That would take them into the middle or the end of the 1980s. The vision was still years from realization, but it was clearly within sight.

Alvy and Ed furtively believed that Disney would be the company to pay for their breakthrough computer-animated film. Every year, they would make a secret trip to Los Angeles, pretending they were visiting relatives so that Alex Schure wouldn't get suspicious. They would show up at Disney head-quarters and say: "Are you guys ready?"

Disney's technologists were enthusiastic, but top management wasn't interested. Walt Disney himself had died a decade earlier. The company was being run by his son-in-law, a former football star, with depressing results. "We knew that if Walt were there, he'd have the vision," Alvy recalls. But Walt was gone, and his successors were struggling.

Alex Schure wanted fervently to become the new Walt

100
The
Second
Coming
of
Steve
Jobs

Disney. In one mansion he had Ed and Alvy working on the far-off future of animation, but in another mansion in the compound he had a hundred people trying to make a Disneyesque film in the old proven way, with artists working meticulously with pencils and paper and ink, a method that hadn't changed much since Disney produced *Snow White* in the 1930s. He recruited experienced animators from the Hollywood studios. He hired background artists and camera operators. And by the end of the decade, they completed their first opus, *Tubby the Tuba*.

It was awful. The music was embarrassingly bad. The story was poorly constructed. There were many technical flaws: shadows, lint. When Alvy and Ed attended a private showing at the MGM screening room in Manhattan, the picture was so boring that Alvy fell asleep. "We were so glad that we weren't associated with it," he recalls.

The *Tubby* fiasco made them realize that they had to fly from their gilded cage. They had complete freedom and they felt they were "pushing the envelope" of technology, but somehow the situation didn't feel right anymore. Alex Schure was never going to be Walt Disney. He had the tremendous will. He even shared their vision that computers would ultimately *reduce* the cost of animation. But he wasn't a creative genius like Walt.

"We saw the movie and we said: 'This guy doesn't have it,'" Alvy recalls.

They knew that they needed a real Hollywood player as their patron.

Then, almost as if on cue, George Lucas called.

■   ■   ■

THE WAY THAT GEORGE found them was circuitous and comical. As the 1970s ended, George saw that Hollywood was still relying on 1940s technology. Rolls of film were still cut and spliced on antiquated mechanical contraptions, and the process was tedious and cumbersome. Could computers somehow make it easier?

That was the visionary part. More urgently, George wanted to speed up the work on special effects for the *Star Wars* sequels. The "light saber" weapons were a real pain in the ass. The actors were filmed holding just the metallic handles of the swords. Then, in postproduction, the glowing laser beams had to be colored in by hand onto the celluloid film frames by the animators at Industrial Light and Magic. It was incredibly slow and boring. Wasn't there some way to get computers to create the simple visual illusion?

George's other big problem was the damned spaceships. Just getting one ship to fly across a movie frame was enough of a trick, since he had to shoot from scale models. But the scenes that showed wartime armadas of hundreds of spaceships flying all over the place—those were the *killers*. Every frame of film—twenty-four frames for every second of running time—had to be overlaid again and again and again. They literally had to cut and paste the pictures of each spaceship onto the tableau. The handicraft was maddeningly tedious. George wondered: Could he get a bunch of computer wizards to figure out a better way?

George himself wasn't immersed in high technology. He didn't know whom to call. For some reason he gave the assignment to his real estate manager, the man who advised him about what buildings to buy in his home area of Marin County, California.

In the winter of 1979, the man drove down to Stanford and wandered around the computer science department, asking whether anyone knew about computers and film. The answer was no. No one! At Stanford, no less! But a visiting professor from Carnegie Mellon recommended one of his former graduate students, a kid named Ralph Guggenheim.

102

The
Second
Coming
of
Steve
Jobs

Ralph was working at an obscure place, the New York Institute of Technology.

The Lucas lieutenant called. He said that he was George's "head of development." Ralph thought that meant the person in charge of stories and scripts. That's what it meant in Hollywood. He didn't realize that this guy was the head of *real estate* development.

The man said: We want you to run George's new computer operation in California. Then almost instinctively he reverted to his everyday real estate huckster's persona:

Marin County is a great place to live, he said. House values there are terrific.

Ralph was overwhelmed.

"I'm deeply honored," he replied. "But I'm only twenty-seven. Let me introduce you to the older guys here."

The Lucas man seemed satisfied. Then, almost as an after-thought, he asked:

"Can you make a spaceship fly around on the screen?"

"Sure, we do it every day."

■   ■   ■

RALPH WENT OVER to Ed and Alvy.

"I just got a call from George Lucas," he told them.

Alvy reacted swiftly.

"Don't say anything," he instructed. "Close the door."

They needed to maintain total secrecy from Alex Schure. Alex was always terribly fearful that someone would steal away the research and technology that he had paid for. The last time someone tried to walk out on Alex, there was almost a fistfight at the lab.

Alvy remembered the situation vividly:

Alex had hired a young Ph.D. named Jim Clark. (Years

later, Jim would become one of the wealthiest and most famous figures in American business as the founder of Silicon
Graphics and Netscape Communications.) For his dissertation
at the University of Utah, Jim had created gear for mounting a
computer display at eye level, the forerunner of the "virtual reality" headsets that would gain popularity in the 1980s. Alex
hired him to come to Long Island and build a new version of
his gadget.

104
The
Second
Coming
of
Steve
Jobs

Alvy liked Jim and thought of him as a "homeboy," since
they had grown up only sixty miles apart: Alvy in eastern New
Mexico, Jim in western Texas. Jim was a brilliant Ph.D., but
he still had the mentality of a tough kid from a hardscrabble
rural town. He was a big, imposing man who had been kicked
out of high school for being a ruffian, which is an impressive
accomplishment in west Texas, a place that is uncommonly tol-
erant of ruffians.

There was raw aggression and clear mistrust between Jim
Clark and Alex Schure. Jim decided to leave. He used a word
processor to compose letters to Stanford and other universities, asking for an academic position.

One day Alex came into the lab and held up a printout of
the letters.

The bastard was spying on them! He must have had a
mole!

"You're fired," Alex said.

Jim reacted violently. He threatened to tear up the computer lab.

Alvy was certain that Jim was about to throw a punch at
Alex. He rushed over to restrain his friend, to calm him down.
He got there just in time to prevent an assault.

For his part, Jim Clark says that he was "really pissed"
when he "found out that Alex was spying," but denies the face-
to-face confrontation.

■　　■　　■

THE ᴇᴘɪꜱᴏᴅᴇ ᴡᴀꜱ still vivid in their memories as they closed the door to the lab.

George Lucas had called Ralph.

Coincidentally, that same morning Francis Ford Coppola's people had called Alvy.

They needed to act swiftly and secretly. Alvy and Ed drove into town, rented an old typewriter, then went to Ed's apartment and very carefully composed their letter to Lucasfilm. "We knew that it was the most important letter of our lives," Alvy recalls.

They flew to California to make their pitch to the Lucas people. George himself, ever reclusive, didn't attend. And Alvy began going to San Francisco to hang out for weekends at Francis Ford Coppola's twenty-eight-room Victorian mansion atop a hill overlooking the bay. The windows framed picture-postcard views of the Golden Gate Bridge. Francis ran avant-garde films in the screening room. There were drugs everywhere. Alvy would watch as Francis maintained several overlapping conversations while cooking spaghetti. Francis felt a sense of competition with his friend George Lucas. He tried to hire Alvy, but Coppola seemed buffeted by intense highs and lows, and his energy was driven too much by cocaine.

They decided to go with George.

They knew that Alex Schure would react violently when he found out, so they came up with a clever scheme for deception. Instead of moving directly to Lucasfilm as a group, they would all take interim jobs as a cover, essentially "laundering" themselves. They were going into a misleading "holding pattern" before landing at their final destination. Alvy Ray Smith and David de Francesco went to the Jet Propulsion Lab in

Pasadena before ultimately joining up again with Ed Catmull at Lucasfilm. Ralph Guggenheim worked for a few months at a documentary film company in Pittsburgh before heading to northern California.

By 1980 they all were together at Lucasfilm. Their office was in a building George owned in San Anselmo, the perfect small town where he lived, which still had an old-time movie house with an art deco marquee. They worked above a laundromat and an antiques store in a second-story suite that they shared with Marcia Lucas, George's wife and editor.

Their honeymoon at Lucasfilm was brief. At first Alvy and Ed felt exhilarated. The glamour of the movie business made it remarkably easy for them to hire the most talented people in their field. They quickly added to their own estimable brain trust and assembled the best team of computer graphics people in the world. The problem was that George Lucas showed almost no interest in computer-generated special effects beyond the original impetus of the light sabers and the spaceships. He didn't yet understand the full potential.

The turning point came when Paramount hired ILM to create the effects for *Star Trek II: The Wrath of Khan* and asked for one particular shot using computer graphics. They wanted a genesis scene, a creative and visually spectacular portrayal of death transformed into life. The ILM people had no experience with computers, so they went to Alvy Ray Smith, who by then was working in an office literally next door in San Rafael.

Alvy realized that this was even more than his first big chance to design a scene in a motion picture. It was an opportunity to make what would also serve as a sixty-second advertisement to George Lucas about how computers could revolutionize film.

Alvy thought about what they already knew how to do with graphics. Alvy had a freakish passion for genealogy and

106

The
Second
Coming
of
Steve
Jobs

embryology, so he was good at making pictures of eggs, zygotes, sperm. One of his colleagues excelled at craters. Another could do mountains, and one even knew how to realistically simulate the appearance of fire.

These early experiments in computer graphics, inspired by the personal quirks of each researcher, all came together in Alvy's storyboard for the scene: A spaceship flies by a barren moon covered by craters. A sperm-shaped projectile shoots out. Then: chaos. Fire covers the planet and melts its surface. Mountains rise. Oceans form. Life reemerges.

The Paramount people loved the idea.

Alvy knew that he needed one more trick. The scene had emotional power, but when George watched movies he wasn't sucked in by the emotions. George focused on the technique, especially the camera work. Alvy knew that if he wanted to impress his boss, he had to conceive of an incredibly acrobatic camera move that would be absolutely *impossible* to film with a real camera, something that could only be done through the otherworldly magic of a computer simulation. In Alvy's big scene, the camera's vantage point would twist and swirl around the spacecraft, then sweep ahead of the wall of flames on the planet.

The day after the premiere of *Star Trek II*, George put one foot inside Alvy's office.

"Great camera move," he said quickly.

Then he was gone.

From that point forward, George's movies relied heavily on computer graphics.

■   ■   ■

NOT LONG AFTER George Lucas became a convert, Disney's executives followed.

108
The
Second
Coming
of
Steve
Jobs

In the autumn of 1984, Disney's board recruited two bosses from Paramount, Michael Eisner and Frank Wells, to take control and attempt to save the company. They needed to do something about animation. Disney's films had been faring so poorly at the box office that its managers had seriously considered abandoning animation entirely. But Walt Disney's brother, Roy, argued passionately for preserving the soul of the company. The new honchos, Eisner and Wells, wanted to save animation but knew they needed to greatly reduce the costs. Soon after they took over, they called Alvy Ray Smith and Ed Catmull at Lucasfilm to talk about going digital.

It was still prohibitively expensive to use computers for the new vision of 3-D animation, but the machines could actually save money if they took on some of the drudge work in the traditional process of 2-D animation. The idea was that Disney's artists would still sketch the characters by hand, but then they'd scan their drawings into computers and use the new machines to help them "ink" over the pencil lines and "paint" the color fields in between. It was as if the humans were creating a children's coloring book, and the machines had the comparatively simple tasks of tracing and then coloring in between the lines.

Essentially, Disney was trying to automate what had long been considered women's work. In earlier eras there had been a blatantly sexist division of labor: the men had the more glamorous, creative jobs of drawing the characters while the lower-paid "ink and paint girls" handled the meticulous grunt work. The women were sequestered in a separate building on the Burbank lot, and Walt himself seldom saw them.

In the new scheme, computers would be the cheap labor.

The approach, which they called the Computer Animation Production System (CAPS), would quickly prove a clear success, saving huge amounts of time and money, although

Disney's people were quiet about it. "For a long time, Disney wouldn't admit to the world that it relied on computers," Alvy recalls. "They thought it would take away the magic."

■   ■   ■

THE DISNEY PROJECT, like the *Star Trek* effect, was a beginning step toward the creative merger of computers and film. In the mid-1980s Ed Catmull still dreamed of creating a full-length movie entirely on the computer, with the kind of three-dimensional animation that he had pioneered in his student film so many years earlier. He and Alvy recruited a small team of artists to work on demonstrations of 3-D graphics. The technology was painfully tricky, requiring a skillful illustrator to learn to become an adept programmer as well. You needed someone whose left brain and right brain were both exceptional. Even then, it took at least a month, and often two or three months, to make a single picture that was akin to a well-composed still photograph. They created a few stunningly vivid images—a pool table, a bouncing ball, the country road to Point Reyes on the Pacific coast—but it was slow, arduous work. The notion of making even a very short film still seemed intimidating.

At a conference Ed met a Disney animator, John Lasseter, who wasn't afraid to talk computers. John's obvious brilliance was balanced by his exceptionally warm, compelling personality, and his almost childlike exuberance. His peers thought of him as one of Disney's most promising young talents. John took Alvy into the Disney archives and said conspiratorially: "What do you want to see?" Alvy had always loved the dancing hippo scenes from *Fantasia* and the pink elephant scenes from *Dumbo*. He was charmed when John pulled out the original sketches and the final animation cells from the movies.

John was disenchanted by the decline of animation at Disney. His frustration peaked after he worked on a test clip (forty-five seconds in all) for a film version of Maurice Sendak's classic children's book *Where the Wild Things Are*. The animators drew the characters by hand, in 2-D, but they used computers to create dramatic 3-D backgrounds. John was terribly excited by the experiment, but Disney's executives—complacent with the old way of doing things—were nonplussed.

110
The
Second
Coming
of
Steve
Jobs

In 1985 John Lasseter switched to Lucasfilm to make short animated films using all the hardware and software tools that had been developed over the past thirteen years by Ed and Alvy and their band.

There was one problem: George Lucas desperately needed to sell their operation.

■　　■　　■

GEORGE HAD TWO BUSINESS MANAGERS, named Doug and Doug, whom Alvy thought of as "corporate dweebs." The Dougs wanted to lay off almost all of the forty-five people in the computer group while Lucas searched for a buyer for the technologies they had created.

Ed and Alvy were appalled. They had put together a remarkable team of people and thought it would be a "sin" to force them to disperse. They mulled founding their own company and taking the whole team with them. But they knew and cared very little about business. "We were a couple of naive technoids," recalls Alvy. He thought of himself as defiantly "anticorporate." He was an artist, a hippie, not some soulless wheeler-dealer.

They talked with their old friend Jim Clark, who had

founded a prominent computer manufacturer, Silicon Graphics Inc., and already become a multimillionaire.

"Why are you still working for The Man?" Jim asked. "Starting a company is real easy. Do it."

Ed and Alvy went to a local bookstore and bought a guide about how to do it. They began writing up a business plan. They figured that they could find a market for the graphics computer they had created for ILM and Disney, a million-dollar machine that stored thousands of digital images. They could sell it to hospitals for archiving x-ray photographs, or to the government's spy agencies, which loved buying new technology.

George put the operation up for sale. Ross Perot's company, EDS (which was then part of General Motors), teamed with Philips, the Dutch electronics giant, and made an offer that was very close to George's asking price of $30 million. To work out the final details and close the deal, each of the four parties—Lucasfilm, EDS, Philips, and Alvy and Ed—planned to send envoys and lawyers to a summit meeting in New York City.

Before they flew east, Alvy and Ed were apprehensive. They had heard strange things about Ross Perot from a credible source, Scott McNealy, the chief executive of Sun Microsystems, a rising young star in Silicon Valley. Scott talked about how he and Ross were supposed to meet at Chicago's O'Hare Airport to shake hands on a deal. The terms had already been negotiated by their people, but the two leaders had never met in person.

At O'Hare, Ross Perot sized up the younger man and asked: "Are you married?"

"No."

"Where do you live?"

"California."

Pixar

That was all that Ross Perot wanted to know.
He stormed away. The deal was off.

■   ■   ■

112
The
Second
Coming
of
Steve
Jobs

THE BIG MEETING was held in the penthouse of the Philips offices on Forty-second Street, looking out on the Beaux Arts sculptures atop Grand Central Terminal. The stress and intensity was almost overwhelming to Alvy: a roomful of high-priced lawyers, arguing over his future. As the meeting ended, it looked as though all the parties were happy with the arrangement. But the EDS negotiators warned that there was one missing element. It wouldn't be a done deal until Alvy and Ed shook hands with Ross Perot.

Ross Perot! If he had rejected Scott McNealy, who was clean-cut and preppy, how would be react to a long-haired bearded wild-assed hippie renegade like Alvy Ray Smith?

They would never know. The next day, the newspapers ran a headline saying that General Motors had forced the ornery Ross Perot to resign from its board of directors.

Perot was out. And the deal was off.

■   ■   ■

ALVY AND ED WERE DESPERATE. There were no other interested buyers, except . . . well, Steve Jobs had remained in touch with them. He seemed like their last chance.

The previous summer, after Steve was ousted from Apple, he thought of buying the Lucas computer group and running it himself. Alvy and Ed rejected the idea. They wanted to run their own show. And they didn't like the notion of "being the first girlfriend after the divorce," as Alvy put it. But now that Steve had gone ahead and started Next, which was consuming all of his attention, they felt more comfortable asking him to invest.

Alvy and Ed went to visit Steve at the Woodside mansion. They wondered why there was no furniture in the place, only a Bösendorfer piano and a BMW motorcycle, testaments to Steve's fascination with German technology. Steve had his personal chefs make them a vegetarian meal featuring a salad of edible flowers. His chefs were a hip young married couple who had graduated from Berkeley and trained at Chez Panisse. Now they lived somewhere in the vast twenty-five thousand square feet of Steve's nearly empty hacienda.

Alvy had some friends at Apple who warned him about Steve's dark side of egotism and temperamental outbursts. But when Alvy would come to visit that December, Steve was unfailingly charming. They'd drive around in Steve's Porsche, talk for a while, go out to dinner. Steve seemed to have the vision and the ability to make things happen.

They had a deal.

The new company needed a name. The gang went out to brainstorm at a burger joint near the office. They wanted a word like "laser," something that seemed high-tech. Alvy proposed "Pixer," which sounded like an infinitive verb, "to pix," to make pictures. Almost there. Spanish verbs often ended in "-ar," so they tried "Pixar." That was it. Pixar.

■   ■   ■

THE NOMADIC TRIBE of artists and computer wizards had finally found a new patron. They joked about how they had gone from one millionaire to another and now to yet another.

Ed and Alvy ran the company together as equals, and from the beginning they guarded their independence from their new owner. They kept their old space in the unmarked Lucas complex in San Rafael, hard by the roach coaches and the loitering day laborers. The office was shabby and cruddy, with a Ping-Pong table and kitschy toys festooned all over, like an undergraduate dorm. Eccentricity abounded. There were outrageous hippies who walked around barefoot and took their dogs to work. A few people truly never bathed. Hardly anyone showed up before noon, though they often stayed as late as midnight. No one expected to make much money. They were there because it was artsy and cool and it was in the bohemian refuge of Marin County.

Steve wanted Alvy and Ed to move the company. For him to get up to Pixar, he had to drive north to San Francisco, plod from traffic light to traffic light on the slow-moving surface streets, then fight the tourists and commuters who crowded the Golden Gate Bridge on the way into Marin. The trip could easily take an hour and a half. Steve told Alvy and Ed to relocate their operation to San Francisco, so with luck he could get up there in only forty-five minutes. But they resisted. They wanted to make it hard for Steve to drop by. And they succeeded. Steve rarely appeared in person. Ralph Guggenheim recalls that Steve visited Pixar's offices "no more than five times between 1986 and 1992, no exaggeration."

"Pixar was geographically inconvenient," recalls Andy Cunningham, Steve's public relations consultant. "We referred to it as 'the hobby.' When Steve ended up buying Pixar, people thought he was crazy. The Pixar crowd was always a very tightly knit group, and Steve didn't mess with them because graphics wasn't his expertise. These guys were doing something highly technical, and frankly I didn't think that Steve understood it. When we did the p.r. for Pixar, Steve wasn't even involved. With Next, he would review every word, every picture. But Pixar was completely run by Ed and Alvy Ray. These guys were adults already. They were self-confident in who they were. Nobody at Next was an adult."

■　　■　　■

THIS ADULT CONFIDENCE AT PIXAR was coupled with swift action that hadn't been seen at Next. In May 1986, only three months after the company spun out from Lucasfilm, they began selling the Pixar Image Computer, a box for storing full-color digital images. The machine was shockingly expensive and extremely esoteric. The price was $135,000 for the box alone, and if you wanted to communicate with it, you needed to plug it into a $35,000 workstation from Sun Microsystems or Silicon Graphics.

But what could it do? The best way to show it off was to make an animated film with the contraption. That role fell to John Lasseter. He still had little experience working with computer animation, but he was learning rapidly. When he was at Lucasfilm he had directed an experimental sixty-second short, *The Adventures of Wally and André B*, with Alvy Ray Smith as producer. (The title was an homage to Louis Malle's *My Dinner with André*.) Alvy conceived of the story as a way to entertain his son, Sam, who was one year old. He described the premise as "a huge bumblebee scares the shit out of a little kid."

John's storyboards had a violence that might appeal to teenagers or immature adults but not to young children. He wanted to explicitly portray the bee biting the child's butt. In the final cut, the actual sting occurred offscreen. Still, Alvy's son was so frightened by the little film that he would cry even if he only heard the opening bars of the soundtrack.

116

The
Second
Coming
of
Steve
Jobs

However sophomoric the storyline, *Wally and André B* hinted at the potential of 3-D animation. The characters were as crudely and simplistically drawn as Mickey Mouse, but like Mickey, they seemed human enough to express the basic strong emotions. And the background shots of a leafy autumnal forest were remarkably beautiful. The light seemed to reflect off of many thousands of individual leaves. The computer-generated effect was stunning. It would have been daunting for human animators to pay attention to such a granular level of detail. But Pixar's software engineers came up with complex mathematical equations that randomized the position and the minute movements of the countless tiny leaves.

For his next film, John found the models for his characters in an unlikely place: the top of his own desk. He had an inexpensive Luxo lamp, a brand that was very popular at the time. The appeal of a Luxo was its easy maneuverability, which made it a fun toy as well as a useful light fixture. The lamp seemed vaguely anthropomorphic, with a swivel head atop metallic supports. It had visible springs and mechanical joints that made it almost infinitely adjustable, even capable of fluid motion at the hands of its owner.

That was all the inspiration John needed. He created a brief scene of a parent lamp watching as a child lamp jumps on a little ball until the ball deflates. The child seems sad for a moment. Then it goes offscreen and returns with an even bigger ball to jump on. The parent looks on, exasperated that its exuberant offspring has failed to learn a lesson.

John and his handful of colleagues in the animation group worked obsessively on *Luxo Jr.* John spent his nights huddled in a sleeping bag under his desk. Pixar's receptionist would wake him up in the morning so he could shower and return to work.

They finished the piece in time for the annual summer

get-together for the computer graphics field, which was called Siggraph (for Special Interest Group on Graphics). Siggraph was a bizarre hybrid of an arts festival and a trade show. It was the year's one-time-only opportunity for the top players to show off their latest work and technical advances to each other. It was where the special-effects experts from the Hollywood studios met the foremost thinkers from the academic computer science departments.

In preparation for the big event, John doubled as the artistic muse for Pixar's marketing team. He created the Pixar logo and the sleek look for the casing of the Pixar Image Computer. He personally designed the Pixar booth on the floor of the convention center. He even designed the *Luxo Jr.* T-shirts that they would give away for free.

As Siggraph began, the show floor was crowded with hundreds of booths, a cacophony of competition. But Pixar's short film quickly emerged as the hit of the show. *Luxo Jr.* was a hypnotic attraction. People were delighted and transfixed as they watched it again and again. The astonishing thing was that John's characters had *personality*. His film had . . . a story! Everyone else at Siggraph was showing demo tapes of special effects. There was reel after reel of lighting patterns, and curtains blowing in the wind, and water flowing over rocks. The other teams called attention to their technical breakthroughs. But Pixar made a real film, a piece of art with emotional impact. "*Luxo Jr.* showed the ultimate potential of the technology," recalls its producer, Ralph Guggenheim. "It showed that this media was subtle enough that people would respond to the characters and laugh."

John Lasseter had scrapped the sophomoric tone of his earlier film. He was developing his ability to tell a story with sophisticated wit, charm, subtlety, and economy, while keeping his playful spirit. He was undeniably a big talent. Ralph entered *Luxo Jr.* in the Academy Awards, and it was nominated for the Oscar for best animated short film.

Still, the point of the exercise wasn't to launch Pixar into the movie business. It was to sell an arcane computer for the outrageously high price of $135,000. "The whole motivation was to show people who wanted to buy our technology that it worked," says Ralph. "Our filmmaking began as a demonstration of the capabilities of our technology. But fortunately it gave John the opportunity to be what he really was: a storyteller."

"The strategy was to promote the technology," recalls Andy Cunningham. "We didn't do anything to position John Lasseter as a 'star.' He was a kid doing fun stuff."

Steve Jobs went to Siggraph and he was pleased by the popularity of *Luxo Jr.*, but what really excited him about Pixar was the hardware. From the earliest days at Apple, Steve had always been a hardware guy. That was his real interest, his overriding obsession. He wanted Pixar to sell lots of computers. The *machine* was supposed to be the real star.

Nonetheless, John Lasseter became an underground celebrity, a minor hero in the insular subculture of animated filmmakers. He secured his reputation the following year at Siggraph with *Red's Dream*, a short film about a little red unicycle that is abandoned in the back corner of a bicycle store on a rainy night and dreams about performing in a circus. *Red's* was longer and much more complex and virtuosic than *Luxo*, and it had an almost surrealistic beauty. Once again, John's work was the convention's unchallenged hit.

John spent much of his time traveling around the world to animation festivals, reveling in his newfound notoriety. He loved the boondoggle aspect of it all. He also hung out in Los Angeles, maintaining his connections in the Hollywood animation scene. Despite his growing profile, his Pixar colleagues

118

The
Second
Coming
of
Steve
Jobs

still thought of him as a humble, easygoing guy. He played on the Pixar softball team in its weekly games in the Lucasfilm league. They'd play at Skywalker Ranch on George's beautiful baseball diamond, a fanatically well-maintained field in the lush foothills, and afterward they'd all go out to a greasy hamburger joint in San Rafael. John was a rare talent but he was one of the gang.

■   ■   ■

EVEN AS AN ABSENTEE OWNER, Steve Jobs exerted an undeniable influence. On a rare visit to Pixar's offices, Steve talked about chips and computers with the Ph.D. engineers, who were visibly awestruck and adoring of him. "I'd watch him address our employees, and the look in their eyes was love," recalls Alvy Ray Smith. "He'd have them twisted around his finger. He's seductive to the nth degree. When I wasn't subject to it, I used to love to see him enter a roomful of strangers and just *take* it. Steve has that talent. I think that it's a talent of the tongue. The closest thing is a TV evangelist. And Steve is *aware* of it."

Alvy and Ed would drive down to Next headquarters in Palo Alto to brief Steve and talk strategy. Beforehand they would work hard to come up with their own clear agenda so they could prevent Steve from taking over. They knew how compelling Steve could be. They agreed on a silent warning signal: if one of them seemed to be falling for Steve's seductiveness, the other would tug on an ear.

Their visits were supposed to happen once a week but wound up taking place only once a month. Steve would make them wait for at least twenty minutes, but then once they had his attention, he would focus intensely for two hours. While

Ed and Alvy protected their close control of Pixar's decisions about technology, they deferred to Steve about marketing and strategy. They didn't know anything about marketing, but that was Steve's forte.

And Steve had a really big idea: he wanted to make the Pixar computer useful to people other than the most brilliant computer scientists. But who? They devoted an especially vigorous effort to create interest in the medical community: Pixar's engineers wrote special software so that radiologists could archive their x rays on the machine. Surgeons could use the computer to create 3-D visualizations of the inside of a patient's body without the need for invasive surgery.

Steve masterminded a tremendous push for sales. In the company's first two years, Pixar increased its staff from 45 people to 117 as it opened sales offices in seven major cities. But the Pixar Image Computer was a very hard sell. "You had to be a rocket scientist to use it," explains Lisa MacKenzie, who joined Pixar as a marketing executive in 1987. When she went on the road to meet with potential customers, she would need to take three brilliant Ph.D.s with her to work the impossible machine. She tried to keep the engineers hidden away behind a curtain, like the Wizard of Oz sequestered in his secret booth.

Even with the smoke and mirrors, there were few buyers. Pixar donated ten machines to leading hospitals, and it sent marketing people to doctors' conventions, but the efforts seemed futile. Medical professionals were very conservative about spending money for expensive technology.

Disney was Pixar's main customer, spending millions of dollars to purchase a few dozen machines for its 2-D coloring system, which its animators were putting to use for the first time for inking and painting the characters of *The Little Mermaid*. A few of the boxes were bought by highly funded research centers in academia and the Washington intelligence

120

The
Second
Coming
of
Steve
Jobs

organizations, which liked to keep up with the latest in technology. But there wasn't much of a market. By early 1988, Pixar had sold only 120 computers.

"Pixar really struggled to find some profitable business in its early days," recalls Pam Kerwin, who joined Pixar as a marketing executive. She thought that Steve's costly move to put salespeople all around the country was "foolhardy," a "disaster." Steve was investing huge sums in marketing, and still the only buyers were the short list of usual suspects: the professors and the spies.

With 120 employees, Pixar was burning through more than $10 million a year. It was *bleeding* money. And all along, the company was accumulating a terrifying debt. Astonishingly, Steve had never given any cash to Pixar, not a single dollar of capital. He had merely gone to a bank and opened a line of credit for the company. His financial adviser Susan Barnes had argued for the strange idea. She thought that the bank's seal of approval would show that Pixar was a real business, not a rich guy's hobby.

It was a great deal for the bank but an incredibly bad deal for Steve and Pixar. The bank had nothing to lose: the line of credit was fully secured by Steve's tens of millions of dollars' worth of Treasury bonds. Meanwhile, Pixar sank into debt from the first week it met payroll, and every week the debt got deeper and deeper. Before long, Pixar's revenues hardly covered the bloated interest payments.

The company was a technical and artistic triumph, but it was a financial disaster.

"We were in debt from the start," recalls Pam Kerwin. "That was no way to run a business. There were no business brains at Pixar." Ed Catmull was a warm, big-hearted soul and a brilliant engineer, but he wasn't a businessman or a negotiator. He was completely nonconfrontational. "It was so cute, how he'd say yes to almost anything," Pam Kerwin says. One time, as an inside joke, someone at Pixar asked Ed to sign an authorization to purchase a sailboat for $250,000. Ed played along and signed.

Ed was a pushover, but Steve wasn't. Whenever Pixar ran out of money, Ed and Alvy had to go back to Steve and ask him to draw more credit from the bank. Before long, Steve made the two founders give back all of their stock in the company in exchange for Steve's continued financing. They had each started with 4 percent of the shares, and they wound up with zero percent. Cruelly and unnecessarily, he reduced them to serving as his hired hands. They accepted the deal. They were motivated by their enduring dream and their commitment to their colleagues, even if there was no hope of ever making real money.

They hesitated to turn to him for more funds. Pixar's employees tried to scrounge by. Lisa MacKenzie recalls that Pixar's people would beg their peers at Sun Microsystems to lend them expensive equipment for free because Pixar never had any cash. They couldn't run the Pixar computer without Suns, and they couldn't afford to buy Suns.

As Pixar hemorrhaged money, Steve said many times that he wanted to shut down John Lasseter's animation group because it was an unnecessary drain on the company. It was only 5 people out of 120, but it didn't produce profits. No one paid to see its shorts.

John wouldn't acquiesce. For his entry in the 1988 Siggraph show, John wanted to make a short film, *Tin Toy*, about a little toy drummer boy marching through the toy-strewn bedroom of a rambunctious and unpredictable infant. To overcome Steve's persistent opposition, he put together what's known in Hollywood as a storyboard pitch. He sketched about one hundred drawings, then filmed them in sequence in a five-minute clip. As

122

The
Second
Coming
of
Steve
Jobs

Steve watched the drawings, John described the storyline in an excited, emotional way.

John was a terrific actor, and his performance won Steve's grudging approval.

John raced against the deadline but he couldn't finish the film in time for Siggraph. They showed it there anyway, inserting a "To be continued" caption just as the narrative approached its climax. Still, Pixar's entry was once again the big hit of the show. What was most astonishing about the film was its depiction of the infant. Humans were the toughest challenge for computer animation. It was one thing when the characters were toys, which are supposed to have a somewhat simplistic, plastic, artificial look, but a person's facial expressions and body movements are extremely complex and demand a much greater sense of nuance and naturalism.

John completed *Tin Toy* in November 1988. It was almost too late. The calendar year was ending, and if they wanted to be eligible for the next Academy Awards, they had to get it shown in a cinema for five consecutive days. Luckily, the film's producer, Ralph Guggenheim, was able to exploit one of his family's connections and arrange for the run.

At the ceremony in April, *Tin Toy* won the Oscar for best animated short film.

For John Lasseter and Alvy Ray Smith and Ed Catmull and Ralph Guggenheim, it was a triumph. For the art and science of computer animation, it was a seminal event.

For Steve Jobs, it was the only good news of 1989.

Crises

3

Steve was still something of a novice in the movie business, but in his other role, as a Silicon Valley entrepreneur, he acted with the showmanship and bluster of a grand Hollywood impresario. He was the master at taking something that might be considered boring—a hunk of electronic hardware—and enveloping it in a story that made it compellingly dramatic.

128
The
Second
Coming
of
Steve
Jobs

He incited a media frenzy before the debut of the Next computer in October 1988. He agreed to let a *Newsweek* reporter witness the backstage drama of the days leading up to the big unveiling at San Francisco's Davies Symphony Hall. Katie Hafner from *Business Week* also wanted an insider's access to write a colorful fly-on-the-wall narrative, and Steve gave his approval. Then, with his characteristic chutzpah, he went ahead and offered an "exclusive" behind-the-scenes look to one of *Business Week*'s main rivals, *Fortune*.

It was as if the world's most eligible bachelor had made dates with three highly desirable women at the same time and the same restaurant, then told the maître d' to seat them in separate rooms so he could hop between tables. And it was as if he knew that when the three women inevitably discovered his scheme, they would still vie for his affections.

At *Fortune*'s story meeting in New York, the magazine's dozen editors talked excitedly about their "exclusive" and how many glossy pages they wanted to lavish on it.

The frothy conversation was interrupted by one of the senior editors.

"I really shouldn't say this," she began tentatively. Her husband was the managing editor of *Newsweek*, and she knew that Steve Jobs had promised the "exclusive" to *Newsweek*, which was planning to run the big story on its cover. And *Newsweek* would get to subscribers and newsstands a few days before the next issue of *Fortune*.

The revelation silenced the group. Another editor smiled knowingly and said: "Steve Jobs always finds a way to convince everyone that he's giving them an exclusive."

Even when they realized that Steve was trying to use his hypnotic charm to manipulate them, the New York editors didn't mind. They would have trumpeted his return even without his enticements. He always gave them the elements of a good story: youth, vitality, idealism, eloquence, showmanship, glamour, seductiveness, rivalry. In a field where the leading figures were important but uniformly dull, he was gloriously colorful.

Steve delivered a bravura three-hour performance at Davies Hall, and the press coverage was extraordinary. "Steve Jobs Comes Back" shouted the headline in *Newsweek*, which said that the Next computer "may be the most exciting machine in years." *Time* wrote that the event was "one of the most widely ballyhooed product launches ever."

■ ■ ■

THE MEDIA SENSATION masked the real situation: hardly anyone would buy Steve's machine.

At the debut he announced that Next would only sell to colleges and universities. The company's promotional T-shirt said "the next generation computer for higher education." But the strategy was disastrous. The Next Cube, as it was known, just didn't move at the campus bookstores, where the Macintosh had experienced its earliest success. It was far too expensive. The Cube retailed for $6,500, and with a laser printer and some necessary extras the total could exceed $10,000. The price was absurdly high, especially since students could buy basic personal computers for $1,500. Steve was trying to sell them Porsches when all they needed and all they could afford were Honda Civics.

The other possibility, selling to the research laboratories and computer centers of academia, was nearly as difficult. Silicon Valley companies like Sun Microsystems simply gave away their machines for free to universities or sold at below cost. The idea was that all those hacker geniuses on campus were the most influential advocates for new technology. Whatever was hot on campus would later become the new standard for the fabulously rich corporate customers. You lost millions giving freebies to Berkeley and MIT and then you made it back many times over by selling for high prices to AT&T and Exxon.

It turned out that Next's strategy was astonishingly misguided.

Next's salespeople and marketing executives began telling a new favorite joke:

Question: What's the "higher education handshake?"

Answer: An outstretched hand with the palm turned open, waiting for a donation.

By the end of 1988, Next's factory was making only 400 machines a month. It was a huge disappointment. Steve had designed his cherished state-of-the-art factory so it could turn out 10,000 machines a month. The Next Cube was the Edsel of computers. In Hollywood terms, it was the equivalent of *Heaven's Gate:* a gifted artist producing a horrendously costly flop.

Steve needed to resort to Plan B.

In March 1989, he abandoned the policy of selling only to higher education, and he announced that Businessland, a national chain of retail stores, would offer the Next Cube for $9,995. Businessland projected that it would sell 10,000 to 15,000 Cubes a year to corporations and business people.

By the end of 1989, the chain had sold only 360.

The Next factory slowed down until it was producing only 100 machines a month. Even that speed was too fast, since many of the unsold Cubes languished in the stockpile.

Steve had envisioned his factory producing $1 billion worth of computers a year. A few Ph.D.s would watch from the sidelines while the machines would be fabricated without ever

130
The
Second
Coming
of
Steve
Jobs

being touched by humans. But even at the rate of mere hundreds a year, not hundreds of thousands, the automation never worked very well, and human hands were everywhere.

■　　■　　■

To THE ENRAPTURED MEDIA and the rest of Silicon Valley, Next seemed like a star, not a huge flop. It was a privately owned company, so it didn't have to publish its quarterly results or give any other disclosures of its sales. Outsiders only saw what appeared to be positive signs. In 1989, *Inc.* magazine named Steve Jobs as the "Entrepreneur of the Decade." A major Japanese manufacturer, Canon, invested $100 million for one-sixth ownership of Next, which looked like a clear affirmation of success. "Next was one of the hottest companies in the valley," says Paul Vais. He recalls that Next's recruiters would raid major firms like Hewlett-Packard and lure away almost anyone they wanted: "You had to be a complete idiot not to hire great people." Throughout the industry, talented professionals continued to take what they considered to be demotions in order to work near the legendary Steve Jobs.

"In 1989, Next was *really* hot," recalls Emily Brower, who at the time was a reporter for *MacWEEK*. After the Davies Hall debut, she heard that Next's public relations firm had a job opening: "Even though I had a reporter's disdain for p.r., I said, well, it's *Next*. The quality of everything Steve does is really high, and I wanted to be a part of that."

Next's staff was growing so rapidly, from two hundred people to five hundred, that the company needed much more space. It moved to two shiny new buildings right beside the bay, a "corporate campus" with an air of prosperity. Steve decorated the new digs with $10,000 leather sofas and elegant black-and-white photographs and bleached oak floors, and he hired I. M. Pei's architectural firm to build a dramatic free-standing staircase off the lobby. "Steve wanted the company to feel larger than life, and sure enough it did," recalls David Wertheimer, who was a Next executive at the time. "It felt like 'here's a company that's really made it,' while in reality it wasn't selling a single computer."

132
The
Second
Coming
of
Steve
Jobs

■   ■   ■

IT WAS DURING this critical time in Next's history, in the first few months of 1989, when the company was on the brink of disaster, that Steve Jobs had a fleeting opportunity to turn Next's initial failure into one of the most stunning successes of modern business. When the rest of the computer industry looked at Next, it was mightily impressed, but not by the achievements that were dearest and most emotionally charged for Steve. The honchos of Silicon Valley didn't care about automated factories. They sent their manufacturing offshore to take advantage of cheap Third World labor. And they didn't care about design or aesthetics. In those fields, Steve Jobs was almost a decade ahead of his time. But the computer titans were utterly in love with NextStep, the software that ran the Next Cube.

What you saw on the screen of the Next looked a lot like what you'd see on the screen of a Macintosh: a mouse freely manipulated a cursor and could click on cute little icons or choose from menu lists or open up several different windows at the same time, showing text in any number of attractive fonts and sizes. The difference was that the Next was even more compelling, even easier to use. John Markoff, a technology reporter for the *New York Times*, thought of it as "a Macintosh on steroids." Meanwhile, in 1989, the IBM personal computer and its clones were stuck with much cruder software that displayed only plain text and forced users to rely on maddening keyboard commands like Alt-Ctrl-F5. Microsoft was refining its new Windows software, which would imitate the approach of the Mac, but Windows was still a horrible mess, and very few people attempted to use it.

The Macintosh was far superior, but John Sculley tried to inflate Apple's profit margins by keeping the Mac's price exceptionally high, so most customers bought PCs instead. The PC makers wanted to license the Macintosh software to run on their machines, but Apple refused. That left IBM and its cloners in a precarious situation. It meant that they were helpless captives of Bill Gates's Microsoft, which had a monopoly on the basic software that ran their machines. Every year computer users came to rely more and more on programs that could only work in conjunction with Bill's software. They were making Bill into a monster of a mogul who would hold great power over the rest of them. To break his lucrative stranglehold, they needed to come up with a whole new approach to software, something that would be so appealing and beneficial that it would compel people to switch. And they thought that NextStep might be their salvation, the great death blow to Bill Gates.

IBM's chief executive said that he wanted to license Next's software. Steve's lieutenants talked at length with IBM's executives despite Steve's persistent objections and reservations about the deal. "He couldn't figure out why IBM wanted to do this," recalls one of the Next negotiators. "He thought that there had to be some ulterior motive."

Steve Jobs and IBM were the oddest of bedfellows. It wasn't just the vicious attack ads that Apple had aired on television during the 1984 and 1985 Super Bowls, portraying IBM

134

The
Second
Coming
of
Steve
Jobs

as an Orwellian Big Brother and its followers as mindless lem-
mings. Steve had clashed with IBM executives ever since he
was twenty-one and Apple was operating out of his parents'
garage. Steve and his close friend Elizabeth Holmes would go
to her parents' house to listen to Benny Goodman albums and
other swing-era big band recordings that were collected by her
father, who was a market analyst for IBM in San Jose. He was
also a programmer, and he would dial in to an IBM mainframe
from a computer terminal in the house. He had an IBM Selec-
tric typewriter hooked up to it for the printouts, since there
was no screen. Elizabeth remembers how Steve and her father
would "lock horns over whether the computer would be for
Everyman." Steve argued that computers would become
smaller and friendlier and then become wildly popular. And of
course he was proved right.

Now, a dozen years later, the head of IBM was turning to
Steve for help. Steve couldn't trust him, but he took advantage
of the opportunity for one-upmanship. IBM sent its envoys to
California with a contract that ran well over one hundred
pages. Steve shook their hands, glanced at the sheaf of papers,
and dropped it in the trash. One hundred pages! Yet another
sign that IBM was ridiculously bureaucratic and outmoded!
Steve wanted a concise contract: five pages, ten at most. He exulted in the role of the little fish telling off the whale. And how
he was going to make them pay! Steve negotiated for IBM to
pay $60 million. It was an extremely high price. Steve was try-
ing to gouge them, and he got away with it. "IBM got *boned* on
that one," recalls Paul Vais, the Next marketing manager. The
$60 million was just to license the first version of the Next soft-
ware. If they wanted the improved version the following year,
they'd have to pay more. They would have to come back to the
table and worry whether Steve was going to throw their contract into the trash.

Even for the hefty $60 million, Steve wouldn't give an exclusive deal to IBM. He remained free to license NextStep to any or all of the makers of IBM clones. And they came to him. Compaq and Dell, two of the biggest cloners, said they would pay mightily to put NextStep on their machines. One of the PC companies even offered $50 million as an initial payment. But there was a catch: the cloners wanted Next to stop making its own hardware. If they were going into a partnership with Steve Jobs, they didn't want to have to compete with him. (Of course, no one realized that the Next Cube was hardly selling.)

The overtures from Compaq and Dell set off intense debates at Next. The software chief, Bud Tribble, was a strong advocate of dumping the hardware and recasting Next as a powerful software company, the new Microsoft. But the transformation was opposed by seven of the ten executives who reported directly to Steve. It appears all seven were driven by simple self-interest: they were the people in charge of hardware design and manufacturing and sales, and their jobs would be diminished or become obsolete under the new scheme.

The decision fell to Steve, and he was still enamored with hardware. He loved designing and making machines. Rather than abandoning the hardware business, he decided . . . to build yet another computer! That's how he would try to save the company.

IBM paid the $60 million but then abandoned its relationship with Next. The man who had been Next's strongest advocate within IBM was Bill Lowe, the iconoclast who was the father of the IBM PC. When Lowe quit and went to Xerox, the responsibility for dealing with Next was passed to another man, Jim Cannavino. Steve Jobs went to New York to meet with the new honcho, who cleared the room of advisers from both sides so they could talk one-on-one. Steve came out of the meeting thinking that he could continue to soak

IBM for large amounts of cash. But he misread his new oppo-
nent. Jim Cannavino never again returned Steve's phone calls.
And IBM never put the Next software on its PC.

In hindsight, it's easy to argue that Steve squandered a rare
historic opportunity to shift the course of the computer business. Looking back, one of Next's founders says sadly: "If IBM
would have embraced Next, it would have been game over for
Microsoft."

136

The
Second
Coming
of
Steve
Jobs

■ ■ ■

SOMEONE HAD TO TAKE THE FALL for the failure of the
Next Cube. Steve turned against the man who had been a
brother figure to him, Dan'l Lewin. In July 1989, Steve stripped
away Dan'l's responsibilities as the vice president of marketing.
Steve would do the job himself.

A few months later, Dan'l quit and went to another technology startup. The departure of someone so close to Steve
was the first signal to the rest of Silicon Valley that something
might not be entirely right at Next.

"Dan'l was one of the nicest guys in the business," recalls a
close colleague, "but Steve gave him the short end of the stick
and blamed him for a lot of the problems."

The first wave of executives was beginning to burn out
from the sheer intensity of working for Steve. "There were
some people who survived at Next and some who would go
poof and explode," says Paul Vais. "If you depended and
thrived on Steve's praise, you would be crushed when he
flamed you with public humiliation, which was inevitable."

Karen Sipprell, who was a marketing manager at Next,
says that Steve's criticism brought out her "maternal instincts"
for protecting her employees. "I spent a lot of my time trying

to shield my team from him," she recalls. "He would often be right in his observations, but he would demotivate them and destroy their self-esteem so they couldn't respond by doing better the next time." Karen would buffer her people, absorbing most of Steve's abuse herself. That was common practice among Next executives, but it had a punishing cost. Karen quit her job soon after her brother survived a plane crash and she realized that she hadn't seen him in an entire year because she had been so fully absorbed by working for Steve.

Next's executives began collecting their favorite examples of Steve's profane, hyperbolic put-downs, which could seem witty and comical so long as you weren't the hapless victim. But even they were stunned when Steve reviewed one employee's work and said: "You've baked a really lovely cake, but then you've used dog shit for frosting."

■   ■   ■

IN HIS PERSONAL RELATIONSHIPS as well as his professional life, Steve needed to be surrounded by people who were tough enough to take his verbal abuse and dish it back. His girlfriend Tina Redse fit that description. When Tina went along with Steve on a business trip to Tokyo for the Asian debut of the Next Cube, she freely displayed her edgy, sarcastic wit. Steve was obsessed with healthy living, but Tina flaunted her bad habits in front of his colleagues. Steve loved the sushi in Japan, and he arranged for his entourage to have a twelve-course vegetarian dinner at a restaurant with a Zen-like minimalist sensibility. Tina shocked Steve's business associates when she smoked and ate steaks. She acted as she wanted, not to please Steve, and he respected her for it. Tina was rebellious and had the strength to spurn him, which is one of the reasons he pursued her over the years.

Even while he was dating Tina, Steve would flirt openly with other women but only until they acquiesced to his charm. He couldn't resist the challenge of pursuit and seduction, but he embodied the old Groucho Marx line about not wanting to belong to a club that would have him as a member. His "seduce and abandon" mode applied to beautiful women as well as to talented executives.

Tina had worked for years in the computer industry but she was developing her own life and identity outside of it, working to help the mentally ill. She was one of the founders and board members of Open Mind, a nonprofit organization that put together resources about mental health. She became a close friend of Gary Bricklin, an intelligent young writer who was confined to a wheelchair because of a nervous-system disorder. Steve bought Gary an expensive new van that was specially equipped for his wheelchair. Tina herself wouldn't accept Steve's gifts, but her friend benefited from his generosity.

Steve's business partner Ross Perot strongly urged him to marry Tina. (Not long before, Ross had balked at doing business with Sun's Scott McNealy because the younger man was a California bachelor.)

Steve was thirty-four, and had been in a relationship with Tina on and off for four years. He hinted to his colleagues that he might propose to her. In June 1989, Steve talked with Heidi Roizen, who told him about her fiancé David, a dashingly handsome surgeon.

"Maybe the next time I see you, we'll both be married," Steve said.

His remark turned out to be only half true. He asked Tina to marry him, and she said no.

When friends asked her why, she said that Steve drove her crazy.

138

The
Second
Coming
of
Steve
Jobs

In the fall of 1989, Steve was invited by a bunch of students at Stanford Graduate School of Business to come speak to their class. One of the organizers was a first-year MBA candidate, Laurene Powell. She had an impressive background: she came from a well-off family and had worked in Manhattan for two years as a trainee at Goldman Sachs, the prestigious investment banking firm. In the spring, when she received her acceptance letter from Stanford, she immediately quit her job and went to Florence, where she studied art history for six months. She flew to northern California just in time for the start of her MBA classes. As she settled back into student life, she confided to her new roommate that she had come to Stanford to meet and marry "a Silicon Valley millionaire like Steve Jobs." During her first semester, she was instrumental in inviting Steve to speak on campus.

The main auditorium at the business school was nearly packed as Steve delivered his standard speech. He talked about Next and where he thought technology was heading. Then, midway through his presentation, he seemed oddly distracted. Laurene was standing at the back left. As she moved into the darkened windowless room, she was dramatically backlit by the intense midday California sunlight streaming in through the open door. The lighting had a halo effect, radiantly framing her magnificent long golden hair.

Laurene made her way toward the stage. She sat right in front of Steve and began looking at him flirtatiously. She was stunningly attractive: in her twenties, an athlete and dancer, alluringly curvaceous but with the long slender legs and lean waist of a model.

As she looked at him, Steve was visibly flustered.

He lost his flow of ideas again and again.

One of his Next colleagues, watching in the audience, was

shocked by Steve's faltering performance. He had seen Steve give dozens of speeches over the years, and Steve was a master of the art. *Never* before had Steve lost his train of thought like this.

When the appearance was over, Steve canceled his business meetings for the day, claiming that he wasn't feeling well. Then he went out with the mysterious woman.

140

The
Second
Coming
of
Steve
Jobs

■   ■   ■

LAURENE POWELL was an astonishingly close match for what Steve wanted in a woman. Like Tina, she was a great natural beauty, exuding a sense of health and naturalness, though people who met them both almost always said that Laurene was even more beautiful. Laurene was a vegetarian. She had eaten "whole foods" and shunned meat since her teens, for health reasons, following the advice of her doctor. She had the kind of brand-name pedigrees that Steve admired: Goldman Sachs was the most prestigious house on Wall Street, and Stanford was arguably the top business school. She was exceptionally bright and showed the kind of sharp focus and ambition that Tina lacked. She had aspirations of starting and running her own company. Like Steve, she melded influences from the California counterculture and the elitist realm of corporate power. At Stanford she rode on the back of the motorcycle of a fellow student who wrote a column on Zen Buddhism for the campus newspaper. At the same time, she dated an aristocratic country-club type. One of her classmates, Tony Swei, recalls: "Laurene was a free spirit who didn't fit into any particular clique." That's exactly how Steve had seen himself during his own student years.

In the days following their impromptu first date, Steve strutted around the office and talked exuberantly about the incredible woman he had discovered. "We *all* heard about Laurene when Steve met her," recalls Allison Thomas, Next's public relations consultant.

Gossip about the relationship spread quickly through the campus and the company. Within a few weeks, Steve and Laurene were seen lunching together at Tressidor, the grand outdoor cafe at the center of the Stanford grounds in a heavily trafficked area near the bookstore. In their business-school courses, one classmate noticed that Laurene began to take a stronger interest in the subject of manufacturing, which was one of Steve's passions.

The rumors took on a nasty edge. The story spread about Laurene plotting to meet and marry a Silicon Valley millionaire like Steve. It made the rounds at Stanford, and then at Next as well. Some of her friends also believed that Laurene had picked out that front center seat *before* Steve's speech and preemptively forbid the others from sitting there.

The Stanford kids looked on with ironic humor as a world-famous figure tried to fit in with their student scene. Steve was only thirty-four, not much older than many of them, but he was still what Ross Perot had called a "white monkey," not really a regular guy. It was especially awkward for Steve that winter, when Laurene joined in with twenty other classmates to rent a ski house in the Sierras. They found a cheap crash pad on Donner Lake, near the Lake Tahoe slopes, for the bargain price of $250 a person for the entire season. They called it The Shelter, and it became a fun social scene for the bunch of twentysomethings.

Any one of the twenty house-sharers might answer the phone. It would be a male voice asking for Laurene. They all knew who it was, but they taunted him for their amusement.

"Who's calling?"

"Steve."

"Steve *who?*"

■   ■   ■

His romantic life rebounded, but the beautiful computer he created was a horrendous flop. And even what his colleagues referred to as his "hobby" was becoming a miserable mess.

Pixar's situation was remarkably similar to Next's. It produced a very expensive computer which it couldn't sell. But it also, like Next, had a brain trust that wrote great software, which offered some hope for salvation: the software tools that John Lasseter had used to model and color and shade the 3-D images in *Tin Toy*, the software that helped them win an Academy Award. That was the really valuable "intellectual property," the legacy of two decades of brilliant and costly research.

At Next, Steve couldn't bring himself to kill the computer and sell software instead. The Cube was his own beloved creation. But at Pixar he acted decisively and without any sentimentality. In 1989 he cut the hardware business, he closed the half-dozen sales offices around the country, and he laid off almost all of the dozens of salespeople he had hired only two years earlier, the salespeople who could hardly sell any of those damn machines. He slashed more than half of Pixar's employees, over time cutting from 125 people to around 60. He had the binge-and-purge approach to entrepreneurship: when he was building a company, he would spend lavishly, and when he was cutting back, he could be brutally austere. What he spared was the brain trust, the nomadic band of Ph.D.s he had taken from George Lucas.

He struggled to figure out how Pixar could make money. Ed Catmull and Alvy Ray Smith would drive down to meet with Steve at Next's new bayside headquarters, bringing along their marketing executive, Pam Kerwin. They would put incredible care into preparing their own agenda, but it just didn't

142

The
Second
Coming
of
Steve
Jobs

matter. Seconds after they sat down around the conference table, Steve would be bounding energetically, writing with Magic Markers on the whiteboard and convincing them about some harebrained new scheme. Steve would talk spellbindingly, and they would be totally captivated by his enthusiasm. It was only when they were back on Highway 101 that they would realize his ideas were crazy.

EVEN AS STEVE was slashing the staff at the failing company, he nonetheless conceived of a grand ambition for it and convinced himself and the others that it could work. If he had to remake Pixar as a software maker, then he wanted its software to be *everywhere*, to be found on *every* personal computer—inescapable, ubiquitous, essential. That's how Microsoft was making its fortune: by creating a "standard." Steve wouldn't say out loud that he wanted to emulate Bill Gates, who was still an envied rival. Instead, Steve would talk about how the success of a company called Adobe offered a terrific model for Pixar. Adobe's PostScript software turned the uninspiring text characters on the screen into a great variety of beautifully shaped "fonts." PostScript was becoming a standard for the industry, a common language of computers. Adobe was profiting mightily by licensing the software to Apple and many other manufacturers of personal computers. Adobe's cofounder and chief executive, John Warnock, was a friend and something of a father figure to Steve. John was a brilliant, gentle, professorial type who had been at the University of Utah with Ed Catmull and Jim Clark at the genesis of the computer graphics movement in the 1970s. Steve had great respect for John, who was one of the strongest influences on his thinking.

John Warnock had given millions of ordinary people the magical stuff to turn their prosaic words into artistic typography. Now, in Steve's new vision for his own company, he would give the masses the mystical power to turn their rough sketches into artistic 3-D images and animations. "Steve thought that he could license Pixar's software on everyone's computer so they could make beautiful pictures," recalls Pam Kerwin.

At first Pam was discouraged by the new strategy. Even as Steve conceived of his defiantly ambitious new software scheme, he cut back mercilessly on Pixar's budgets and staffing. Pixar's engineers created a version of their software to run on Macs and PCs, but with little money for marketing and a sales force that hardly existed anymore, who would sell it?

It didn't matter. Before long, the Pixar people realized that Steve's new vision wasn't going to work. The problem was that Steve didn't seem to grasp that the technology was incredibly difficult to use. John Lasseter had pushed the engineers to make the software easier for artists to work with, but it was still extremely complicated. To create 3-D pictures you needed gifted artists who were also technical virtuosos, which is rare, or gifted artists who were technophilic and could work closely with the programmers. It took a Disney star like John Lasseter collaborating with a bunch of computer science Ph.D.s. This just wasn't something that ordinary people were going to play around with at home for their own amusement.

Besides, the general population wasn't yet very sophisticated at using computers. In 1989, the typical PC owner didn't even have a graphical user interface with a mouse, windows, pull-down menus, and icons. Microsoft wasn't even close to releasing the first viable version of its Windows software. Except for Macintosh users, people were still staring at a single font of fluorescent text on a dark screen. The Mac's exceptional graphics capabilities were creating the boom in desktop pub-

144

The
Second
Coming
of
Steve
Jobs

lishing, but that meant that people could lay out newsletters or magazine pages on the computer, which is remarkably basic compared with the artistic and technical challenges of creating 3-D animations.

Steve always had profound faith that as computers got better and better, their magic would become accessible to regular folks. His faith usually proved visionary, but in this case he was embarrassingly wrong, or at the very least he was decades ahead of his time, which is too far ahead for an investor pouring millions of his own dollars into a company.

"The fundamental problem was that the market for 3-D was always small because it's highly sophisticated," says Adobe's John Warnock. "It's just hard stuff, extremely hard, but that's why the Pixar engineers get off on it. Artists usually don't relate to it. Three-D is a different mindset. You have to be a storyteller, cameraman, modeler, artist, and a mathematician as well to some extent. You have to create algorithms and procedures. If you're Ed Catmull you can do that stuff, but if you're almost anyone else, you can't."

Looking back, John Warnock says that what Steve Jobs was trying to do at Pixar was like "trying to mass produce a Stradivarius." A virtuoso like Midori could play one of the perfectly crafted violins and produce tones of subtle, nuanced beauty. But giving Strads to millions of music students wouldn't make them into Midoris. And giving Pixar's software to everyday artists wouldn't make them into Oscar winners like John Lasseter.

One of Steve's most cherished beliefs was that people could do great things if you gave them great tools, which was a noble sentiment, and often true, but it was also true that in many fields people also needed extraordinary talent and hard training to do great things. That was the case with 3-D computer art, but Steve stubbornly persisted. "Steve was always trying to figure out why the Adobe model didn't work for Pixar," recalls Pam Kerwin.

■   ■   ■

146

The
Second
Coming
of
Steve
Jobs

IN THE LATE 1980S Steve had wanted to kill Pixar's five-person animation team because it didn't turn a profit. They saved their jobs by winning the Oscar for *Tin Toy* in the spring of 1989, but even afterward, Steve implored them to find a way to make money. Ralph Guggenheim, who managed the small group, came up with a strategy: They would hire themselves out to make television commercials, which would bring in plenty of cash while they kept improving the state-of-the-art in 3-D animation. Then they would try to produce a half-hour television special, probably for the Christmas season. And eventually, they would fulfill Ed's dream—now entering its third decade—of making a feature-length film with computers.

Steve approved the plan. It also appealed to the ambitions of John Lasseter, who was being recruited relentlessly by his former employer, Disney. John was still in his thirties, and he told Ralph that he didn't want to spend the rest of his life winning the Oscars for short films. He wanted a chance to win for best director of a feature film. Ralph's plan gave them a way to sustain themselves until they could break into features.

As John worked on his next wonderfully creative short for Siggraph, *Knick-Knack*, which carried forward his obsession with children's toys, Ralph negotiated a deal with a San Francisco advertising studio called Colossal Pictures. Despite its grandiose name, Colossal was actually a smallish startup, but it had gained notoriety for its "blendo" technique of blending animation with live-action video. Pixar could craft the animation while Colossal shot the live actors and then combined it all into a seamless creation.

They signed the deal in July 1989. The following month, the Pixar crew went to the Siggraph convention, where Steve was scheduled to receive an award for computer graphics visionary of the year and to give an acceptance speech. Steve refused to show up for the rehearsal of the awards ceremony, so Lisa MacKenzie, a Pixar marketing executive, went in his place. Later, when it came time for his actual speech, Steve wasn't there.

Lisa's boss, Barbara Barza, began to panic.

"Where's Steve?" she asked.

"He went to change his shirt," Lisa said.

"You let him?"

Steve reappeared only moments before the appointed time, and Lisa rushed to brief him about what he was supposed to say. Steve seemed completely distracted.

"Yeah yeah yeah," he said dismissively.

The award was announced, and he went to the microphone.

"I'm Steve Jobs, and I am *not* the president of Apple Computer," he said snidely.

The Pixar entourage was shocked. This is *our* world, they thought, and Steve is making nasty, arrogant remarks about the stupid old rivalries in *his* world. "I was embarrassed and appalled," recalls Lisa MacKenzie. "We were trying to have this pride of association with Steve, but he was being a jerk and belittling Siggraph, this organization that we hold dear." The Siggraph crowd wasn't a bunch of college kids who saw Steve as a cult hero. It was filled with hot shot professors and hot shot Hollywood special-effects gurus. This was their cherished community, and Steve wasn't really one of them.

"They weren't going 'Ooh ooh, Steve,'" Lisa recalls. "They were saying 'What the hell is *he* doing here?'"

■ ■ ■

STEVE WAS DEEPLY MOODY and maddeningly erratic. He was as entirely unpredictable as a young child. He could be petulant, misbehaving as if he simply didn't know better, or he could act with an unaffected charm that seemed wonderfully innocent, almost naive. And when the Good Steve reappeared, it was easy to forget the torments of the Bad Steve.

148
The
Second
Coming
of
Steve
Jobs

He acted just like a wide-eyed kid during an especially memorable business trip he took with Next's top salesman, Todd Rulon-Miller. The two men were together in Detroit, making sales calls, when one of their appointments canceled. Suddenly and unexpectedly they had some free time in a very unfamiliar city. What should they do? They looked around and saw that they were in front of the world headquarters of General Motors.

Steve entered the impressive high-ceilinged lobby and walked up to the receptionist, who was licking envelopes, seemingly bored and distracted.

He said that he'd like to see Roger Smith, the chief executive officer.

Todd was astonished. This was like a scene from the wild gonzo documentary film *Roger & Me*, in which the liberal journalist Michael Moore, looking like a random crazy guy off the street, would appear at GM lobbies and ask to meet right away with the head of the nation's biggest corporation. And, of course, the brazen filmmaker would be thrown out.

Now, in a moment of life imitating art, another seemingly random crazy guy was standing there, and the receptionist was visibly nervous. She called for the security guard.

"Sir?" asked the guard.

"Call Roger, he'll take my call," Steve insisted with easy confidence.

They gave him a telephone and dialed the number for Roger Smith's assistant.

"Mr. Smith is busy," she said.

"Tell him Steve Jobs is in the lobby. He'll see me," Steve said, winking at Todd.

A few moments later, they were escorted to the top floor, a palace of corporate baroque, where they waited uncomfortably in front of the armed guards and attack dogs.

Roger Smith came hustling down the hall.

"Steve, how are you!" he exclaimed.

They went to Roger's private office, which was strewn with cardboard boxes. Roger had just turned sixty-five and announced his retirement. This was his final week on the job, and he was busy packing his books and personal belongings.

"We want to sell you computers," Steve said enthusiastically.

Roger called in Bob Stempel, his successor as CEO, who talked business with Steve for three-quarters of an hour.

When the Next executives were back on the street, Todd said: "You're amazing!"

"Huh?" Steve replied, as if he often dropped in unannounced on famous people.

"How did you get us in?"

"Oh, I met Roger before, twelve years ago."

■   ■   ■

SOON AFTER THE GM VISIT, Steve's innocence and exuberance didn't play nearly as well during a sales call at Disney. Although the visit was intended as a fairly routine pitch, it wound up as an edgy confrontation with tough moguls who would play a vital and unexpected role in Steve's future.

Steve and Todd flew to Los Angeles for a meeting with Disney's No. 2 executive, Frank Wells, and its head of feature films, Jeffrey Katzenberg. The chief executive officer, Michael Eisner, stepped in for a few minutes to listen as Steve Jobs made his presentation.

Steve's people had set up two Next machines on a table. One had a black-and-white monitor for running utilitarian business software. The other had a color monitor for showing off the latest in computer graphics.

Steve performed with his usual dazzling eloquence and enthusiasm for an hour and a half. His sales spiel was compelling, but then he veered way off topic and began describing his grand vision: he wanted to give millions of ordinary people the ability to create incredible pictures and even animated characters on their computers. He would make it possible for regular folks to express themselves with the artistry of Disney's animators.

Jeffrey Katzenberg held up his hand, signaling that Steve should stop.

The room fell silent. Jeffrey let the sense of anticipation build as he walked over to the two computers.

He pointed to the black-and-white computer.

"This is *commerce*," he said. "Maybe we'll buy a thousand of these."

Then he gestured toward the color monitor, which was showing a demonstration of Pixar's graphics software, the magical tool that Steve wanted to give to the world.

"This is *art*," Jeffrey said. *"I own animation, and nobody's going to get it."* His voice was fierce and intimidating and commanding. "It's as if someone comes to date my daughter. I have a shotgun. If someone tries to take this away, I'll blow his balls off."

■   ■   ■

150

The
Second
Coming
of
Steve
Jobs

JEFFREY KATZENBERG WAS RIGHT: he dominated the animation business. And his formidable power was indeed threatened, but not in the way implied by Steve's implausible vision.

The real danger was that many of Disney's most promising talents had left during the studio's dismal years in the 1970s and early 1980s, when it turned out a series of embarrassingly mediocre movies. Disney hadn't been able to hold on to rising young stars like Tim Burton, an animator who quit in 1985, at age twenty-six, and quickly became famous for directing three live-action hits (*Pee-wee's Big Adventure*, *Beetlejuice*, and *Batman*) all for a rival studio, Warner Bros.

Tim had studied at the traditional feeder school for Disney animators, "Cal Arts" (the California Institute of the Arts), where he was a contemporary of another young genius, John Lasseter. Now Tim was a cult hero and John had an Oscar. That sent a clear message to Cal Arts students that you could achieve great success away from Disney.

When Jeffrey came to Disney in the fall of 1984, he resolved to lure back some of the talent that the studio had so foolishly squandered. He talked with Tim, who agreed to make *The Nightmare Before Christmas*, and he kept trying to rehire John, who resisted the overtures.

I want to do computer animation, John said.

You can do it at Disney, Jeffrey countered.

But John explained that he couldn't do it on his own. He didn't know how to program computers. He needed to work together with the engineers at Pixar, who were constantly writing software and inventing technology so he could realize his creative ideas.

If you want me, John said, you have to hire my whole team.

■   ■   ■

As the summer of 1990 ended, the Disney executives told their Pixar colleagues that they were finally willing to talk about making a feature film with 3-D computer animation.

John Lasseter, Alvy Ray Smith, and Ed Catmull went together to Disney's headquarters in Burbank for a meeting with Jeffrey Katzenberg. They arrived at the Team Disney building, a postmodern temple lined with huge fanciful sculptures of the Seven Dwarfs in the place of columns.

152
The
Second
Coming
of
Steve
Jobs

Alvy was strongly impressed by his first encounter with the movie mogul.

"Jeffrey was charming, persuasive, and highly articulate," Alvy recalls. "I was really taken by how much like Steve Jobs he was. They were like the *same guy*."

Jeffrey was open and forthright as he warned the Pixar people about what they could expect about working with him on a film.

"I'm a tyrant and I have strong beliefs," he said. "You don't have to listen to me, but if you're wrong, there are consequences."

Afterward, the Pixar delegation was taken to meet with some of Disney's animators and directors, who were encouraged to talk freely without Jeffrey in the room.

Jeffrey *is* a tyrant, they said unflinchingly. But he's almost always right.

■   ■   ■

John Lasseter wanted to go ahead, but still, nothing happened. The two companies needed to negotiate detailed terms, but months passed without a meeting. The problem was that Disney had a huge fiefdom that still created animated films the old way, with hundreds of people who might easily believe that their jobs were threatened by Pixar's strange new high-tech approach. They were also threatened by the very idea of hiring an independent outside contractor to do the work that they had always done better than anyone else.

Jeffrey Katzenberg wanted a Pixar movie, but the idea was opposed by his lieutenant, Peter Schneider, who ran feature animation. Now the Pixar people were afraid that Peter was dragging his feet and trying to kill the deal. Their optimism began to fade.

■   ■   ■

FOR A SHORT TIME, a new sense of hope for Steve's career came from the Next side. He was readying for the public debut of the new, second version of the Next computer in September 1990. He wanted to re-create the excitement and buzz of the original Next unveiling two years earlier, and he even rented the same impressive venue, Davies Symphony Hall in San Francisco.

The new machine was called the NextStation, and its most striking differences were visible at a casual glance. The computer's outer casing was still made of the sleekest blackest magnesium, but it was now shaped like a rectangular pizza box, a more conventional design that was easier and cheaper to manufacture than the Cube. And the monitor displayed color, an overdue improvement over the old monochrome monitor.

Onstage at Davies Hall, Steve's most dramatic moment came when he showed a clip from *The Wizard of Oz* on a computer's screen. The clip began with Dorothy living in a black-and-white world. She opened the door, and suddenly the tableau exploded in color.

The audience went berserk at the stunt, applauding wildly.

Hardly anyone had ever before seen a movie playing on a personal computer. Computers weren't that powerful yet.

It was simply hard to believe, and for good reason: it was a hoax. The movie wasn't coming from inside the black computer box. It was coming from a laser disk player hidden behind the curtain. It was all smoke and mirrors, like the Wizard of Oz himself.

154

The
Second
Coming
of
Steve
Jobs

The NextStation was *supposed* to be capable of playing a movie stored in digital form on its own disk drive. But that required a special new video chip, and Next's supplier hadn't come through and delivered the chip. So Steve went ahead anyway and faked it all.

Steve's slick trickery wooed the handpicked crowd at the event, but later, in the outside world, the response to the NextStation was underwhelming. The new machine wasn't going to save the company. It wasn't a technological breakthrough, and it didn't have a clear target market: if you were a businessperson who mainly needed to run spreadsheets, you'd do perfectly well buying a standard Intel-Microsoft PC for thousands of dollars less than a Next. Steve's prices had come down, but he still wanted to command a premium for his famous name and his aura. At $7,995 for a color NextStation or even $4,995 for a low-end model with a black-and-white monitor, Steve's new machines were two to three times more expensive than a PC that was perfectly serviceable for the needs of the average user. And if you wanted high performance computing, you'd get a Sun Microsystems workstation, which was faster than a NextStation. Sun used RISC, a newer, more advanced approach to microchip design, while Next's engineers had stuck too long with what they were familiar with: the slower CISC chip design that Apple had always used in the Macintosh.

As the year ended, Next's 1990 revenues came to only $28 million. By the standards of the computer industry, that was insignificant. Sun Microsystems, which was started in the mid-1980s by a bunch of Stanford classmates, already had annual revenues of $2.8 billion, making it one hundred times bigger than Next.

The Sun guys had acted swiftly, sold cheaply, and built a huge business. They hadn't obsessed about the aesthetics of their machines. They put circuitry into bland beige boxes, and their corporate buyers just didn't care. They didn't try to make the software visually attractive and easy to use. Their customers were technical wizards—engineers, scientists—who *liked* the fact that they had to speak in tongues to get the things to work the way they wanted. That proved they were genius types, members of an elite technical priesthood. They *liked* that mammoth companies had to depend on their mystical skills. Sun had no style, no panache, and its leader Scott McNealy was a no-bullshit MBA, not a visionary or an aesthete. Sun was the anti-Next, and it had triumphed even before Next's executives realized that the two companies were competing in the same market.

■　　　■　　　■

WITH THE FAILURE of his two ventures, Steve's money was beginning to run out. Pixar was a money sink. He had bought the company for $10 million, and it had accumulated a debt of $50 million. Sixty million, lost in four years! If Pixar was a hobby, it was an extremely expensive hobby, and Steve couldn't afford it. Pixar was getting strangled by the huge debt. It could hardly cover the interest charges or even pay for the upkeep of its building.

Steve got off easier at Next, where he had plunged only $12 million of his own cash, since he tapped others for most of the funding: Perot for $20 million, Canon for $100 million. (Though the investors had a voice as members of the board, Steve ensured his unilateral control by keeping half the stock for himself.) But Next had eaten through almost all of its capital and once again it was nearly broke.

Between Next and Pixar, he had spent $72 million of his personal fortune. He was left with about $25 million in reserve. His bid for vindication had been devastating financially. If only he had held on to his Apple shares, he'd be worth over $450 million.

And his remaining $25 million of savings was in great jeopardy. Steve had 570 people on his staff at Next and 80 at Pixar. His "burn rate"—the amount of money it took to meet the payrolls and overhead and keep the companies running—was more than $60 million a year. It was highly unlikely that even someone with Steve's blinding persuasiveness could attract new investors from the outside, since his companies had such dismal financial histories. If Steve tried to sustain the businesses, he could easily squander the rest of his personal fortune in a year or so. He had already burned through his "fuck you money." Now he had to struggle to protect the safety net that supported his lifestyle: the Woodside mansion, the New York penthouse, the German sports cars. He needed to cut back drastically. At the very least, he needed to pick one venture and kill the other.

Steve's torment was transparent to his executives, especially as Christmas approached and he reviewed the disappointing results and numbers from the closing year and made his plans for the new year. Pam Kerwin, the marketing chief at Pixar, recalls: "Steve tended to get scared about things in December. I always feared December."

In December 1990, when Alvy Ray Smith and Ed Catmull were out of town on extended trips, Steve resolved to slash Pixar.

156

The
Second
Coming
of
Steve
Jobs

"Steve was totally freaking out," says Pam Kerwin. "Because of the huge Pixar debt, Steve worried that he wouldn't be able to tap his personal funds to bail out Next. Pixar and Next blew up at the same time, and it was obvious that his real love was Next."

Steve called for a massive retreat, laying off thirty of Pixar's eighty employees. When he had to make cuts and save money, he was characteristically extreme: he didn't want to give severance pay to *anyone*, not even the longtime employees who had been there since the Lucasfilm days, people who had spent a full decade there and done exceptional work.

The layoffs hit in February 1991. The finance department was cut from ten people to only one. Steve kept the brilliant animation team, which at least was bringing in some money by making TV commercials. And he retained the brain trust of engineering geniuses, thinking that maybe he could somehow merge their operation into Next.

And then he told Pam Kerwin to sell off the company's assets, the software programs it had developed. When Pam was done, she'd be out of a job, too, and the company would shut down. By that point, she recalls, "Steve kind of lost heart with everything."

■   ■   ■

STRUGGLING TO KEEP his two companies alive, he confronted a crisis in his private life.

Laurene was pregnant, and she wanted him to marry her. He refused.

She was so angered by his rejection that she moved out of his house.

Her departure was brutally wounding to him. When he came to the office, Steve seemed "crazy," recalls a Next colleague. His emotional state was volatile and fragile. His executives tried to stay away from him as much as they possibly could.

Steve's friends wondered whether he had fully gotten over his love for Tina Redse, who had spurned his marriage proposal less than two years earlier. They thought it odd that Steve had maintained such a close friendship with Tina all through his courtship of Laurene, which he discussed openly. "He would call Tina and they would talk, and then Steve would say, 'I have to go because I'm going out with Laurene,'" recalls a mutual friend.

Now Laurene was carrying his child.

It was as if he were being tested: he was nearly thirty-six, and he was confronted with the same moral issue that he had faced at twenty-two, when Chris-Ann was pregnant with Lisa.

At twenty-two he had been young and immature, obsessed with his work and his sense of destiny. Had he changed in fourteen years? In that time he had come to know his natural mother and sister, he had buried the adoptive mother who had loved him, he had gradually learned how to be a caring father to his daughter. He was still maniacally driven in his career, but he had already made his mark in the world and just as quickly been relegated to its margins.

He relented.

He agreed to marry Laurene.

158

The
Second
Coming
of
Steve
Jobs

■   ■   ■

THEY SET A WEDDING DATE for only a few weeks away, March 18, before her pregnancy would become particularly noticeable. Steve made the arrangements rapidly but with his relentless aesthetic perfectionism and maniacal attention to detail. He chartered a bus to take the wedding party on the four-hour drive from Palo Alto across California to Yosemite National Park. Then the entourage would enter the Ahwahnee Hotel, a romantic old lodge of wood and stone at the foot of a spectacular cliff of gorgeous blue-gray granite.

The ceremony was held in a small room. There were only a few guests: Laurene's family. Lisa. Mona Simpson. Bill Fernandez, Steve's best friend from high school.

The audience sat in chairs facing a wall of floor-to-ceiling glass panels, which reflected a magnificent outdoor tableau. They could see the expanse of the Yosemite Valley covered by dense evergreen forests and framed by the snow-covered peaks of the Sierras.

A virtuoso was playing classical guitar. During his flurry of planning, Steve had asked around to find who was considered the best classical guitarist in northern California. People told him about a Stanford professor with a superb reputation. Steve tried to hire the accomplished musician, who turned down the offer, saying that he didn't want to leave his family. So Steve arranged for the man's family to come along for a vacation at Yosemite.

Between interludes of guitar music, the ceremony was conducted by Kobin Chino, a Zen Buddhist monk who had been Steve's guru and friend since Steve was in his late teens. Kobin was a lovable, poetic, romantic personality who was known for speaking very slowly (even in his native Japanese) and giving unintelligible lectures. Like the other Japanese priests in California, Kobin was treated with great deference by his American followers. He was a renegade who rebelled against the strict discipline and burdensome responsibilities of being a priest. He was the Steve Jobs of Zen.

Kobin shook a stick with streamers and sashes. Incense burned. A gong sounded.

Bill Fernandez thought the ceremony was "simple and wonderful." He recalls: "It was not ostentatious. There were no great orations. It was understated and beautiful. Steve's style is very Spartan, and this had the spare elegance that's characteristic of him."

Afterward, Steve told the guests that they were all going to take a walk together through the valley. He provided backpacks and pullovers from the North Face, a popular store for outdoor sports gear. Then they traipsed through the snow for about a half mile. Walking together was how Steve bonded with people. Throughout his teens he would take long walks with Bill Fernandez and talk about philosophy and life. In his twenties, he loved walking the Stanford hills with John Sculley. When he wanted to hire someone, or talk about a deal, or prevent an executive from leaving, he would always suggest a walk. And a wedding walk was so unique, so unconventional, so unexpected that it was positively Jobsian.

160
The
Second
Coming
of
Steve
Jobs

■   ■   ■

AS IF HE WERE A CHARACTER in a moral fable, whom fate rewarded for his noble actions, Steve's decision to marry Laurene and raise their child together was soon followed by a crucial turnaround in his career.

Disney wanted to pursue the deal.

It was a corporate marriage instigated partly by fear and jealousy. When the Disney talks had stalled, the Pixar guys took meetings at Paramount and Warner Bros. They tried to make their Hollywood excursions as conspicuous as possible, so Disney would find out.

The strategy succeeded, and now the Disney talks were back on.

Steve flew to L.A. and returned to the Team Disney building, where Jeffrey Katzenberg had so effectively intimidated
him in their previous meeting. He was wearing his bohemian-
artist's uniform of a black turtleneck and blue jeans. He sat at
one end of the very long table in the conference room adjacent
to Jeffrey's private office. Jeffrey was far away at the other end.
A trio of Pixar executives—Ed Catmull, Bill Reeves, and Ralph
Guggenheim—sat along the length of the table. They watched
the confrontation as the two moguls parried and tested each
other. "It was like being spectators at Wimbledon," Ralph recalls. "It was prince of the San Fernando Valley meets the
prince of Silicon Valley."

Jeffrey began by asserting a sense of authority.

I want to make something clear, he said. If you're talking to
us, you talk *only* to us.

Before the summit Jeffrey's people had been arrogant and
condescending to Steve's people. Their attitude implied that
Pixar was *nothing* and Disney was going to run the show. Now,
as the two princes finally met face-to-face, Steve tried to act
tough. His bravado masked even the slightest indication of
how desperately he needed the contract. He was in a position
of weakness but postured as though he were negotiating from
strength.

I've put $50 million into this company, he said, and I'm not
giving this away cheaply. You're not going to get any of our
technology. And I want a three-picture deal.

Jeffrey countered by showing his own formidable resolve.

Pixar isn't going to get a percentage of the video sales,
Jeffrey said. That's nonnegotiable. If you don't like those
terms, we can shake hands right now and leave.

Steve stayed.

For all of Steve's chutzpah and posturing, he was at an
extreme disadvantage. Jeffrey had great knowledge about

Hollywood and animation, while Steve had very little. The discussion turned to the issue of the movie's budget. Disney would finance the production and keep 87.5 percent of the profits, so its interest was to keep the costs down. Pixar had a 12.5 percent share of the net, but its greater interest was to secure an ample budget so it could afford to make the film without taking a loss itself or compromising on the quality.

Steve put out a number: $22 million.

We *never* make animated films for that much, Jeffrey said. Do it for $5 million less.

Steve acquiesced.

Much later, Steve and the Pixar executives learned that Jeffrey had snookered them shamelessly. Disney's animated features typically cost $10 million *more* than Steve's proposed figure! Jeffrey was getting them to make a movie for $15 million less than he would have spent! They had left $15 million on the table because they didn't know better.

Even so, it was a secret coup for Steve Jobs. He had saved Pixar.

With the financial terms all set, there was one more step toward a green light: Pixar needed to pitch a story premise. John Lasseter began brainstorming. One of his greatest obsessions was toys, the subject of his last two short films. And he liked one of the most reliable Hollywood genres, the "buddy movie." Why not . . . a buddy movie about toys?

Jeffrey loved the idea. In May 1991, they closed the deal for *Toy Story*.

Back at Next, Steve went to his vice president of sales, Todd Rulon-Miller.

"You're not going to believe what I just did!" Steve said. "I just cut a deal to make three movies for Katzenberg!"

Todd couldn't share the enthusiasm. He remained skeptical.

162

The
Second
Coming
of
Steve
Jobs

"Steve," he said. "*Tin Toy* was only three minutes long and it took you a year . . ."

Steve wasn't paying attention. His eyes were glazed over.

■   ■   ■

THE SWEETNESS of the Disney deal was offset by the bitterness of Steve's ongoing struggles, especially as he clashed with two of his most essential and strong-willed executives.

Susan Barnes, Next's chief financial officer, was preparing to leave in the spring of 1991, becoming the second of Steve's five cofounders to abandon him. "I've done all I can financially," she told him. "It's just not working." She gave him two months notice, saying that she had accepted a position at Richard Blum & Associates, an investment banking firm in San Francisco run by the husband of California senator Dianne Feinstein.

"Don't tell anyone," Steve implored her. Before she left, he wanted to carefully craft a press release so that Next would save face. "How do I explain why the CFO quits without it looking bad for the rest of the company?" he challenged her. Then he suggested that Susan should say publicly that she was leaving Next because she wanted to spend more time with her young children. (She had married Next's software chief, Bud Tribble.) Susan opposed the idea. She wasn't going to work any less vigorously in her new position. She wasn't opting out for the "mommy track," and she wouldn't lie to the press.

Her new employers had little patience for arguing with Steve over the spin. They didn't like Steve's draft of the press release, so they went ahead and put out their own.

Steve was incensed.

Susan went to his office to try to appease him.

"Put me on the board," she suggested. That would show that she still believed in Steve and his company even while she took a position elsewhere.

"Good try, but no," he said.

A few moments later, when she got back to her own desk in the other building, her voice mail didn't work anymore. Her e-mail didn't work, either. Steve had cut her off.

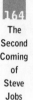

■   ■   ■

STEVE'S CONFRONTATION with Susan Barnes was cordial compared to his rift with Pixar president Alvy Ray Smith. Their explosion came after years of simmering tension. In Pixar's early days, Alvy felt free to speak back to Steve. "That's bullshit!" Alvy would exclaim, and Steve seemed to like it that someone stood up to him. But then Alvy began exploring the nebulous border between Steve's grudging appreciation and his intolerance. An early danger signal came when Steve was working intensely on the Next Cube and Alvy criticized Next for being so far behind schedule. Steve interpreted the comment as a personal affront: "He identifies with the machine," recalls Alvy, "and when I insulted his machine, I insulted him."

"Alvy and Steve never got on very well," says Pam Kerwin. "Alvy is not aggressive like Steve, but they have similar personalities: charismatic. Emotional. They were never really comfortable with each other, and Alvy started to think he didn't have a place in the company."

Alvy knew that he had crossed the border one day during a Pixar board meeting, when he inadvertently preempted Steve's authority. "An unspoken law with Steve Jobs is he *owns* the whiteboard," Alvy says. "That's his stage, and you just intuitively knew not to mess with it." When Alvy casually began writing on the board, Steve reacted furiously.

"You can't do that!" Steve protested, as if he were a selfish child guarding a toy.

Their faces were only inches apart as Steve screamed at him. Steve resorted to petty invective. He even insulted Alvy's southwestern accent. Then he stormed out of the room.

"It was ugly," Alvy recalls. "Steve turned on me with everything he had."

Alvy was stunned. He needed to sort out what had happened, so he took his family away to a rented beach house at Sea Ranch, a three-hour drive up the winding Pacific coast.

"What did I do?" he plaintively asked his wife.

After enjoying two decades working in a group of brilliant researchers and creative artists who shared power and treated each other as equals, with respect and consideration, Alvy refused to accept his role in what he thought of as a "master-slave relationship" with Steve Jobs. "I knew that I couldn't have a person like that in my life," he recalls.

Alvy decided to quit.

Steve didn't want him to leave Pixar. He came into Alvy's office, took out a sheet of paper, and drew a line that slanted upward, then down, and then up again. This was the "hero-asshole roller coaster," Steve explained. In the beginning, Alvy was a hero. Now, he was an asshole. But if he tried harder, maybe he could become a hero again.

Steve was willing to give him another chance.

Alvy wasn't persuaded by the bizarre pep talk. He left Pixar in 1991 and founded his own company, Altimira, with plans to make 3-D graphics software. His product would reflect the same basic idea as one of Pixar's products, but he wouldn't steal any of Pixar's software code. He would write his own code from scratch. Since the inspiration came from his work at

Steve's company, he offered to give 10 percent of the new venture to Steve. If Alvy's startup succeeded, Steve would be very well compensated. It was a good deal for both sides.

Alvy lined up well-known venture capitalists, who were ready to finance his new company. He needed Steve's cooperation so the investors wouldn't fear a legal morass. But Steve simply didn't trust Alvy. He thought that Alvy was trying to screw him somehow. Instead of the 10 percent stake, Steve demanded a $25 royalty on every copy of Altimira's software, which would make it very hard for Altimira to turn a profit.

"Steve had me by the balls," Alvy says. "My venture capitalists weren't going to close the deal without Steve. They all wanted to out-negotiate Steve. But when Steve is irrational, you can't negotiate with him."

With his fate in limbo, Alvy was overcome by intense, debilitating stress that undermined his physical health and his closest personal relationships. He went to two psychiatrists and a marriage counselor. He suffered an attack of chest pain and found himself being wheeled through the corridors of Marin General Hospital, where the doctors rushed into action, suspecting that he was in cardiac arrest. It turned out to be a bizarre lung problem. He was convinced that the weird malady was somehow induced by the tension of dealing with Steve Jobs.

■　　■　　■

BEFORE LONG, the brain drain resumed at Steve's companies.

Bud Tribble was next. When he had married a fellow cofounder, Susan Barnes, the other insiders joked that the news would have to be disclosed to Next's investors, because it increased the company's "risk factors": if one spouse-executive quit and felt mistreated by Steve Jobs, the other might leave, too.

166
The
Second
Coming
of
Steve
Jobs

That's exactly what happened.

"I didn't see how we were going to be successful," recalls Bud. The problem was that Steve's passion was for the physical machine while Next's real asset was its intangible software. "Next's hardware was not head-and-shoulders above Sun and the others," Bud says. "I didn't think that Next was going to change. I concluded that building factory and hardware boxes was in Steve's blood. He loved spending time in the factory."

Bud wanted his work to have an influence on the direction of the industry, and he saw that Sun was becoming a leader. He placed a call to the office of Sun's chief, Scott McNealy. Within five minutes, Scott returned the call from a car phone. They wanted him.

Steve tried forcefully to convince Bud to stay at Next. After many intense conversations, they found themselves talking on the phone late on a Sunday night.

"You can't talk me out of it," Bud said firmly. "I'm going to Sun."

Early the next morning, when Bud tried to enter the engineering building at Next's headquarters, he found that his security passcard no longer worked. Steve had cut him off.

■   ■   ■

ALONG WITH THE UPPER-LEVEL DEFECTIONS, a little of the mythology of Steve Jobs's companies was starting to wear off. In February 1991, the *San Francisco Chronicle* savaged him for the deep cutbacks at Pixar. In April, *Forbes* published a tough-minded article that began: "The discouraging results at Next, Inc., show that Steve Jobs, whatever his greatness as a visionary, is not much of a manager." The story showed persuasively that Steve had made public statements grossly exaggerating Next's sales figures, and that even those inflated numbers were incredibly disappointing.

But despite the emperor-has-no-clothes tone of some of the press, most of the media continued to treat Steve Jobs as a living legend, giving a generous benefit of the doubt to Next. In August, *Fortune* celebrated the tenth anniversary of the IBM personal computer with a cover photo of Steve Jobs and Bill Gates at Steve's empty Woodside mansion, where they sat together for a lengthy interview. Bill truly belonged on the magazine's cover: unlike Steve, he had played a role in the creation of the IBM PC, and he had since become an industry leader with a net worth of $4 billion. But it was still Steve who symbolized the romance of entrepreneurship and technological vision.

168
The
Second
Coming
of
Steve
Jobs

■   ■   ■

THE FOLLOWING MONTH, Laurene gave birth to a healthy son, Reed Paul Jobs. The name Reed was for Steve's alma mater, Reed College. Paul was the name of Steve's father and his own middle name.

Laurene thought that the Woodside house was too isolated and remote for raising a family, so they moved to Old Palo Alto, which had much more of a sense of neighborhood and community. Palo Alto was a flat-terrain town where neighbors saw each other on the sidewalks and stopped to chat under the canopy of overarching trees. You could walk a few blocks to the main street, University Avenue, and do all of your errands on foot. The Jobses bought an understated 1920s brick house in a vaguely medieval style. It was one of the larger homes in the area, which was filled mostly with two-bedroom wooden Craftsman bungalows that had been built early in the century for Stanford professors. But like the modest bungalows, their house was situated very close to the street on a small lot. The home, like the town itself, was idyllic and charming but not excessive or ostentatious. Palo Alto was filled with doctors, lawyers, and other upper-middle-class professionals, not CEOs, and it didn't have the snobby cachet of nearby enclaves like Atherton.

During and after her pregnancy, Laurene helped to run an entrepreneurial venture called Terra Vera (for "green earth"), a gourmet natural-foods startup. She cofounded the company with one of her Stanford classmates, J. J. Mullane, who was known on campus as a militant vegetarian. Together they produced organic salads and healthy burritos filled with tofu, beans, and rice. Laurene collaborated on strategy while J. J. drove the truck and did more of the leg work. As a bootstrapping measure they weren't afraid to rely on a little nepotism: Terra Vera began catering Next's parties and events, and its foods were sold at the cafe across from Next's headquarters. Eventually, the young entrepreneurs talked their way into small contracts supplying their goods to major supermarkets such as Safeway, the dominant chain in northern California, and Whole Foods, the local gourmet store, where Steve himself would walk over to to shop for the family's fresh fruits and organic vegetables.

Laurene became immersed in motherhood and her own thriving career. She knew many of Steve's business associates, especially the ones who frequently called on him at the house, and she occasionally dropped by his office, but she wasn't visibly involved in his companies. She wasn't striving to become a partner in power, a Hillary Clinton type.

But beneath the image of the perfect family, some of Steve's close friends and colleagues thought that early on the marriage was troubled. They believed that it took a while for

Steve to commit to the relationship because he truly loved Laurene, not because he felt a moral obligation to marry her. Eventually, however, he became known as a devoted husband and father and was exuberant about their son. Laurene maintained a certain independence but she was consistently supportive of Steve as he struggled with his career.

170

The
Second
Coming
of
Steve
Jobs

■   ■   ■

AFTER HE SIGNED THE DISNEY DEAL, Steve's role at Pixar once again receded to that of owner and distant overseer. He tried to push his way into the process of making movies, but the Pixar people conspired to keep him away. They respected his skills as a negotiator but not his instincts as a novice filmmaker.

With Alvy Ray Smith gone, Ed Catmull took the title of president. He was a quiet, scholarly type whose colleagues thought he was a "fish out of water" in business. Even though he avoided arguments, his demeanor concealed a fierce resolve. Ed was masterful at serving as a buffer between Steve and the rest of the company, especially the small team that was starting preproduction on *Toy Story*, which was led by director John Lasseter and producer Ralph Guggenheim. Ed drove down to Next's headquarters once every four to six weeks to brief Steve, who only rarely showed up in person at Pixar's offices. Steve's attitude was that the Pixar people should "go to school on Disney's dime." He liked the idea that they were being paid to learn about the movie business from the masters. So long as he didn't have to spend much of his own money, his anxiety was temporarily appeased. But the situation was difficult for Pixar, since Disney was only paying the direct expenses for making *Toy Story*, and the rest of the company—the programmers, for instance—was "on nickels and dimes," recalls Pam Kerwin, who had stayed on to run the software business.

While they chafed about the tight resources, the Pixar people enjoyed their independence from their owner. Steve was always saying "give me an org chart," but there never was a hierarchical chain of command. There was only a trio of executives—Ed, Ralph, and Pam—and everyone else sort of reported to them. Steve didn't believe that there was really such a loose, unstructured, egalitarian arrangement. He thought they were trying to obfuscate the real situation to make it harder for him to intervene. He asked for an org chart, and when Steve asked for something, he didn't forget. He would keep asking.

Steve couldn't understand the Pixar culture because it was so different from what he had created at Next. The two companies were like control groups in an experiment. Next was a cult of personality revolving around a visionary but mercurial dictator. Pixar was a collegial, egalitarian group that thrived on open collaboration. Ed would run the meetings but he never dominated the conversation. Everyone was encouraged to contribute, whether they were administrative assistants or Ph.D. engineers. "Everyone's opinion was expected," recalls Pam Kerwin. "There were quite a few really weird people without social skills, but it was a very accepting environment. You could ask anyone anything, even the most experienced technical person, and they'd stop and take the time to explain." It was the kind of sixties-inspired corporate culture that Steve had idealized earlier in his career, but with a communal aspect that couldn't possibly exist under his own overpowering leadership.

Pixar's founders, Ed and Alvy, had hired people who were very much in their own image: brilliant people who were nonetheless sweet, gentle, and considerate rather than arrogant and competitive. John Lasseter was a huggy guy who exuded warmth and affection for his colleagues. Ralph

Guggenheim was a New York Jewish intellectual and a real mensch. Pam Kerwin, a former schoolteacher, was a cross between a loving, supportive mother figure and a long-haired Marin County hippie chick. They played with each other's kids and felt like a family. Pam's husband was astonished that Steve Jobs didn't have "his own man" at Pixar, watching over the investment and running the place.

The Pixar people had harmonious relationships from years of working together. What they didn't have was experience making a full-length feature movie. Luckily they knew what they didn't know. Telling a compelling story on screen for seventy-five minutes is much harder than sustaining a single gag for two or three minutes. To learn more about narrative, John flew to Los Angeles to take a weekend-long crash course on story structure that was advertised in *Variety*. The teacher, Robert McKee, was something of a cult figure in Hollywood, more for his famous course than for his own screenwriting (he had sold many scripts but none had ever been made into a feature film). McKee was a former stage actor, and he could deliver a marathon twenty hours of lectures and make it seem enthralling and inspiring rather than tiresome. His course served as continuing education for up-and-coming Hollywood types and the younger agents and directors. Well-known actresses who wanted to write would sit next to waitresses and video-store clerks who were furtively working on spec scripts. When the weekend was over, they would emerge fluent in the cryptic language of Hollywood insiders, talking about the "arc of a character" or the "inciting incident" or the problem with the "second act" of a screenplay. John Lasseter was so enthused with the course that he sent a half-dozen colleagues to L.A. to take it.

For nearly a year, John and his team worked on the story for *Toy Story*. They put together production schedules and budgets and created a thirty-second example of what the film

172

The
Second
Coming
of
Steve
Jobs

would look like. It was just a gag involving the two main characters—Woody, a ventriloquist's dummy, and Lunar Larry, an astronaut figurine—but it showed off the kind of astonishingly hyperrealistic and luminous three-dimensional look that John envisioned.

John presented the clip to Peter Schneider, Disney's head of feature animation, the man who had opposed the film originally. (Since then Jeffrey Katzenberg had co-opted Peter by putting the production under Peter's fiefdom, even though Jeffrey retained the ultimate power.)

Peter wasn't normally an effusive personality, but when he saw the thirty-second demo clip, he said that he was "astounded." What Pixar could do was breathtaking.

Disney's honchos approved the start of production, but they were nervous about entrusting the film solely to Ralph Guggenheim, who had never worked on a full-length feature. So they brought in a Hollywood veteran, Bonnie Arnold, to serve as the coproducer. Bonnie had earned associate-producer credits on a number of live-action films—*Dances with Wolves*, *The Addams Family*, *The Last of the Mohicans*—and she was ambitious to move up to full producer.

Ralph wanted to show Bonnie that the Pixar crew was as highly respected in its own world as the Disney people were in theirs, that Pixar was the very best at what it did. So that summer he took her to the Siggraph conference, where Pixar was adulated.

Almost everyone here is a Ph.D., he said.

Bonnie said that she was used to managing people who weren't so well schooled.

"What's the difference between a gaffer and a grip?" she asked, setting up the punch line: "A high school education."

Bonnie was an expert at dealing with tough crew members and solving gritty crises. When the latrine wasn't working on one of the western locations for *Dances with Wolves*, she was the one who got it fixed. For her, filmmaking was an unremitting physical battle. For the Pixar people, it was something that you did at a desk with a computer.

When she arrived at Pixar's headquarters, Bonnie began setting up her office.

"I need a typewriter," she said.

Her new colleagues were surprised. They all had computers. Why a typewriter?

"I have all these forms to fill out," she said. Many actors worked on a shoot for only a day or two, and the producer needed to type out the forms to process their checks.

Don't worry, the Pixar people told her. We're all on salary here. We're Ph.D.s.

As Bonnie settled in, Disney sent an accountant to work full-time on the film.

"What can we get you?" Ralph asked.

"First, I need a typewriter," he said.

The Pixar people were exasperated. They were running a high-tech operation. It was bad enough that they had to buy a typewriter for Bonnie. Use *her* typewriter!

"What else can we get you?"

"I need a safe."

A *safe*! Why?

"For the ten grand in cash." The reason was very simple: Whenever there was a problem on a film set, the producer would open up the safe, pull out a pile of $100 bills, and hand out the bribes to the Teamsters. That was the quickest way to solve a problem.

The Pixar guys had an Oscar, but only now were they getting an education in the real workings of Hollywood. The culture clash was extraordinary. Pixar epitomized the mellow feel-good ethos of northern California, while Bonnie was

174

The
Second
Coming
of
Steve
Jobs

frighteningly L.A., a transplant from the realm of power and fear. The Pixar culture was unfailingly polite, with great respect for the individual. Bonnie was the kind of character who'd shout, "Get out of here, I don't like your face!"

Bonnie fired her administrative assistant without cause, just because she didn't like the person. "I was shocked," recalls Pam Kerwin. "I thought: Oh my God, we're going to be in court in two seconds." It took a while for the Pixar executives to realize that Bonnie hadn't done anything wrong by the standards of Hollywood, where it's OK to fire people arbitrarily because you have to act quickly and there's no time for drawn-out diplomacy. Besides, everyone belongs to the union and there's always another film ready to shoot.

The bad feelings about Bonnie only worsened when she installed an intercom system to announce meetings that would begin in ten minutes. A loudspeaker! The Pixar people cherished the peacefulness of their environment, where they could work without such jarring disturbances. Now their quiet sanctuary was compromised. And Ph.D.s didn't come running down the hallways when someone barked on a loudspeaker! After a while, though, they got used to the system and realized that it was a very good idea. Bonnie knew how to get things done, and they came to respect her and even to like her. She brought a more pragmatic mindset to the laissez-faire bunch of intellectuals. Her experience managing big projects proved invaluable as Pixar hired nearly one hundred people to work on the film.

After a while, the Pixar geniuses learned to take a certain amusement in Bonnie's Hollywood psychology. On one rainy day Bonnie was pacing nervously in the lobby of the Pixar building as she waited for a bunch of Disney vice presidents to arrive. Pam Kerwin looked out the front window and saw a limousine steering through the downpour.

"Hey, Bonnie," she said. "Your VPs are here. Maybe I should run out with an umbrella?"

Pam was kidding. At Pixar, everyone treated each other as peers. No one bowed down to authority or rank. No one demanded deference.

She watched, astonished, as Bonnie ran out into the rain and held an open umbrella beside the door of the limo.

176

The
Second
Coming
of
Steve
Jobs

■   ■   ■

MEANWHILE, AT NEXT, the situation improved somewhat, but not nearly enough. In 1991, Steve lured a hotshot executive from Microsoft, Mike Slade, to become Next's director of marketing. Mike was a cocky, fast-talking, profane, irreverent, charismatic figure who was unafraid to stand up to Steve. He galvanized the company, instilling a new sense of esprit de corps. That year Next's sales quadrupled to $127 million, though it was still bleeding money and it still had only a fraction of 1 percent of a market dominated by Sun.

Steve's Japanese partners at Canon tried to protect their $100 million investment by putting in another $30 million to cover Next's losses and sustain it into the next year. But it turned out that Canon was throwing good money after bad. Next sold only twenty thousand computers for the entire year of 1992, fewer than Apple sold in a single week. Canon had to sustain Next by giving it a $55 million line of credit.

The infusions of Japanese money came at a high price: Canon pressured Steve to bring in a more experienced manager from the outside to run the company with him. He hired Peter van Cuylenberg, a British executive who had spent sixteen years at Texas Instruments. The new man would share a new "office of the president" along with Steve.

A mass exodus began. Mike Slade thought that Steve's new hire was pompous and treacherous. After only one year as the vice president of marketing, Mike quit. His unexpected departure was devastating to morale at the company. Then Todd Rulon-Miller, the vice president of sales, quit as well. Then Steve received the resignation of Rich Page, his hardware guru. Rich was the fourth of Steve's five cofounders to leave.

Steve himself came close to quitting. "He got right at the edge there—emotionally, psychologically," recalls a colleague. "Right to the edge." He told a friend that he contemplated giving up entirely, handing the keys to the company to Canon, and abandoning his career so he could spend his time playing with his baby son, Reed.

But he couldn't leave. He felt trapped. He couldn't face the shame of walking away from a conspicuous failure, the embarrassment of conceding that he *couldn't* do it again.

In a meeting at Next headquarters, Steve looked around at the remaining members of his executive staff and he told them bitterly: "Everyone here can leave—except me."

■   ■   ■

THE GREATEST INSULT came when his handpicked new partner, Peter van Cuylenberg, tried to betray him. Peter called Scott McNealy at Sun Microsystems. He proposed that Sun should buy Next, kick out Steve, and then install him, Peter, as the head of the operation.

Scott McNealy had no reason to feel loyalty toward Steve Jobs. For the past year, Next had been running vicious attack ads against Sun as a desperate ploy to gain attention. But Scott didn't seem disturbed by Steve's effort to pick a fight: "Who cares about Next?" he told a reporter. He said that he worried about IBM and Microsoft, not about Next.

Scott was a brutally tough competitor but he also had a sense of honor.

He called Steve and told him about Peter's betrayal.

Steve was outraged.

It was history repeating itself, the horrible John Sculley episode all over again.

178

The
Second
Coming
of
Steve
Jobs

■   ■   ■

IT WAS BAD ENOUGH that Peter van Cuylenberg had turned out to be a frightening reincarnation of John Sculley. Soon, a kind of living ghost from the Apple years returned to haunt and torment Steve. It was as if Steve were being punished for his past sins.

In December, Steve's car windshield was broken by a vandal, as were sixteen windows in his house in Palo Alto. A few days later, Laurene saw a man sitting on the curb across the street and holding a bag of rocks.

The man wasn't a stranger. He was Burrell Smith, who had been the chief hardware designer of the Macintosh. Burrell had been a legendary figure at Apple, a brilliant engineer who pushed himself incredibly hard to fulfill Steve's demanding visions. But after Steve unfairly criticized and humiliated him in front of the Macintosh team in 1985, he had left Apple and never returned, not even to pick up his final paycheck. In the following years, his mental health deteriorated. In 1990, he suddenly lost control and vandalized a church in Palo Alto, knocking over two statues and breaking the panes of stained glass. He was diagnosed as a bipolar manic-depressive with a "chemical brain imbalance." After eighteen months of taking lithium, he seemed to have recovered and he went off the medication.

Now he was losing control again.

He lived only a few blocks down Waverly Street from Steve and Laurene.

■　　　■　　　■

IN EARLY FEBRUARY 1993, a smart, ambitious young reporter at the weekly trade magazine *InfoWorld* got a tip from a Next insider that the company was killing its computer. The reporter, Cate T. Corcoran, conferred with her editor, who said that he heard that someone had tried to order a NextStation and the order had been rejected. Then she talked to the magazine's gossip columnist, who found a third source to confirm the story, a disgruntled executive who had recently left Next. With three sources, they could safely break the news.

On Monday, February 8, *InfoWorld* revealed that Next was shutting its factory and getting out of the hardware business. Even though this was a big scoop, the editors didn't play the story as the issue's lead. Next simply wasn't important enough for the lead.

The following day, the story was picked up by *The Wall Street Journal* and the two daily newspapers in San Francisco, the *Chronicle* and the *Examiner*. On Wednesday, Steve Jobs confirmed the rumors. He announced that Next was making massive layoffs, cutting its staff from 530 people to about 200. Canon was taking over the factory. Next would focus instead on selling its software to run on other machines. Steve would try to salvage a much smaller company out of the ruins.

That day, *InfoWorld*'s Cate Corcoran went to Next's headquarters for a one-on-one interview with Steve, whom she had never met before. She was in her mid-twenties. She was escorted by two p.r. women, around her own age, who were exceptionally pretty and slender and beautifully dressed. She thought: Even Steve's people are incredibly stylish.

They took her to a large empty conference room. Steve arrived. Cate was still inexperienced as a reporter, and she didn't know that you're supposed to schmooze first and ask some easy questions to establish a rapport before turning to the harder questions.

180
The
Second
Coming
of
Steve
Jobs

"Does the hardware shutdown mean that Next is a failure?" she asked point-blank.

Steve sunk his head into his folded arms on the table.

He rubbed his fingers into his temples.

"I don't want to do this interview," he said softly. "I don't want to do this interview." He seemed so fragile, depressed, and withdrawn, and she felt empathy for him.

He got up and began to walk out of the room.

As he got to the door, she called out, trying to cajole and coax him back.

He returned and sat for an interview.

Was he truly depressed, she later wondered, or was it all a big manipulation?

■ ■ ■

STEVE WAS CAPABLE of manipulating people, but this time it surely wasn't an act. He was truly emotionally distraught. "It was gut-wrenching for him," recalls Todd Rulon-Miller. "Steve loves hardware and designing factories. He was a hardware freak."

"The transition was *devastating* for Steve: laying off half the company he had built, abandoning this beautiful hardware, acknowledging that the world didn't need another computer," recalls Karen Steele, who was Next's communications manager at the time. "One of our p.r. objectives was *not* to be mentioned as 'failing' and 'fledgling.' It was a humbling experience for Steve. He said he'd eat crow if he had to. I saw him in a humbled capacity with people he had treated poorly in the past."

Steve's longtime public relations consultant, Allison Thomas, resigned the account. They needed p.r. advice. Karen Steele convinced Steve to try to rehire Andy Cunningham.

It was an embarrassing act of contrition. After Steve had criticized Andy's work and dumped her in the late eighties, she went on to build her reputation as the smartest publicist in Silicon Valley, and her firm had grown from three people to well over a hundred.

Karen made the call.

"I'm surprised," Andy said. "Does Steve know you're calling? Are you aware of the history here? We had a falling-out. I will not work with the same Steve as he was before."

Steve called her, and he seemed remarkably humbled and reformed. Astonishingly, she agreed to take his business again. Her old friend Susan Barnes said to Andy: "It's telling that Steve kept firing you and you kept coming back. There's a piece of Steve that's so brilliant it's hard to resist working with him."

■   ■   ■

EVEN AS HE APPROACHED HIS NADIR, Steve's charismatic personality and his immutable pop-culture legend had a powerful attraction on other entrepreneurs in Silicon Valley. He developed a very close friendship with the software mogul Larry Ellison, who liked to come over to Next's offices and play with the machines there. Now that Next desperately needed to restore its credibility, Larry agreed to join Steve's board of directors.

Larry was the cofounder and chief executive of Oracle, which was second only to Microsoft for its size, wealth, and power in the software business. While Steve was trying to forestall his own financial collapse, Larry had become a multi-billionaire. While Steve was struggling to stay at the margins of the industry, Larry was taking a place near its red-hot center. The irony was that, despite all that, Larry was the one who worshiped Steve. He yearned to emulate Steve's charisma and celebrity. Larry was powerful in the business but he remained a virtual unknown to the public. The problem was that Larry made costly arcane software for the elite technological priesthood, not cheap gizmos for the masses. His business was absurdly profitable but dreadfully prosaic. Now that he had the money, he wanted the fame and glory, too. He wanted to be recognized by millions of people as one of the great technological visionaries. He wanted to be an icon like . . . Steve Jobs!

Steve and Larry had much in common to serve as the basis for their friendship. They were both born out of wedlock and put up for adoption. (Larry's mother was a teenager in New York City who sent him to be raised by relatives in Chicago.) They both struggled for many years to accept and understand why they had been abandoned by their birth parents. They both came from modest economic backgrounds, though Larry liked to exaggerate and romanticize his youthful deprivation. They were both tall, handsome, and slender. They had elegant, austere, minimalist tastes in fashion and design, and a mutual fascination with the Far East. Larry would dress in dark Savile Row suits for work and black silk Japanese sport shirts with black slacks for leisure. He wore an expensive kimono as

182

The
Second
Coming
of
Steve
Jobs

he walked barefoot by the rock gardens and koi ponds of his secluded mansion, which looked like the home of a feudal Japanese warlord, with shoji screens and samurai armor and a
moon-observation platform. From Next's offices Steve could
see Larry's corporate headquarters rising a few miles away
along the bayshore wetlands, a cluster of sleek rounded towers
of emerald reflective glass, the most magnificent architecture
in the valley.

In 1992, Larry began trying to seduce reporters from
the major national publications into writing about his glamorous lifestyle and his technological vision. His timing was
good: with Steve in so much trouble, the media needed a
new high-tech hero, someone with the glamour and color
that was sadly lacking in Bill Gates. In 1993 *Fortune* dismissed
Steve as a "snake-oil salesman," then put Larry on its cover and
let him tout himself as the lone visionary who would merge
Silicon Valley with Hollywood and create a new era of interactive media. It was a breakthrough for Larry, his first appearance as the cover boy for a major magazine. Then he rented a
huge Hollywood studio at CBS as the setting for a speech about
his far-ranging visions. One of Steve's colleagues who attended
the lavish event recalls: "I found myself thinking: Here's a
guy who's desperately trying to be like Steve Jobs. There was
a part of Larry that wanted to be like Steve, to have that *power*
over people. Larry had nothing to be apologetic for, but even
though he was worth three billion dollars, while Steve was
worth mere millions, Steve still had a big influence on him."

■   ■   ■

STEVE'S COMMUNICATIONS EXECUTIVE, Karen Steele,
got up at six o'clock on the morning of May 25, 1993. It

promised to be a very big day for them. Steve was addressing the annual Next convention, a combination of a trade show and an evangelical revival meeting for Next's most loyal customers and enthusiasts. In his keynote speech he was planning to announce that Larry was joining the board of directors and helping him save the company.

Karen picked up her copy of *The Wall Street Journal* and saw a front-page story about Next. The article was a brutal put-down. It said that Steve was taking "a steep fall from a very lofty perch. His NeXT workstation seems destined to become a high-tech museum relic. He himself is fighting to show that he still matters in the computer industry."

Karen saw Steve as he prepared to go onstage in front of a thousand people.

He had read the article.

"It could have been worse," she said, trying to lighten the mood.

"Yeah," he shot back. "If you were me."

184
The
Second
Coming
of
Steve
Jobs

■   ■   ■

IT DID GET WORSE. The following day Steve and Laurene and their nanny made a report to the Palo Alto police about the man who was harassing them, Burrell Smith. Their nanny said that she had seen Burrell ride up to the house on a bicycle and throw a cherry bomb, which exploded against the wall. Steve filed for a temporary restraining order to keep Burrell from coming within one hundred yards of his family, nanny, home, car, and office.

Burrell was arrested and taken in handcuffs to the Palo Alto municipal court.

A judge issued the restraining order.

■   ■   ■

THE NEXT LAYOFFS proceeded bitterly. Some three hundred people cleared out of the headquarters by the bay. The place became a "wasteland," recalls Emily Brower, a public relations executive.

In September, a bunch of salvagers and used-furniture dealers went to the Next factory for an auction of its contents. They bid on 715 lots that were laid out on the barren cement floor. They bought the Herman Miller chairs, the trash cans, the paper shredders, all the surplus Next Cubes and laser printers and oversized computer monitors.

Steve's dream was being liquidated.

■   ■   ■

IT GOT WORSE AND WORSE. Soon after the blowup at Next came the great trauma at Pixar.

The crisis snuck up on them. The work on *Toy Story* had been going extremely well. The director and creative visionary, John Lasseter, reported to Jeffrey Katzenberg at Disney. Their relationship was harmonious and productive. "John really respected Jeffrey and Jeffrey really respected John," recalls Pam Kerwin. As John's team developed the story, they sketched out hundreds of storyboards, which they pinned to the walls all over the building. Then they would film a series of storyboards, making a "reel" to get a crude approximation of what the actual film would look like. John would go to Burbank and play the reel for Jeffrey, filling in the voices for all of the characters and acting out their physical gestures and movements. These "pitches" were one of the most vital parts of the whole process, the key to honing the storyline. John was a masterful actor, emotional and compelling, and he looked for those same talents in his animators. Their art wasn't just being able to draw well, it was making the drawings come alive with vivid characterization. "When John hires people, he doesn't care if you had formal training in animation or computer graphics," says Alvy Ray Smith. "He wants to know if you can *act*."

John's team started with high-level plot concepts, which they constantly changed, deepened, and refined depending on Jeffrey's reactions to the pitches and reels. Jeffrey was a superbly instinctive editor, with an unerring ability to find the weaknesses in a plot, but he wasn't a script doctor. He didn't presume to fix the flaws that he pinpointed. "Jeffrey could tell you that something wasn't working but he wouldn't be able to tell you why," says Pam Kerwin. "He would say, 'This stuff isn't working for me,' not 'Do this instead.' "

As John went back again and again to Burbank, Jeffrey remained unhappy.

The story just didn't work.

The problem was that the hero, Woody, wasn't an appealing character. Woody was originally conceived as a ventriloquist's dummy. Now he was a cowboy figure. He lived in the bedroom of a boy named Andy, and he was Andy's favorite toy. Woody felt threatened when his owner got another toy, a spaceman (originally "Lunar Larry," now "Buzz Lightyear") that was newer and niftier. The story hinged on the bantering rivalry between Woody and Buzz, who would ultimately become the best of friends. It was the classic plot of a buddy movie. But somehow the Pixar animators had erred as they tried to adopt the old formula. The comical interplay between the two toys was too mean-spirited. Woody especially came off as an annoying, nasty, complaining, bullying, hateful character.

Pixar began the actual work of animation in July 1993, but

186

The
Second
Coming
of
Steve
Jobs

through the summer and early fall, Jeffrey Katzenberg was still unhappy with the storyline. John Lasseter and his colleagues kept coming back with new ideas, but nothing seemed to work. The repeated rejections were frustrating and painful.

In November, Peter Schneider screamed at Ralph Guggenheim. He said that Ralph and Bonnie were terrible producers and that he would fire them if they were employees of Disney and not Pixar. Then he called Steve Jobs and demanded that Steve get rid of Ralph. Steve resisted.

Only Steve could hire or fire at Pixar, but Disney had creative control over the film. On November 17, Jeffrey Katzenberg shut down production on *Toy Story*.

Pixar looked as desperate and moribund as Next.

Steve Jobs was at the nadir of his career.

I n 1993, when Next was finally revealed as a blatant failure, the news media that had adored Steve Jobs for so many years now turned on him with the resentment and bitterness of a spurned lover. One of America's most highly respected business journalists, Joseph Nocera, published an extraordinary *mea culpa*, criticizing himself for having fallen for Steve's charm back in 1986, when he spent a week as a "fly on the wall" at Next and wrote an effusively flattering profile of Steve for *Esquire*. Nocera had watched as Steve humiliated employees in meetings and obsessed over seemingly trivial details, such as what brand of juice to put in the company's refrigerator, but he had nonetheless written a positive piece.

Now that Steve's character flaws had produced a failed company, the journalist went back and reread his old notes. He published a new article, in the October 1993 issue of *GQ*, saying he was "ashamed" by how he had been seduced: "Like so many others before and since, I spent most of my time falling for Jobs. He knew exactly which buttons to push; that seems obvious to me now."

Nocera wrote that Steve Jobs was by far the most charismatic person he had ever met, even after a decade of covering business leaders. He concluded: "The real tragedy of Jobs, I think, is that of all the people he deceived with his powerful aura, no one was more hypnotized than Jobs himself. No one bought into the myth of Steve Jobs more than Jobs."

A couple of weeks later, *Fortune* profiled Steve as part of a scathing cover story titled "America's Toughest Bosses," writing that he was "brilliant and charming but explosive and abusive" and that his "inhuman drive for perfection can burn out even the most motivated worker." At the end of the piece, the reporter added: "Though Jobs declined to be interviewed for this article, his office did make available several current Next employees who wanted to tell you that Steve is going through a 'major personality change' . . ."

Not surprisingly, the *Fortune* reporter remained skeptical of the sugar-coated corporate spin. But in reality, this man who was so fond of abusive tirades and seduce-and-abandon roller-coaster rides was beginning to soften.

192

The
Second
Coming
of
Steve
Jobs

Steve's famous intensity had greatly diminished. Much of the time he withdrew from the turmoil of his career and retreated into the comfort of his family life. He called truces in some old wars. His ex-protégé Susan Barnes rejoined his circle of friends, but when she called his office to set up a meeting with him, it was hard to find a time when Steve would be in the office, even though he wasn't traveling. He was hiding out at home. The assistant suggested Tuesdays, which was the one afternoon when Steve kept regular office hours.

Sequestered safely at his house and his thriving small garden in Old Palo Alto, he loved playing with his two-year-old son, Reed. He would take Reed over to Bob Metcalfe's farm in the foothills of Woodside, where Bob's wife, Robyn, kept unusual species of animals, even a white llama. The place was a delight to the little boy. When Reed began to talk, Steve recorded the child's exuberant high-pitched voice as the outgoing message for his own answering machine. People who called for Steve would hear: "This is REED!"

At thirty-nine, Steve was finally ready for the pleasures of parenting. His friends and colleagues all knew that he was just crazy about the kid, and they believed that fatherhood and marriage were mellowing him out at least somewhat and making him more mature.

He tried to ignore the onslaught of bad press, using his old psychological defense of pretending the man in the magazine articles was "some other guy named Steve."

"At the low moments, Steve was so ridiculed and abused," recalls his friend Todd Rulon-Miller. "Steve was beaten down and bedraggled. But he showed a strength of character and will. He drew on an inner courage and resolve. I don't know how he did it."

■ ■ ■

HIS PATIENCE PAID OFF.

The crisis at Pixar, while real, wasn't as hopelessly dire as the Pixar executives had believed. It turned out Disney often halted the production of its feature films midway through the animation process and took the time to rewrite storylines that weren't working. What seemed so apocalyptic to the Pixar novices was really just Disney's normal way of doing things. And Hollywood types lashed out in emotional rages all the time. No big deal.

Pixar's leaders did have reason to worry, though. While production was stopped, there were some one hundred stranded people who had absolutely nothing to do. Pixar needed to pay their salaries and keep them happy and engaged creatively while *Toy Story* languished in turnaround hell. The company managed to reassign some of its artists and engineers to work on television commercials as a moneymaking temporary diversion.

After months of nervous brainstorming, John Lasseter and his core brain trust came up with a clever fix for the problems in the plot of *Toy Story*. They decided to add new scenes at the beginning of the film that portrayed Woody as the leader of all the toys in the bedroom, the character who took responsibility and looked out paternalistically for the others. This way Woody seemed admirably selfless, a good-hearted, likable guy. Then, when Buzz Lightyear arrived and Woody's ego was threatened by the shiny rival, the audience could more easily understand and forgive Woody's moments of selfishness.

Jeffrey Katzenberg approved the story changes. In April 1994, he ordered the production to start up again. For the Pixar team, it was a huge relief, though as work resumed they faced unremitting deadline pressures and high expectations. The place was still frenetic, recalls Ralph Guggenheim: "We knew we were on the edge of horrible failure or great opportunity."

194
The
Second
Coming
of
Steve
Jobs

■   ■   ■

STEVE SPENT LITTLE TIME at Pixar and his influence on *Toy Story* was minimal. A film depends on its director as the creative visionary and the benign dictator. John Lasseter had those roles, and it would have been foolish and unworkable for Steve to undermine John's authority with the production or the crew. John answered only to Jeffrey Katzenberg and Disney, but Steve at least wanted to be in the loop. John obliged by showing Steve the story reels, but only after he had shown the Disney honchos. Steve would make comments and suggestions on a take-it-or-leave-it basis. John would say "yeah yeah yeah," humor Steve a little, and then follow his own artistic vision. He kept Steve apprised of milestones. He gave Steve a recording of an early version of the Randy Newman songs for the soundtrack. Steve listened as he drove around in his Mercedes sports coupe along with one of his Next colleagues. He didn't like the music very much, but he withheld his criticisms.

The coproducer of *Toy Story*, Ralph Guggenheim, was convinced that until the production neared its completion, Steve didn't really appreciate the film's extraordinary potential.

Then, in January 1995, came the crucial moment that changed Steve's thinking. Disney was staging a press conference in Manhattan to create some advance hype for the animated films it would debut later in the year: *Pocahontas*, which was scheduled for a summer premiere, the best time for releasing animated films, and *Toy Story*, which would open on Thanksgiving weekend.

John Lasseter and Ralph Guggenheim flew to New York for the event. They were overwhelmingly impressed by the costly setup. Disney had erected what Ralph thought of as "an unbelievable huge fucking tent" right in the middle of the Great Lawn in Central Park. Inside there was a ninety-nine-seat screening room. The movie screen was surrounded by cutouts of Disney's most famous creations—Mickey Mouse, Donald Duck, Pluto, Snow White, the Seven Dwarfs—as well as images of Woody and Buzz Lightyear. *Their* inventions had already been enshrined in the pantheon of Disney's beloved characters!

"My God!" Ralph exclaimed.

At the far end of the tent they saw the "green room," the lounge for VIPs, decorated with beautiful furniture. Waiters in white jackets would serve canapés there. In the tent's clear plastic center, a podium was set up for the press conference, which would be hosted by the mayor of New York, Rudy Giuliani. That was the kind of pull that Disney exerted.

They called Steve in California and told him to get on a plane.

The next day, the Disney brass showed up in full force: The big chief, Michael Eisner. The link to history, Roy Disney. Joe Roth, the new studio boss, who replaced Jeffrey Katzenberg (who had clashed with Eisner and left to become the cofounder of DreamWorks SKG). Peter Schneider and Tom Schumacher, the heads of feature animation.

Steve Jobs joined them in the screening room.

They watched a sneak preview of clips from *Pocahontas*. The director gave a talk. The heroine's lead animator explained the artistry that went into the film. The composer Alan Mencken sat at a piano and performed what promised to be another batch of hit songs.

"It was a *tour de force* presentation," Ralph recalls.

Then Ralph and John got up and talked for twenty minutes about *Toy Story*. They showed one of the most memorable sequences from the movie: a bunch of little plastic green army men statuettes escape from their bucket and march through the bedroom.

Steve was incredibly excited. The mayor, the Disney brass, the press conference: it all validated the movie's worth. Despite the many years that had passed, Steve was still insecure in his

196
The
Second
Coming
of
Steve
Jobs

own aesthetic judgments and relied on informal surveys of other people. The Disney guys were the gurus of animation, and here they were, promoting Pixar's film along with their own grand production. It was exactly the validation that Steve needed.

"Steve went bonkers, he was just so excited," Ralph recalls. "That was *the* moment when Steve realized the Disney deal would materialize into something much bigger than he had ever imagined, and that Pixar was the way out of his morass with Next."

It was the great revelation for Steve: finally, he saw how he would redeem his career. He realized that his salvation would come not from Next, his own creation and passion, but from Pixar, his supposed "hobby," the frustrating money sink of a company that he had wanted to close down, the asset that until then he had still wanted to sell off.

The Central Park event went so well that Michael Eisner asked John and Ralph to fly back to California with him and his wife, Jane, on their private Gulfstream jet.

After nine years of struggle and uncertainty, Pixar had finally arrived.

■   ■   ■

No LONGER RESIGNED to merely watching the Pixar drama from off in the wings, Steve thrust himself forward as an actor on center stage. He stripped the title of president from Ed Catmull and appropriated it for himself, adding chief executive officer as well. The gesture was more than symbolic: Steve was trying to take over the running of the company.

For years his rare appearances at the Pixar building were like Elvis sightings. He had been the distant investor, the absentee landlord. Now, he yearned to be a star player in what seemed destined to become the blockbuster movie of the holiday season.

At Apple and Next, Steve had been accustomed to everything revolving around himself. But when he descended on Pixar, he found that everything revolved around another man: John Lasseter. John had become the vital creative force and the spiritual leader, the very soul of the company. John was the one whom everyone—artists, engineers, marketing people— looked to for guidance and approval. John made the decisions. The culture was a reflection of John's smart, warm, quirky personality. He nurtured and touched and hugged people affectionately and inspired a sense of family and acceptance. In some ways he was like an arrested adolescent, and he loved to have all kinds of toys and random pop-culture kitsch strewn around the cluttered offices.

John and Steve were both exuberant, persuasive, and charismatic, but they were polar opposites in their aesthetics and their instinctive leadership methods. Steve adhered to deprivation diets, strived to remain bone-thin even into his middle age, and dressed nearly every day in black. John was a chubby guy who scarfed greasy hamburgers and wore outrageously colorful Hawaiian shirts. While Steve decorated Next's offices with stiff black leather couches that cost $10,000 apiece, John filled the Pixar screening room with comfy mismatched thrift-shop sofas that were falling apart. John's style was homey and playful. Steve's had once been playful but now it was serious, austere, and elegantly minimalistic. John motivated his people through a sense of mutual love and respect. Steve used to inspire extraordinary love, but more and more he had come to rely on intimidation and fear. Now that he was successful again, he was reverting back to his terrifying old self, as if he had never been softened or humbled by his long period of failure.

198

The
Second
Coming
of
Steve
Jobs

He was Bad Steve again. And John was . . . the *anti-Steve!*

Steve's sudden presence provoked wariness and anxiety at Pixar. When he tried to intervene in creative matters, he inevitably clashed with John, whose positions were always backed by the other executives, Ed Catmull and Pam Kerwin and Ralph Guggenheim.

Before long Steve tried to push the balance of power in his favor by bringing in his own man. He hired Lawrence Levy as the chief financial officer. Lawrence was bright and appealingly young (thirty-six) and he wasn't a backstabber. In his previous job as the No. 2 guy at a Silicon Valley startup, Electronics for Imaging (EFI), he had proven that he could get along in the shadows of a strong-willed entrepreneurial founder. Lawrence had taken EFI public and then driven up its stock price. He was the kind of smoothly competent fellow who evoked the trust and confidence of Wall Street's securities analysts. Steve interviewed and hired him with the explicit idea that Lawrence would soon become Pixar's chief executive officer and that he would take the company public the following year.

Pixar's old guard weren't surprised that Steve would want to have "his own man" there as his eyes and ears; indeed, they wondered why he hadn't done it years ago, why it took so long for him to wise up. Still, it was an affront that Steve's guy wasn't going to just keep a watch on them—he was going to be their *boss.* The Pixar veterans were enraged. They felt it was a brutal insult for Steve to bring in an outsider to displace their patriarch and technological visionary, Ed Catmull. *Toy Story* was the realization of a dream that Ed had been pursuing with unyielding faith for nearly a quarter century. Pixar was Ed's brainchild.

"People jumped to Ed's defense," recalls Pam Kerwin. "There were meetings with people saying plaintively: 'Ed, why can't you be the head?'"

But Ed remained characteristically self-sacrificing and

diplomatic. He had never cared about titles or authority or formal structures, and neither had Alvy Ray Smith. When they cofounded Pixar in 1986, neither had wanted to be called "president."

Now, as he faced his loyal supporters, Ed joked about that episode from the venture's early history. "We all drew straws to see who would head the company and Alvy and I lost," he said. "I asked Pam to do it and she said no. I asked Molly"—the office's beloved sheepdog—"and she said no."

Then he added: "We tried to scare off Lawrence, but he's coming anyway."

As Steve tried to assert his power and authority, the Pixar veterans resorted to more passive forms of resistance. The executive row was a hallway near the front of the building and it had only three offices, which were occupied by Ed, Pam, and Lawrence. They wouldn't let Steve take any of the offices. There wasn't room, they said. When he came up for the day, they made him into a squatter, forcing him into a corner of Lawrence's space.

Pixar's remoteness from Steve's home in Palo Alto still afforded a degree of insulation and protection. In the early 1990s, when the company had been kicked out of its original building by the landlord, George Lucas, who needed the space, it had moved right across the San Rafael–Richmond Bridge to Point Richmond, on the eastern edge of the bay, a few miles north of Berkeley. But the new location was just as far from Silicon Valley, and it still took Steve an hour and a half to drive there. If anything, the traffic was even more unpredictable and maddening on his new route. Once again Steve argued that they should move the company to San Francisco. The Pixar executives were shocked and dismayed by Steve's thoughtless narcissism. They were working frantically seven days a week to meet the deadlines for *Toy Story*, and Steve was

200

The
Second
Coming
of
Steve
Jobs

so insensitive that he dared propose moving the company in the middle of it all, just so it would be more convenient for him! Besides, it would have been foolish to move Pixar forty-five minutes to the south because John Lasseter lived so far to the north, in the old village of Sonoma, amid the wine country.

In Steve's new incarnation as Pixar's president and CEO, he insisted on holding an "executive committee" meeting once a week, with tiresome briefings that would last for hours. At first he tried to schedule it for the midday, but Ralph and John objected. They needed to work on the movie during the day! Steve was interfering with production!

Steve compromised and ran the meetings between four and seven o'clock. Then he presided over a working dinner, and then he accompanied John and the other executives into the screening room to watch and comment on the dailies. Steve would dominate the conversations, seemingly unaware that John didn't really want or need his advice. John put up with the marathon sessions to humor Steve, but they were unnecessary and draining for him. John would awaken before sunrise and leave home before seven every morning to get to the office in time for the *real* dailies at eight. That's when he watched the film clips with the other artists. *They* were the ones he relied on for advice and criticism, not Steve Jobs. But Steve would selfishly detain John there with him until ten or ten-thirty at night, extending John's workday to a brutally taxing fourteen hours. John would fall asleep during the late-night screenings. When Steve finally released him, John would look so worn and bleary-eyed that Pam Kerwin worried that he would kill himself as he was driving home on the dark country roads. Eventually, John's wife, Nancy, had to insist on a curfew for him.

■   ■   ■

202
The
Second
Coming
of
Steve
Jobs

STEVE'S MOOD WAS EFFUSIVE as he celebrated his fortieth birthday in February 1995. Laurene threw a surprise party for him in San Francisco at Larry Ellison's second house. Larry still lived in his samurai-style mansion in the suburbs, but he had recently bought a *pied-à-terre* in the city on the same block as the Getty residence. He was one of the few new-money types in Silicon Valley who wanted to hobnob with the insular old-money types in town. The others were put off by high society's snobbery and exclusivity, though they enjoyed a kind of reverse snobbery in their own tight circles, where they had the status and power.

Larry's lot was magnificent: it was on the best block of the best neighborhood, at the top of the hill in Pacific Heights, with panoramic postcard views of the city and the bay. He had torn down the rotting old house, which was built by a nineteenth-century sugar baron. In its place he was finishing a brazenly modern structure of glass, steel, and concrete. The society columnist for the *San Francisco Chronicle* quipped that the street-side exterior resembled a sleek espresso machine. The city's elite all wanted to get a look inside.

Steve's oldest friend, Bill Fernandez, found the address and walked past the lineup of valet-parking attendants. Inside, he was astonished when he came up to the floor-to-ceiling glass walls suspended above the edge of a cliff. Half the house was torn up and filled with dust and rubble, but Laurene had hung curtains that hid the construction work. The curtains were a clever variation on the party's Moroccan theme. Dozens of guests nibbled on vegetarian hors d'oeuvres as they sat cross-legged on the floor or sprawled like sultans on plump throw pillows. Bill Fernandez talked with a balding disheveled middle-aged computer hacker, who turned out to be Steve's buddy William Randolph Hearst III, the grandson of the megalomaniacal publishing magnate who inspired *Citizen Kane*.

The crowd was silenced for Steve's moment of glory. One of the Pixar executives presented Steve with a large framed poster of Buzz Lightyear and Woody. It was a blowup of a still from *Toy Story*, signed by many of the animators and the technical crew.

Steve said that he was very touched.

The scene was tantalizing but cryptic. The crowd began buzzing with gossip:

What the hell was Steve up to? When and how did he get into the movie business?

■   ■   ■

AROUND THE SAME TIME, a group of *Newsweek* writers and editors met at the magazine's headquarters on New York's Madison Avenue to deliberate about the candidates for a splashy feature on the fifty most important people in technology.

Two of the writers, Steven Levy and Katie Hafner, nominated Steve Jobs.

"Everyone else in the room said, 'Huh?'" Katie recalls. "It was sad."

Steve had once been seen as the single great figure of the computer revolution. Now, the wags of the New York media hardly considered him one of the top fifty. And there was no doubt about who was No. 1. Bill Gates was preparing for the release of Windows 95. Steve's loyalists printed a T-shirt that said "Windows 95 = Next 88." If anything, the tag line overstated the virtues of Windows, which still wasn't as easy to use as Next's old software. But the bragging rights were small consolation for the hangers-on at a desperately struggling company. Now Windows had tens of millions of customers while Next had only tens of thousands. Windows dominated the computer industry. The only viable competitor in the consumer market was Apple, which accounted for 8.3 percent of global PC sales at the beginning of 1995. Apple's market share had remained fairly steady through the 1990s, but its still-profitable position was about to be threatened by the formidable one-two punch of Microsoft and Intel. The new version of Windows 95 made PCs almost as intuitively easy to use as Macs. And Intel was preparing for the debut of its Pentium chip, which would give PCs about the same bang-for-the-buck in speed and power as the Power PC chip provided for the Macintosh. Together, Microsoft's Bill Gates and Intel's Andy Grove lorded over the industry and commanded the kind of attention and celebrity that had once belonged to Steve Jobs.

204

The
Second
Coming
of
Steve
Jobs

The gatekeepers of the business press had already dismissed Steve, but they didn't know about the plans he was secretly developing for his dramatic comeback.

Steve's scheme was clever and audacious. He wanted to take Pixar public immediately following the opening of *Toy Story* in late November. He would exploit the Hollywood hype and glamour surrounding the film's debut as a shrewd way of promoting the stock. Hey, you liked the movie? Buy the shares!

The problem was that Pixar wasn't nearly ready for an initial public offering (IPO), at least not by the usual standards imposed by the investment bankers who specialized in those kinds of deals. The wizards of Wall Street always wanted a startup company to make money for a while before they agreed to sell its shares on the open market. No profits, no public offering. That was the unwritten but abiding rule at the leading brokerage houses.

Pixar had always lost money. Even with Disney paying most of its costs, Pixar was still losing more than $2 million a year. It had accumulated a deficit of $47 million from nine years of losses. And even if *Toy Story* was a big hit, Pixar's slice of the profits would be small at best and they wouldn't come for a long while. It was an ugly scenario.

Steve talked with his financiers in San Francisco and his lawyers in Silicon Valley. They told him that he was deluded. They thought that his scheme just wouldn't work.

But that summer of 1995, something bizarre happened. Netscape Communications, a software company that was only a year old and had never made a profit, nonetheless went public. There was so much media hype and water-cooler buzz about Netscape's product, the Mosaic web browser, that hordes of small-time investors clamored to buy shares. The stock's price shot from $28 to $58 on its first day of trading, and the company's founder, Jim Clark (an old colleague of the Pixar guys), made a paper profit of $565 million.

The Netscape deal was a pivotal moment in the modern history of Wall Street. It was the forerunner of a radically new conception of investing and stock promotion.

Steve wanted Pixar to be one of the first companies to follow Netscape's example and emulate its extraordinary success. But there were other obstacles to taking Pixar public. For starters, John Lasseter expressed doubts about the idea. He was afraid that a publicly owned animation studio might have to compromise its artistic vision, creativity, and originality as it succumbed to Wall Street's pressure for generating ever-higher revenues and profits. He wanted a studio that was driven by storytelling, not sales figures.

Steve decided to go public anyway, but for unexpectedly Byzantine reasons, he couldn't do it without first securing the cooperation of John, Ed, Ralph, and Bill Reeves, who was the technical director of *Toy Story*. The foursome had Steve at their mercy thanks to one of the wrinkles in the 1991 deal between Disney and Pixar. Disney had insisted that Pixar's key people must sign employment contracts, which would commit them to make *Toy Story* and two more films over a seven-year period. This way, if Disney wanted to produce a sequel or a spin-off, it could engage the same creative team. Employment contracts were a common practice in Hollywood but they remained an alien concept in Silicon Valley, where people cherished their freedom to switch jobs and start companies.

206
The
Second
Coming
of
Steve
Jobs

It wasn't trivial to entice the four men into long-term deals that would tie them up for what might be the most productive years of their creative lives. So Pixar had sweetened the deal by setting up a profit-sharing program, which would cut them in on a small piece of the action on their films. That's what clinched the Disney deal.

Now, in 1995, Steve's bankers told him that he had to eliminate the profit-sharing arrangement. In a public company, the profits are supposed to rebound to the benefit of thousands of shareholders. It would look bad if Pixar's earnings were always getting siphoned off by a few of its filmmakers and little was left over to enhance the stock price.

There was an alternative: public companies could reward their executives with stock options as a potentially lucrative incentive. This way, the key employees received windfalls only if they drove the stock price up and made money for the rest of the shareholders.

If Steve wanted to take Pixar public, he would first have to get Ed, John, Ralph, and Bill to swap their profit-sharing points in exchange for a pile of stock options.

A very big pile of stock options.

Tens of millions of dollars' worth of options.

Or they could block the deal.

They had Steve Jobs by the balls, and they knew it.

■   ■   ■

JOHN LASSETER hired a pit bull of a Hollywood lawyer and sicced her on Steve. The negotiations lingered on for months. But as autumn came and the debut of *Toy Story* neared, Steve finally acquiesced.

John would gain control of 800,000 shares. If the IPO went as planned, the stock would start trading at $14 a share, meaning that John's stake would be worth $11.2 million. Steve was holding on to 30 million shares, which would be worth $420 million. And the rest of Pixar's 140 staffers would get . . . very little.

Steve wasn't being generous at all with his employees. He was trying to keep as much of the stock for himself as he possibly could. He held on to 80 percent of the company.

Ralph knew what was going to happen. It was all too painfully obvious: the "prospectus," a Securities and Exchange Commission (SEC) filing that set forth all the terms of the deal, was going to arrive from the printers one day in October, and everyone at Pixar would read it that very first day and be outraged by the cruel disparities.

"There's going to be blood in the hallways," Ralph warned. He tried to push Steve to act more magnanimously toward their other colleagues. Steve could easily afford to give a $50 million gift to the rank and file and still keep the vast majority of Pixar's stock for himself, which would ensure his unilateral control. But Steve wouldn't consider it.

No one was certain why Steve wouldn't spread the wealth more widely. Some of his colleagues thought it was because he feared ever slipping below 50 percent ownership and losing control of the company, as he had at Apple. Other observers, like Alvy Ray Smith, snidely said that Steve wanted to improve his chances of becoming a billionaire so he could call his best friend Larry Ellison and say that he had joined the club. And some people said that Steve was a fearsome negotiator who simply never gave away more than he had to.

■   ■   ■

208

The
Second
Coming
of
Steve
Jobs

MEANWHILE, an army of attorneys and auditors descended on Pixar and struggled to put together detailed financial statements to show the SEC. Pixar was an honest operation, but it wasn't run like a real company. It had somehow gotten by without a financial executive for the four years between the layoffs in 1991 and the arrival of Lawrence Levy in 1995. Steve had cut the entire financial department except for one hapless employee who wasn't even a certified public accountant. For a while she had tried keeping the books on a personal computer but she had trouble getting the software to work. For years Pixar had been run on an improvised "home checkbook" approach. The auditors were appalled: *this* was a company that wanted approval from the SEC to sell six million shares to the general public?

■   ■   ■

FOR THE FIRST HALF OF 1995, Steve remained a media outcast, shunned by the cadre of powerful editors in New York. His new public relations counselor, Kamini Ramini, would occasionally call her contacts at *Business Week* or *The Wall Street Journal*, who told her that they just weren't interested anymore in Steve Jobs.

Later, when the media types began to hear the buzz about *Toy Story*, Steve saw a chance to rehabilitate his image. He had to go to New York for business in September, so he asked for informal meetings at several major publications for while he was there. This time, they said yes.

One morning he spoke in front of a dozen reporters and editors at the *New York Times*. Afterward, a writer on the technology beat, Steve Lohr, said that he wanted to profile him for the Sunday magazine, the showcase for the newspaper's longest articles.

Steve Jobs was reticent. He wanted coverage about his professional comeback, but didn't want to allow a powerful reporter to question him about his personality and his private life. When no one was writing about him, he had craved the exposure. Now, when he felt he was on the verge of triumph, when a dozen staffers turned out to see him at the *Times*, he was turning cavalier toward the press. He was once again living the Groucho Marx joke about not wanting to belong to any club that would have him for a member. He wanted media adulation but he also wanted to dominate and control the situation, as he had always done during his heyday. The posture of humility and diplomacy from when he was at the nadir in 1993 and 1994 was giving way to his old style of arrogance and narcissism.

The Bad Old Steve reappeared the following month as he reneged on his promises to Stewart Alsop. Stewart was the editor in chief of *InfoWorld*, a widely quoted pundit and the organizer of Agenda, an annual conference that was attended by four hundred of the most influential people in the computer industry. Bill Gates was always the star attraction. Stewart would schedule Bill as the "anchor," the final speaker on the third and final day of the gathering at a swanky resort hotel. This year, though, Stewart switched the place and date of the event, from southern California in September to Phoenix in October, and Bill couldn't make the new date. Bill was going to China in October to meet with the premier.

Stewart invited Steve Jobs to take the place of Bill Gates and be the star of the show, but he had a condition. He insisted that Steve attend the entire conference, like Bill had. Bill didn't just fly in and fly out. He always stayed around and took part in the discussions. He schmoozed in the hallways and he got into long intense debates with executives and reporters and he hung around drinking late at night in the hotel lobby. That was partly why Agenda was such a sought-after invitation. If Steve wanted to be the new star, he too would have to promise to stay in Phoenix for the entire conference.

Steve promised.

A week before the conference, Stewart was called by one of Steve's assistants, who was asking about the schedule for flights in and out of Phoenix. Stewart groaned. The next day, the assistant called again saying that Steve would arrive the night before his speech. When that night came, she called again, asking what private airport was closest to the hotel, since Steve was planning to touch down just before he had to go onstage.

Stewart was exasperated. The phone rang again, but this time it was Steve himself, calling from aboard a private plane that was leaving New York to take him to Phoenix.

Stewart told him not to bother.

"You're fired," he said.

Bill Gates at the top of the world was easier to deal with than Steve Jobs struggling to make his way back.

■   ■   ■

ON OCTOBER 11, the Pixar prospectus was published, and the blood began flowing through the hallways.

Only five people were going to become fabulously rich from the deal.

"The other hundred and thirty-five people at the company were pretty much screwed, and there were really bad feelings about that," recalls Pam Kerwin. "The people who had been there since the Lucas days got together and expressed a great

210

The
Second
Coming
of
Steve
Jobs

deal of dissatisfaction." Steve took many people on walks around the block to try to calm them down. But the bitterness remained. No one begrudged the idea of giving great rewards to Ed or John, but a bunch of the technical geniuses thought that they had made at least as important a contribution as Bill or Ralph. The unsung heroes were getting only 50,000 shares apiece, not 800,000 shares. Those 50,000 shares were worth $700,000, which was a lot more than anyone had ever hoped they'd make at Pixar. They hadn't come there for the money, but now that truckloads of money were being dumped on the place, it was a viciously divisive issue.

Many people at Pixar who had been the best of friends suddenly stopped talking to each other. It was a sad breakdown. For two decades they had been like a family. They threw big parties and dined at each other's homes and bought presents for each other's babies. Their kids played on the same soccer teams. Their spouses were close friends.

Now, the money wars were destroying all of that. Pixar had been such an idyllic creative and social environment. Now it was turning into a business.

The foursome of Ed, John, Ralph, and Bill felt so bad about the rift that they considered giving some of their own shares to their colleagues. But there were legal and tax complications, so it turned out that they couldn't easily redistribute their newfound wealth.

Ralph felt that he was caught in the middle: his colleagues resented him for his rich windfall, but his strident lobbying on their behalf provoked the anger of his temperamental boss. "I thought that I was fighting the good fight, but I lost face with Steve," he recalls.

Steve had been especially parsimonious with Pam Kerwin, who had made a vital contribution to the company. Pam produced the two interactive *Toy Story* software packages for young children, which had seventy-five minutes of original computer animation, nearly as much as the seventy-seven minutes that John Lasseter had created for the actual movie. Her people had exhausted themselves to finish the PC products in time for the release of the film. Pam often stayed at the office all night and slept for no more than fifteen minutes at a stretch. She motivated dozens of people to put in brutal hours. And now Steve was trying to shaft her!

212
The
Second
Coming
of
Steve
Jobs

Pam told him that she had received an offer to become the CEO of another company, and she was going to accept it.

Steve tried to talk her out of leaving. He met her on a Sunday and took her on a long walk. He knew that it would look very bad for Pixar if one of the company's officers, a vice president, were to quit right before the IPO.

"Stay here for your fuck-you money," he told her.

He gave her a big raise in salary, and she stayed.

■　　■　　■

WHILE THE PIXAR PEOPLE were fighting over all the money they were sure that they were going to make, the honchos at Disney were fiercely divided in their opinions about *Toy Story* and its financial prospects.

Michael Eisner hated the title, which he thought was "too juvenile." The Disney marketing executives disagreed with him. They thought it was a great title, descriptive and succinct. (Besides, wasn't the movie *supposed* to appeal to children?) Eisner's new No. 2, Michael Ovitz, was downbeat on the picture, too. *Toy Story* had been Jeffrey Katzenberg's baby, and now that Jeffrey had turned into a traitor, the Disney bosses brutally denigrated his judgment. Their criticisms seemed at least somewhat justified when they screened a sneak preview for a test audience and no one laughed at the opening scene. John

Lasseter had to rush to create a replacement during the final frantic weeks before the premiere.

One of the key players at Disney, the public relations executive Terry Press, was highly enthused by *Toy Story* and thought it would be a huge hit. She told Mike Ovitz that it would earn $150 million in domestic box-office receipts. Ovitz laughed at her. She also clashed with the Disney executive who licensed children's toys and other consumer products around the movie characters. Astonishingly, Disney's toy people said they didn't "get" *Toy Story!* They disliked the fact that many of the film's stars—Mr. Potato Head, the Green Army Men—were existing toys rather than new properties that were owned by Disney. Still, they didn't rush to fill the store shelves with figurines of Woody or Buzz Lightyear. The film was about to open, but there were hardly any *Toy Story* toys for kids.

Disney's marketing honcho, Dick Cook, was a lonely believer in the film, and he put together a $100 million campaign, with the vast majority of the money coming from partners like Burger King and Frito-Lay, which sponsored the promotional tie-ins.

Steve Jobs was awestruck by Disney's marketing power:
One hundred million dollars!
And Disney's top guys didn't even like the movie.

■   ■   ■

IT HAD BEEN twenty-three years since Ed Catmull made his first crude computer-animated film. Now he was about to see the realization of the dream that had driven his entire career.

For the world premiere of *Toy Story* on November 22, Ed flew to Los Angeles with his youngest son (he had three), his little daughter, and Pam Kerwin. They arrived early at the El

Capitan theater, where a row of paparazzi were awaiting the entrances of Tom Hanks, who did the voice for Woody, and Tim Allen, the voice of Buzz Lightyear.

They walked around the corner to the nearest Burger King. The fast-food joint was plastered with *Toy Story* paraphernalia and filled with kids slurping sodas from Buzz and Woody cups. That's when it really hit them, when they had the visceral sense of what they had created. They had known about the promotions—they had approved the art—but it was still thrilling and surreal to see a bunch of kids clamoring for images of their characters.

"We just froze and said, 'Holy shit,'" recalls Pam.

214
The
Second
Coming
of
Steve
Jobs

■   ■   ■

THE EL CAPITAN SHOWING was the real premiere of *Toy Story*, but the following evening Steve Jobs held his own "premiere," a private screening and reception for the people he really wanted to impress, the techno-moguls of Silicon Valley. It was his way of signaling that he was back on top.

"We called it the 'Apple wasn't a fluke' party," recalls Pam Kerwin.

Pixar rented a grand ornate prewar movie palace in San Francisco, the Regency. Near the marquee it set up klieg lights and positioned a bunch of TV cameras. As the VIPs made their entrances—Larry Ellison from Oracle, Andy Grove from Intel, Scott McNealy from Sun—they were photographed as if they were Hollywood celebrities, even though it was all for show. The real paparazzi had shot the real stars (Tom Hanks, Tim Allen) the night before at the real premiere. But the computer guys didn't know better. For them, this was as close as they ever came to Hollywood treatment, and it seemed very glamorous.

Alvy Ray Smith entered the theater. He passed the lineup of guests in tuxedos, who were waiting for their free popcorn, and he took a seat. Even though he was *persona non grata* with Steve, he remained a very close friend and confidant of Ed Catmull and the other Pixar executives, who made sure that he was there to share the occasion with them.

As he watched the film, Alvy was enthralled. "This was a twenty-year dream," he recalls thinking. "Only it took seventeen years longer than we thought it would."

The movie ended to a standing ovation. Then Steve got up and addressed the crowd. He was glorying in the spotlight.

"This was Steve's return to center stage and, my, did he hog it," recalls Julie Pitta, the correspondent for *Forbes*. "Steve was onstage by himself and Silicon Valley was there to pay him homage. He was not going to share the stage with John Lasseter, who was kept very much in the background."

The Disney executives marveled at how Steve upstaged the film's director and creative genius. Steve was still a novice to Hollywood, but he had already mastered two of its vital lessons: he knew how to take the credit and how to show up for the photo.

■   ■   ■

THE GUESTS WALKED two blocks down the street to the site of the party, a magnificently ornate Bernard Maybeck building that had been a Cadillac showroom in the 1920s but had been vacant and decaying for years. Disney's party squad had instantaneously spiffed up the abandoned space as if they were preparing a soundstage for a fantasy film. There were islands and islands of beautiful food.

The invitation had said "creative black tie," giving some

leeway to the Silicon Valley types, most of whom despised formality and pretentiousness. Stewart Alsop showed up in blue jeans and a blue blazer, which he ironically "dressed up" with a white shirt, red bow tie, and red cummerbund. He looked around one of the building's tall ornate columns and saw that Scott McNealy was wearing the same combination. The *Fortune* correspondent, Brent Schlender, one-upped them with his tacky patterned golf pants.

Michael Eisner didn't come but he sent Mike Ovitz in his place, the way that the president might send the vice president or first lady to the coronation of the king of a very small country.

Laurene Jobs had given birth to her second child only three months earlier, but she looked astonishingly slender in a slinky little black cocktail dress. She wore her blond hair to the middle of her back, and she radiated healthiness with her tan skin and toned limbs. Scott McNealy's wife, Anne, had also recently given birth, and she looked utterly exhausted. She was there nonetheless, playing the role of the good corporate wife.

Larry Ellison was accompanied by an ornamental anonymous blonde but he seemed to be interested only in his best friend, Steve Jobs. He stood besides Steve and helped receive the guests, as if the two of them were the bride and groom at a wedding banquet. Steve was elegant in a tuxedo with a beige silk waistcoat, his idea of a "creative" twist.

The pundit Stewart Alsop was known as a court-jester type even when he was sober, and he helped himself to Disney's free booze and quickly got a little drunk, which eliminated his inhibitions almost entirely. He went up to Steve and Larry and said:

"Have you heard my asshole theory?"

"No," Larry replied.

"If you look at the really big companies that are still run by their founders, they're all assholes."

216
The
Second
Coming
of
Steve
Jobs

Larry thought over the idea for a moment.

"Did you just call me an asshole?" he asked, more aston-ished than outraged.

"Not in a bad sense," Stewart said, delighted that he could taunt the billionaire.

■   ■   ■

TOY STORY RECEIVED EXULTANT PRAISE from the film critics, and it earned an impressive $29 million in U.S. box-office receipts during its first weekend.

Early on the morning of November 29, Ed Catmull and Pam Kerwin met in downtown San Francisco at Pixar's invest-ment bank, Robertson Stephens & Company. They rode up the elevator to a high floor and found the trading room, where well-groomed twentysomethings huddled in front of consoles stacked with computer screens and telephone lines. The finan-ciers had set up a table with glasses of fresh Odwalla carrot juice, which they knew was Steve's favorite beverage. (Steve liked Odwalla's organic juices and fruit shakes so much that he kept a refrigerator full of them at the office and he had become a friend and an informal business adviser to the company's president. When a child died from drinking Odwalla's com-pletely natural, unpasteurized apple juice, the executive had called Steve out of a meeting and asked him how to handle the crisis.)

The trading in Pixar's stock was scheduled to start at 7 A.M. California time, a half hour after the markets opened in New York. Just moments before seven, Steve Jobs came running through the hallways, making his entrance as dramatic as pos-sible.

The original plan had been to start the trading at a

relatively low $12 to $14 a share. Lawrence Levy, the chief financial officer, argued for this cautious approach, but Steve wanted to take a bigger risk and try for a huge hit. At his insistence, Robertson Stephens set the opening price at $22. Now the market would decide who was right.

The clock struck seven and the phone consoles began lighting up. Seemingly everyone wanted Pixar stock. The price shot from $22 to $49 in the first half hour.

218
The
Second
Coming
of
Steve
Jobs

The threesome looked at each other as they silently multiplied the share price by their number of shares. "We were just completely freaked out," recalls Pam Kerwin.

Steve Jobs was worth nearly $1.5 billion.

■   ■   ■

BY THE BEGINNING OF 1996, Steve had already made two of what would be his three most valuable contributions to Pixar. First, he had bankrolled the venture through nearly a decade of struggle and uncertainty until it became a financial success. "Pixar failed nine times over by normal standards," recalls Alvy Ray Smith, "but Steve didn't want to fail so he kept writing the checks. He would have sold us to anybody in a moment, and he tried really hard, but he wanted to cover his loss of fifty million dollars." Hallmark had looked at buying Pixar. In 1994 Steve tried to sell the company to Microsoft, which had just bought Alvy's startup and hired Alvy as a research fellow. But no one would cover Steve's loss and make him whole. He had held on out of desperation. Steve always had a penchant for changing his mind and walking away from good deals because he wanted better terms, and usually that habit was self-destructive. He would lose contracts that Next and Pixar sorely needed because of his stupid stubbornness. But ultimately, his character flaw was his salvation.

Steve was what Alvy called "an accidental visionary," and Steve nearly confessed as much to *Fortune*'s Brent Schlender. "If I knew in 1986 how much it was going to cost to keep Pixar going, I doubt if I would have bought the company," he said.

Steve's second stunning contribution to Pixar was the decision to take the company public when all the lawyers and bankers said it wouldn't work. His audacity paid off magnificently.

Before long, the speculative fervor around Pixar's stock dissipated and the share price fell from the forties to the twenties. Steve's tenure as a paper billionaire was short, but he remained a near-billionaire. Pixar kept $123 million of the $132 million proceeds from the public stock sale (the other $9 million was taken by the investment bankers). That meant that Pixar went from $47 million in the red to $76 million in the black.

Now that he had a huge box-office hit and a position of financial strength, Steve was ready to make the third of his three inimitable contributions to Pixar. He called Disney and said that he wanted to renegotiate the terms of their partnership.

The 1991 deal between Disney and Pixar was heavily weighted in Disney's favor, which wasn't unusual. Disney's executives had reputations as fierce negotiators who had the power to demand a domineering "master-slave" relationship with their contractors.

Now Steve wanted a relationship of equals, and he had the nerve to insist on it.

As he prepared for his talks with Michael Eisner, he had three objectives. He wanted Pixar and Disney to split the production costs fifty-fifty for Pixar's future films, and he wanted to share the revenues fifty-fifty as well. He wanted Pixar to have creative control over the movies. And he was especially intense about wanting equal billing, with the Pixar logo just as large as the Disney logo on the posters and ads and video boxes. Steve saw the potential for making Pixar a brand name that resonated with parents and children, a name that could sell all kinds of lucrative consumer products tied in to films. He realized that the Pixar brand, like the Apple brand or the Disney brand, could become a pop-culture icon, and that had a far greater financial potential than the box-office profits.

He had a one-on-one lunch with Michael Eisner.

Eisner was stunned.

"When Steve laid out the terms he wanted, Disney thought it was outrageous," recalls Pam Kerwin.

The Disney executives lacked respect for Steve. He was a novice in their world, and they weren't particularly impressed by his famous achievements in his own world. They thought that Hollywood was much tougher than Silicon Valley. In the movie business you had to fight viciously every day for survival, while in the technology business you were mightily rewarded by Wall Street for even the slightest accomplishments.

The culture clash was pronounced and comical. The hardened Hollywood types thought that Steve's rhetoric and persona—the allusions to sixties counterculture and Zen—were just an act. They could easily see right through it. "All that vegan feel-good shit cloaks that he's so cutthroat," says a Disney executive who worked closely with him.

Though they weren't impressed by Steve, they respected and admired John Lasseter. Disney's animators began saying that John could become the new Walt Disney. The Disney brass saw that they had grossly underestimated *Toy Story*, which played to crowded theaters through the holiday season and ultimately reached $160 million in domestic box-office receipts, a high figure by any standard and a superb one for a film that only cost $27 million to produce. Disney rushed to make Buzz and Woody toys but couldn't get them to the stores in time for the Christmas shopping rush. A well-placed Disney insider says that the company forfeited the opportunity for

220

The
Second
Coming
of
Steve
Jobs

"hundreds of millions of dollars" in toy sales. "We had a few items but nowhere near what we needed to have."

Eisner knew that John Lasseter was the golden goose—and Steve Jobs had him.

Through the stock deal, Steve had made John a multimillionaire. More importantly, John ran his own fiefdom at Pixar, a company he built in his own image with people he had picked himself, a place where he was the crown prince. If John had switched over to Disney, he might have been just another talented animator there.

John was the trump card for Steve to play at the right moment. When Michael Eisner balked at Steve Jobs's proposal of a fifty-fifty partnership, Steve threatened that he would make a deal with another studio as soon as Pixar finished the two films that it owed Disney. John's seven-year employment contract only obligated him to work exclusively with Disney for another three years. Then Pixar would be free to collaborate with Eisner's bitter archrival, Jeffrey Katzenberg at DreamWorks, or with any of the other studios.

Steve's ego made him hard to deal with, but the smooth, diplomatic Lawrence Levy played good cop to Steve's bad cop in the talks with Disney, and the strategy succeeded.

Michael Eisner acquiesced. Steve got exactly what he wanted: the fifty-fifty partnership, the equal billing. Pixar agreed to make five feature films for Disney over a ten-year period. John Lasseter was awarded creative control, and any other new Pixar director who made a blockbuster film would then have control over his or her movies in the future.

Hollywood insiders were shocked that Disney had given away so much. Steve had challenged the most fearsome negotiators in American business—and won. The other Pixar executives marveled at his extraordinary chutzpah and what he had done for them. "There was no way Disney would treat another tiny company the way they treat Pixar," says Pam Kerwin. "It's because of Steve. Pixar wouldn't have made it without Steve. He made huge contributions." Looking back at Steve's foresight about the public stock offering and the power it would give him with Disney, Ralph Guggenheim says: "Steve is a truly visionary guy who sees directions and eventualities."

Such were Steve's invaluable roles at Pixar: banker, negotiator, wheeler-dealer. For those virtues he was greatly appreciated there. But as Steve redoubled his efforts to immerse himself in the company's day-to-day management and the creative process of making movies, his presence was viewed as an unwarranted and disruptive intrusion.

"There was great apprehension when Steve tried to take over the running of the company," recalls Pam Kerwin. "But a funny thing happened. Steve's charisma and his 'reality distortion field' didn't work at Pixar. We were too mature to get hooked in."

When Steve brought one of his own people from Next to work at Pixar, the transplanted executive soon felt befuddled. "I don't get it," he said. "At Next, Steve said 'Jump' and we said 'How high?' At Pixar, they say, 'Oh, it's Steve.'"

Every Friday, Steve would assemble the entire Pixar staff in the lunchroom, with the crowd overflowing onto the lawn, and he would deliver a speech, trying to assert his leadership. But the hearts and minds of the Pixarians belonged to John Lasseter. "People were not moved by Steve," says Ralph Guggenheim. "You could see that it was hard for Steve, sharing the spotlight with John. Both Steve and John loved the spotlight. It seemed like a competition for whose DNA would be imprinted on the company's culture."

Steve was in danger of strangling the golden goose.

Luckily, it was too late for him to change Pixar. John's personality was already infused throughout the place. Pixar be-

222

The
Second
Coming
of
Steve
Jobs

came a weird cross between an artists' colony and a teenagers' clubhouse, holding yoga classes in the morning and tai chi at lunch and poker games at night. Only John could inspire something as wonderfully quirky as Pixar University, the three-month training program for new hires, which culminated in formal graduation ceremonies with hilarious themes: the students would all wear huge hats or they would all dress like cheerleaders or they would all march down the aisle backward and then listen as John delivered his commencement address from the end to the beginning.

While John's wacky spirit colored the culture, his storytelling artistry gave him a sense of authority and an ability to sweet-talk people into following him. Steve still owned Pixar, but the company really belonged to John and to Ed Catmull, who commanded the respect and the love of the Ph.D. engineers who remained so vital to the films.

"Steve is different at Pixar than anywhere else because Steve is not Steve at Pixar," says Pam Kerwin. "Steve was an icon at Apple but he's a banker at Pixar. It was *our* technology and John's creative vision, and Steve didn't have a hands-on role."

Steve's most embarrassing moment came at a meeting when he discussed the proposed design for a new corporate campus in Emeryville, a warehouse district next to Berkeley. Steve commissioned a Japanese architect, who conceived of a stark structure of poured concrete. It expressed Steve's austere aesthetic, not John Lasseter's playfulness or his tattered hominess. The animators said that the plans looked too grim. Then Steve dropped the real bomb: he said that there would be a single bathroom in the new complex. Only one bathroom for four hundred people. That way, it would serve as the central meeting place, the locus for informal discussions. Not the lunchroom. Not the lounge. The *bathroom.*

One of Pixar's managers was a lactating mother, and she voiced her objections. It was bad enough at the current campus in Point Richmond, she said. The buildings were low and sprawling, and it took too long for her to get down the long hallway to the women's room. Why make the situation so much worse at the new headquarters?

Pam Kerwin seconded the objection.

224

The
Second
Coming
of
Steve
Jobs

Steve suddenly exploded. He made put-downs about people who have to go to the bathroom frequently—especially women. His tone was acerbic and challenging.

A bitter fight broke out. Everyone else, including John, opposed his scheme.

Steve's anger turned into sad resignation.

"Can't I just win *one* thing," he said.

The meeting adjourned, and John took Steve aside and convinced him to apologize to the rest of the group.

"It was the stupidest thing to fight over," recalls Pam Kerwin, "but that was the only thing Steve had control over in the company: the design of this building."

By late 1996, Steve came to grudgingly accept that he wasn't really wanted or needed at the animation studio. He realized that he wasn't John and he couldn't be John.

He had to find a new outlet for his own energy, creativity, and ego.

He desperately needed something else to do.

■   ■   ■

IN NOVEMBER 1996, Steve's sister Mona Simpson published her third novel, *A Regular Guy*. It was a thinly veiled portrait of Steve and the women in his life: the story of a narcissistic, workaholic tycoon who is insensitive about the emotional needs of his lover and his young daughter.

Mona's book was eagerly anticipated by readers and critics even before they knew it would be about her famous brother. Her first two novels, *Anywhere But Here* and *The Lost Father,* had made her a literary celebrity. She was profiled in *People. Granta* named her one of the twenty best American writers under forty. She taught at Columbia, Bard, and NYU and received a fellowship from Princeton and a grant from the National Endowment for the Arts. Her private life had flourished as well: she married a writer for *The Simpsons,* gave birth to a son, and set up residences in Santa Monica and the Upper West Side of Manhattan.

Mona exploited her personal experiences for the material in her fiction. After publishing books about the emotional struggles of growing up with a demanding mother and an absent father, it wasn't surprising that she would decide to write about her brother.

She wrote slowly and meticulously, and she spent the first half of the 1990s, a full five years, trying to recapture the emotional details from Steve's world in the early 1980s. She had been part of that world while she was living near Berkeley, where she had gone to college, and supporting herself as a freelance writer for the alternative press.

When *A Regular Guy* came out, Mona was besieged by reporters who wanted her to talk about the real-life parallels to Steve, but she refused, saying it would be unfair. "There is some biographical truth in what I do, but I want the license to make things up—which I do," she told the *Los Angeles Times.* "I remember a lot, but I don't think I remember a lot necessarily accurately."

Meanwhile, the *New York Times* asked Steve whether he felt exploited or betrayed by his sister. "Of course not," he said dismissively. "It's a novel." How much of himself did he see in Tom Owens? "About 25 percent of it is totally me," he said.

That's not what Steve's friends believed. The few people

226

The
Second
Coming
of
Steve
Jobs

who knew Steve well thought that the fictional protagonist, Tom Owens, was much closer to 100 percent Steve Jobs. Nearly all the major characters were easily identifiable and drawn with extraordinary accuracy. It wasn't just that Mona had captured the emotional and psychological truths about Steve and the women—his daughter and her mother and his girlfriend—close to him. It showed how he was a narcissistic workaholic who didn't give them enough love until he was ousted from his company and finally humbled. She hardly bothered to change or disguise the actual details, and even the names of the characters, places, and companies were closely modeled on the actual names. Steve's girlfriend Christina became "Olivia." His daughter Lisa became "Jane." Sculley was switched to "Rooney." Apple morphed into "Genesis" and the Macintosh into "Exodus." Palo Alto equaled "Alta." Cafe Verona was "Cafe Napoleon." Steve's adopted sister Patti reappeared as "Pony."

In real life, Steve had given an expensive specially equipped van to his girlfriend's friend Gary Bricklin, who was confined to a wheelchair. In the novel, Tom gives a van to his girlfriend's friend "Noah Kasdie." In real life, Steve often embarrassed Tina by flirting openly with attractive women, then retreated when they began to return his interest. In the novel, Mona creates a composite character, "Julie," as a proxy for those women.

Mona hadn't needed to disguise her characters because so little was known publicly about Steve's private life. After Steve's dark side was documented by Michael Moritz, who published his Apple book, *The Little Kingdom*, in 1984, Steve had withheld his cooperation from biographers, and he tried to block journalists from writing feature stories that focused on his personal life rather than the latest achievements of his companies.

Most critics mentioned briefly that *A Regular Guy* was loosely based on Steve's life and then proceeded to judge it on its own terms as a literary work (the reviews were mixed). Several newspaper reporters even asserted, erroneously, that Tom Owens was modeled on Bill Gates as well as Steve Jobs.

The truth was that long passages from Mona's book could have been published intact in a biography of her brother, beginning even with the first sentence: "He was a man too busy to flush toilets." (That had been true during the early days of Apple.) Steve's friends and close colleagues saw so much in the book that they knew was true that they had to wonder about the rest. In one scene, the Steve character has sex with a sixteen-year-old virgin, then feels somewhat guilty but does it again. An invented scene, or real life?

Mona wouldn't discuss her sources, but she did make one confession to a reporter. She was called at her office at Bard College by Lisa Picarelle, who was writing a profile of Steve for a computer industry trade publication. Mona revealed that the book had ended her close relationship with Steve. He still called her occasionally because he hadn't much family and he thought it was important to keep up a connection. But he *had* felt betrayed.

The media attention about *A Regular Guy* passed quickly. One month after its publication, Steve Jobs was back in the news for an entirely different reason.

He was going back to Apple.

During Steve's long exile, Apple lost almost all of the qualities that had made it such an astonishing success during his heyday there. Apple's software had once stood out as innovative, original, and uncommonly easy to use, but it hadn't changed all that much in a decade, and in that time Microsoft had managed to imitate it—and to fight off Apple's legal challenges to its copycat ways. Apple was celebrated for the industrial design of its machines, its bold aesthetics, but somehow its products had come to resemble the bland beige boxes of every other computer manufacturer. Apple gained notoriety by having a youthful, charismatic, mediagenic leader, but its board of directors succeeded in bringing in a string of top executives who had none of those characteristics. The greatest asset that Apple still had was a strong brand, an image that connoted creativity and nonconformity. But that aura was a legacy from an earlier era, and it was deteriorating badly. Apple's stewards were trying to coast on a reputation that no longer matched up with the reality. And, arrogantly, they were demanding a premium price for products that no longer were much better, or different, from what hundreds of other PC makers were offering.

Apple seemed bound for bankruptcy. Its stock price had fallen from $60 a share in 1992 to $17 a share at the end of 1996, a period when other computer stocks were rapidly doubling or tripling. The company's annual sales had plummeted from $11 billion to $7 billion. Its market share fell from 12 percent, which had made it the leader, to 4 percent, which made it an also-ran. Apple had lost $1 billion in the past year and seemed on a course to lose billions more. For years, the CEOs—first John Sculley, then Michael Spindler—had been trying to sell the company. They shopped it to the big players in global electronics—Philips, Siemens, Kodak, AT&T, IBM, Toshiba, Compaq, Sony—but they couldn't find a buyer.

John Sculley had initially cast himself as a marketing guru, a master of image and advertising. But after he ousted Steve Jobs, he went native in Silicon Valley and yearned to prove himself as a technologist. As he struggled to master the intricacies of engineering, he lost touch with what had endeared the Apple brand to millions of enthusiasts: the cool, young, hip

232
The
Second
Coming
of
Steve
Jobs

image that appealed to creative individuals rather than their corporate overseers. In 1993, as Apple's profits began to tank, the board forced him to quit.

While Sculley wasn't a true pop-culture hero like Steve Jobs, at least he was a dynamic guy who enjoyed the spotlight and tried fervently to become a visionary. His successor, Michael Spindler, a German-born Apple veteran, was known as a behind-the-scenes, nuts-and-bolts manager. Spindler was an odd choice to run a business built on charismatic leadership and cultural panache. He was standoffish and indecisive. He despised the media and disliked making public appearances. He was also the wrong man to lead a company in crisis. Spindler couldn't deal with stressful situations: his colleagues would see him literally shake and shiver.

Apple's fleeting opportunity to ensure its long-term survival came in 1995 as Sun Microsystem's Scott McNealy proposed merging the two companies under his own proven leadership. But when McNealy saw that Apple's loss for the fourth quarter was going to be even worse than expected, he drastically lowered his bid.

On January 8, 1996, Spindler checked into the hospital with heart palpitations. His doctor said that he had to quit his job soon or he was going to die. On January 31 the board of directors replaced Spindler with one of its own members, Gil Amelio, who was a veteran executive from National Semiconductor, which was well known to Silicon Valley insiders but unknown to the general public. National didn't sell to consumers—it manufactured microchips for the big computer manufacturers. Running a behind-the-scenes component supplier wasn't exactly the best training for a CEO who had to promote a retail product to a mass audience of mainstream consumers. But Amelio craved his moment in the national media limelight as the head of a company with a famous name. He refused to yield control to the outspoken McNealy. The Sun deal was off.

It was ironic that just when the press was beginning to hype a new wave of remarkably young, change-craving, self-made, speed-crazed technology entrepreneurs who harkened back to the old Steve Jobs mythology—players like Marc Andreessen (from Netscape), Jerry Yang (Yahoo), and Jeff Bezos (Amazon.com)—the Apple board members insisted on hiring CEOs who were in their own image: aged, cautious old-school managers mired in the ways of lumbering corporate giants.

Gil Amelio was the ultimate wrong guy. In 1996, his first year as CEO, Apple lost $1 billion. It looked like Apple was in a vicious death spiral. There wasn't a clearly articulated strategy for restoring market share. Even many of Apple's most loyal fans held off from buying new Macintoshes because they didn't know what was going to happen to the company.

Apple's breakdown was captured in a joke told by Chris Espinosa, who had joined the company in the late 1970s, when he was a teenager, and was still there in the late 1990s. He said that there were four kinds of Apple employees, and each kind reflected the personality of one of the four men who had led the company. There were "artists," who were passionate about being different and creating innovative products, like Steve Jobs. Then came the "wanna-bes," epitomized by John Sculley, who wanted to be at Apple because it was so cool. They're the worst, the joke said, because they contribute nothing. Then there were the "nuts-and-bolts types," who were implementers, not innovators, like Mike Spindler. And finally, there were the "social climbers," like Gil Amelio. They were bad, too, but at least they were easy to spot and they were always gone in a year or two.

That, indeed, was about how long Gil would last.

234
The
Second
Coming
of
Steve
Jobs

■   ■   ■

EVEN BEFORE COMING TO APPLE, Gil Amelio's track record was blemished and his egotism was an embarrassment. Many observers believed that National Semiconductor's problems only worsened during his tenure as CEO, but he went ahead nonetheless and published a book about the "turnaround" he had supposedly engineered. "He was totally out of his depth," recalls Louise Kehoe, the *Financial Times* correspondent, who had followed his career for many years. "I was astonished that he could be appointed to run Apple."

Gil's plan for Apple, while flawed, was fairly simple. He wanted the Macintosh's software to be able to compete with Microsoft's Windows NT, an expensive program for corporate clients that needed to link together many machines into smoothly functioning networks. Apple had spent billions of dollars on research and development over the years, but somehow it had failed to create an alternative to Windows NT, at least one that worked. The only choice, he felt, was to buy someone else's software.

By November 1996, Apple was nearly ready to close a deal with Be, a startup founded by Jean-Louis Gassée, a former Apple executive who had tried to cast himself as a silver-tongued technological visionary, sort of a Steve Jobs type with a Gallic flavor. Be was a very small, struggling company, but it had the kind of software that Gil wanted.

On the Friday before Thanksgiving week, a mid-level manager at Next, acting impulsively, without the knowledge of his bosses, left a voice message for Apple's chief technology officer, Ellen Hancock, saying she should consider Next instead of Be.

The following Monday, she called the Next manager. On Tuesday, representatives from Apple and Next held a conference call. On Wednesday, they had an all-day meeting in the Next boardroom. They adjourned for Thanksgiving and resumed talks the following week. It was only on that Wednesday

that one of the Next executives told Steve what they were
doing.

"Guess what," said the VP of sales, "we're talking to Apple."

"Apple *who*?" Steve replied.

It was no secret to Steve's friends that he quietly yearned to
go back to Apple, which was still the key to his own identity. A
few months earlier, Steve had been talking to one of his loyal
colleagues from the early days at Apple who had followed him
to Next. When the colleague, marketing executive Karen
Steele, told him that she was returning to Apple after all these
years, he replied wistfully, "It must feel like you're going
home."

236
The
Second
Coming
of
Steve
Jobs

■   ■   ■

ANOTHER MOMENT that revealed Steve's strong emotional
attachment to Apple came when he was giving a talk to the
Stanford Graduate School of Business's High Tech Club at the
home of a student. For three hours he sat in the lotus position
on the floor in front of the living-room fireplace, answering
questions good-naturedly. Afterward, the host, a young MBA
candidate named Steve Jurvetson, asked the legendary figure
to autograph his Macintosh keyboard, which had already been
signed by Apple cofounder Steve Wozniak.

Steve Jobs said that he'd do it, but only if first he could
remove all the unnecessary keys that his successors had added
in a foolish effort to make the Mac more like a Microsoft-
Intel PC. He despised the long row of so-called function keys
(like "F1") and the cluster of navigational arrow keys, which
were clunky alternatives to the more intuitive process of
using a mouse to explore menus and icons. So Steve Jobs
pulled his car keys out of his pocket and began scooping

into the computer keyboard, violently disgorging all the keys that offended him. "I'm changing the world one keyboard at a time," he said with a straight face. Only then, when he had mutilated the apparatus, did he take a pen and scribble his autograph on it. He was making a statement: he still had an intensely proprietary feeling about Apple's computers, and he yearned to restore the company in accordance with his vision.

■   ■   ■

GIL AMELIO wanted Apple to buy Next. He liked Next's software and he grasped the potential public relations value of Steve Jobs, the living legend, returning to the company he co-founded twenty years earlier and serving as some kind of ambassador of goodwill.

"I'm not just buying the software," Gil told his colleagues. "I'm buying Steve."

He thought, with shocking naivete, that Steve could be controlled, that Steve would willingly serve as a figurehead. That Steve wouldn't try to promote an agenda of his own.

On Monday, December 16, 1996, *The Wall Street Journal* published rumors about the negotiations, and journalists from dozens of media outlets began calling to try to confirm the story. It looked like the deal would be done sometime during that week, since the weekend marked the beginning of the Christmas holiday.

Christopher Escher, Apple's p.r. director, told Gil that the official announcement should be made early in the week, before the beat reporters went on vacation. "Let's not do it the night before Christmas," he said jokingly.

He was chosen to write a draft of a letter from Steve to

Apple's employees. It wasn't hard for him to predict what Steve would want. "Steve likes big, dramatic, advertising-copy kind of shit," he recalls. "Dramatic bullshit about 'returning to the journey.' Self-dramatizing. Self-glorifying. Oedipus returning to Colonnus."

Christopher submitted the draft.

Steve called him and said that he liked it.

238
The
Second
Coming
of
Steve
Jobs

■   ■   ■

As Christmas neared, they set a price of $430 million, astoundingly high for a failing company. A single issue was blocking the closing of the deal. Gil insisted that Steve sign an employment contract committing him to work for Apple for a certain period of time.

Steve stubbornly refused.

The deal was constantly flipping, off and on and off again. Twice Christopher Escher ordered satellite trucks to the Apple campus to broadcast the press conference to news organizations and to Apple's employees, and twice he had to send the trucks home.

On Friday, December 20, the beat reporters were thoroughly irritated by Apple as they waited impatiently at their offices in San Francisco and tried to rearrange their travel plans for the holiday.

Christopher ordered the satellites once again. The press releases were waiting to go out on the wire services. The website was ready to go live with the news. The p.r. department's question-and-answer teams were poised for the onslaught.

At the tower that housed Gil's office and the Apple boardroom, executives from both sides were milling around the hallways, thinking about the ski runs they were missing at Lake Tahoe and the tee times they had forfeited at Pebble Beach.

Finally, late in the afternoon, Steve appeared in his usual casual attire—the black turtleneck and blue jeans—and he summoned them all into the boardroom.

Steve brought in his attorney, Larry Sonsini, the most powerful lawyer in Silicon Valley. He let the anticipation build, then he launched into his dramatic performance.

"Ever since I was a child," he began, "I never wanted to disappoint anyone."

He told the sad story of how, one time, when he was a child, he let down his parents.

"Isn't that right, Larry," he prodded.

"Yes," said the lawyer.

"Pixar and my family matter the most to me in my life," Steve continued. "And I don't want to disappoint anyone. Isn't that right, Larry?"

"That's right," Larry echoed on cue.

Steve couldn't commit to a contract because he wouldn't dare let them down.

Christopher Escher sat at the table, incredulous. Steve was laying on "a thick line of bullshit," he thought. "His chutzpah was incredible." But it was working. Steve seemed as though he were willing to walk away from it all. That was his brilliance as a negotiator.

Gil wanted the deal more than Steve did. Gil acquiesced. Steve could be an "informal adviser" at Apple, with no contractual commitments. The deal was done.

■   ■   ■

THEY CALLED THE REPORTERS, who rushed down from San Francisco for the press conference.

Gil took the stage first, made a few remarks, and then introduced Steve.

239
Apple

Steve entered not from the wings but rather from the back of the auditorium, prolonging his solo moments in the spotlight as he walked lopingly down the aisle.

As he stood by Gil's side, Steve looked as though he couldn't wait to leave. Gil was trying to play the elder master. Steve was signaling that he wasn't a dog on a leash.

Gil explained to the crowd that Steve had stayed up two nights in a row and that he was too desperately tired to say anything.

240
The
Second
Coming
of
Steve
Jobs

Nonsense, thought Louise Kehoe, the *Financial Times* correspondent, who was in the audience. "It was clearly an excuse for Steve not to say anything *specific*," she says.

After the presentation, Louise made her way onto the stage. She saw that Steve recognized her, but she deliberately went over to talk with Gil first.

Aren't you concerned that Steve will want power? she asked.

"Steve is here to help," Gil said, seemingly unconcerned.

"I had these same conversations with John Sculley," she said.

Then she turned to Steve.

"What are you up to?" she said accusingly. "What are you doing?"

Wasn't he going to try to take over Apple?

"Oh no, Louise," Steve said. "I have a family. I have other interests."

■   ■   ■

WHEN THE APPLE EXECUTIVES returned from their vacations, they once again found themselves in the spotlight. On January 3, 1997, Gil told Wall Street's analysts that Apple's sales fell more than 30 percent in the final three months of 1996 from the same period in 1995.

The Macintosh had bombed at Christmas.

On January 7, Gil and Steve were slated to share the keynote speech at Macworld, an annual ritual that drew some eighty thousand of Apple's enthusiasts to San Francisco.

The Apple faithful were anxious to see their cult hero and hear his plans for saving the company. But Gil went on first, and he went on and on. He had thrown out his scripted text, and instead he rambled ad lib for two hours, repeatedly losing his train of thought. But he was seemingly oblivious to how thoroughly he was embarrassing himself.

Steve Jobs was backstage, holding his head in his hands.

"What did you think of that?" Steve asked Christopher Escher.

"It was excruciatingly painful."

"I agree," Steve said.

Then Steve took the stage, and thousands stood up and cheered.

■   ■   ■

ONE OF STEVE'S FIRST actions as "informal adviser" was to accompany Gil on a diplomatic mission to Microsoft to meet with Bill Gates.

Steve found himself standing in front of Microsoft's head-quarters in the suburbs of Seattle. At his side was his old friend Heidi Roizen, whom Gil had appointed as Apple's liaison to its software developers.

They both wore stick-on security name tags that identified them as visitors.

"It's strange," she said. "Ten years ago who would have thought that we'd be together wearing Apple badges?"

As the meeting began, Bill Gates seemed unfocused, as

though he had more important matters to think about and this was merely an unwanted distraction.

Steve was charming and hypnotic.

"Bill, between us, we own one hundred percent of the desktop," Steve said, meaning that Microsoft and Apple together controlled the market for PC operating-system software.

Bill shook his head in amazement. Steve's tone made it sound as though Bill had 50 percent and Steve had 50 percent and combined that made 100 percent. The reality was that Bill had 97 percent and Steve had only 3 percent. Bill was the one who controlled the industry by himself. But Steve could stare at him and talk as though they were equals! The absolutely incredible chutzpah!

Steve said that he wanted Microsoft to start writing programs that would work together with Rhapsody, the upcoming fusion of Next's software with Apple's.

"Steve, I really don't think it's good policy for Microsoft to bet on products that aren't there yet," Bill said.

"You made a bet on me before and it turned out well," Steve quickly shot back.

After the meeting, Bill talked privately with Heidi, who was his old friend. Bill was in awe of Steve's magnetism and the effect that it had even on him.

"This guy is so amazing," Bill said. "He's a master at selling."

■   ■   ■

WITHIN WEEKS, Steve began executing what clearly had been his plan all along: he shrewdly manipulated the media in an attempt to discredit Gil Amelio and to promote himself as Apple's would-be savior. He turned to his most loyal and

242

The
Second
Coming
of
Steve
Jobs

reliable supporter in the press, *Fortune*'s Silicon Valley correspondent, Brent Schlender. Brent was known for his coziness with techno-moguls like Bill Gates, Andy Grove, Scott McNealy, and especially Steve. The moguls gave him an insider's access, and he almost always responded by serving as their advocate and unofficial mouthpiece. To some, it seemed to be a slightly unsavory relationship, but business journalism was a highly competitive field, and *Fortune* needed the techno-titans on its cover the way that *People* needed Princess Diana.

In late February, Brent published a long article titled "Something's Rotten in Cupertino." He wrote that Gil's inexperience in the personal computer business helped explain "why the company's products and marketing efforts still seem so chaotic." He faulted Gil for "dithering" and for making "vague public pronouncements." He asserted that Steve had a plan that could turn around Apple, that Steve was seriously considering a takeover, and that Steve's billionaire friend Larry Ellison would help him raise the money.

Steve himself couldn't have written a more eloquent manifesto for a coup.

■　　■　　■

IN MARCH the Jobs family went to the big island of Hawaii for a week of vacation at Kona Village, where the guest rooms were huts with no phones or televisions. The resort was favored by couples who wanted to lay idly on the beach while their children were taken away for the whole day and kept busy with hikes and contests. Laurene looked beautiful in a bathing suit with a sarong draped around her long legs. Steve had just turned forty-two, and when he exchanged his black shirt for bathing trunks he showed a bit of a middle-aged bulge. He was no longer a heartthrob to teenage girls. His hair was thinning, he was starting to go bald on top, and he wore glasses, but he was still a handsome man.

The other vacationers were very social, engaging each other in long chats and exchanging copies of novels. Steve and Laurene kept to themselves, though they ran into Lisa MacKenzie, a former Pixar executive. She was alarmed when she saw how the Jobses made it hard for Reed to fit in with the other kids. Reed won the children's fishing contest, but Steve wouldn't let him accept the award, which was a bunch of nickel candy. Reed could only eat healthy food. As an alternative prize, Steve took Reed to the resort's gift shop and bought him something for $10. The other kids thought the scene was weird.

Reed could order fruit smoothies from the bar but no candy, no ice cream. For the entire week, Lisa kept thinking how much she wanted to slip a Tootsie Roll to the boy.

Steve enforced a strict diet for Reed, but in other ways he was an indulgent parent. When they went together on a sail-boat for a whale-watching trip, Reed was scared by the rough water. Steve asked the captain to turn around and return them to the resort. The captain refused, noting that there were several other paying passengers and that the waters would calm down. Steve proceeded to call for a rescue boat to come out and get them.

Steve was accustomed to being the captain of his own ship. He only knew how to lead, not how to follow.

■   ■   ■

LATER THAT MONTH, March 1997, Larry Ellison confirmed to the *San Jose Mercury News* that he was thinking

244
The
Second
Coming
of
Steve
Jobs

of making a hostile bid for Apple and then giving the company to Steve to run. But Larry wasn't sure. He asked the paper's readers to send e-mail to him if they supported the idea.

Larry's public posturing was bizarre. If you really want to take over a company, you don't broadcast your intentions, which drives up the stock price and makes the deal more expensive. And you don't indulge in Hamlet-like indecision in front of the media.

Even more embarrassing, the e-mail address that Larry gave out didn't work. He said to use saveapple@oracle.com, but Oracle's software could only accept addresses with a maximum of eight characters before the @ sign. So he had to change it to savapple@oracle.com. Larry was supposed to be some kind of technical genius, but he didn't know one of the simplest facts about his own company's internal computer systems.

Larry didn't need to finance a takeover because Steve was maneuvering so effectively toward a palace coup. The crucial blow came when Apple announced that it lost $708 million in the first three months of 1997. The company had lost a total of $1.6 billion in the first year and a quarter of Gil Amelio's tenure as chief executive. Gil had to go. The Macworld scene and the press coverage had shown that there was great enthusiasm for Steve. And the board of directors needed something dramatic to lift the stock price.

On July 9, the board ousted Gil.

Steve thrust himself into the power vacuum and quickly took control. He purged the board of members who had watched ineffectually during Apple's long decline. Then he installed three of his own loyalists, including Larry.

There was turmoil and uncertainty among the thousands of Apple employees as Steve seized power, since no one knew what he was going to do, not even Steve himself. "Steve didn't have a plan at all," recalls Heidi Roizen.

Nonetheless, Wall Street's analysts were thrilled by the coup. Investors quickly bid up Apple's stock from $13 a share to $20. But many of the industry's leading figures remained skeptical. Michael Dell, the highflyer of computer makers, said that if he were running Apple, he would "shut it down and give the money back to the shareholders."

Steve was offended by the flippant remark, and he sent e-mail to the rival mogul. "CEOs are supposed to have class," he wrote. "I can see that isn't an opinion you hold."

246
The
Second
Coming
of
Steve
Jobs

■   ■   ■

THE SUMMER 1997 Macworld convention in Boston was scheduled for early August, only a month after Steve installed himself as Apple's untitled but de facto leader. He called a meeting for a Saturday morning with the team of a half-dozen people who were producing the event.

"OK, I think you know who I am," he said as he entered the room. "Who are you and what can you do for me?"

They went around the table. One man said he was an outside consultant who ran trade shows, and he had staged Apple's last big conference for its software developers.

"That was the worst thing I've seen in my life!" Steve exclaimed. "We don't need your services. It's nothing personal. I'm sorry you had to come in on a Saturday, but we don't need you." The man left.

Two hours into the meeting, Steve paused dramatically.

"What I'm going to say now can't leave this room," he said. "If it does, I'll fire you. So look around and see if you can trust the other people. If not, leave now."

They all stayed.

Steve revealed his news: Microsoft was investing $150 million in Apple and promising to continue writing software for the Macintosh for at least five years. And Bill Gates would probably come to Boston in person to share the stage for the announcement.

■   ■   ■

APPLE'S DECLARING A TRUCE with Microsoft was trivial and unnecessary, as if Monaco proclaimed that it wouldn't attack France. Microsoft had long ago conquered almost all the territory and Bill Gates was happy to give Apple a separate peace. Microsoft had been making good money by selling software for Apple's machines for two decades and it had no reason to stop.

The announcement wasn't very significant, but August is the slowest season for news, and Steve and Bill were two of the best-known personalities in American business. Steve offered *Time* the exclusive behind-the-scenes story. Meanwhile, Steve's admirers at *Newsweek*, Katie Hafner and Steven Levy, kept trying to schedule a meeting with Steve during Macworld. Steve promised them a special interview, but they later discovered that a *Time* reporter was following Steve everywhere: the airplane, the hotel, backstage.

Newsweek's editor, Maynard Parker, was furious when he found out.

"How did this happen?" he demanded.

"Steve was up to his usual tricks," Katie Hafner recalls. Steve had tried to give out multiple "exclusives" a decade earlier, during the Next debut. He hadn't changed at all.

Time rewarded Steve by picturing him solo on its cover.

Newsweek also put the story on the cover, but it exacted revenge against Steve by running Bill's photo instead.

What clinched the cover placements was an unexpected but memorable tableau of the two moguls. The bizarre scene came about because Bill didn't want to fly to Boston, so he decided to address the convention via a live video feed instead. His image was projected on a huge screen at the auditorium, and it dwarfed the life-sized figure of Steve.

248
The
Second
Coming
of
Steve
Jobs

The symbolism was simple and compelling: Steve, the counterculture iconoclast, finally being co-opted by Bill, the ominous Orwellian Big Brother. The audience booed and jeered at Bill's image, and Steve scolded them as if they were unruly schoolchildren.

Many of the Apple cultists felt betrayed, but Wall Street's investors were reassured by Bill's display of support. That day, Apple's stock rose 33 percent to $23 a share.

■   ■   ■

ON SEPTEMBER 16, 1997, Steve announced that he would serve as the "interim CEO." He moved into a conspicuously small office, close to the boardroom. He inherited Gil's secretary, Vicki, and told her that he didn't like the pens that Apple kept in stock. He would only write with a certain type of Pilot pen, which he proclaimed was "the best."

He took to walking around the Apple campus barefoot in cutoff shorts and a black shirt. One day he accosted Jim Oliver, a Wharton Ph.D. who had been Gil's assistant.

"What do you do here?" Steve demanded.

"I'm wrapping things up."

"You mean that in a while you won't have a job?" Steve shot back. "Well, good, because I need someone to do some grunt work."

What a strange way to motivate people, Jim thought. Then again, it was a chance to work for a legendary figure.

It turned out that the "grunt work" would give Jim a close-up view of Steve's deliberations about how to save Apple. The job was to take notes at the meetings where Steve would review every part of the company and decide what to keep and what to kill.

The gatherings were held in the boardroom, which was in the only high-rise office building on the low-slung campus. It had a panoramic view of the expanse of Silicon Valley. Steve would call in the head of a product team and all of its key players. Anywhere from a dozen people to three dozen would crowd around the long wooden table. They had to show Steve all of their existing products and expound in detail about their future plans. If they made physical products, like monitors, they had to bring models of their upcoming lines. If they wrote software, they had to run Steve through the features of their programs.

Steve's attitude wasn't confrontational. He wanted to absorb a vast amount of information before he took action. Still, there was always an undercurrent of tension, and Steve would occasionally upbraid people if they didn't seem to realize the urgency of the situation. Gil had made extensive cuts, but Steve was going to cut a lot more. Steve said that he would keep only the great products and the profitable products. If something was unprofitable but strategic, its managers would have to argue for its continued existence.

During the first review meeting with a group, Steve would listen and absorb. In the second meeting, he would ask a series of difficult and provocative questions. "If you had to cut half your products, what would you do?" he would ask. He would also take a positive tack: "If money were no object, what would you do?"

The series of group meetings helped Steve to get to know

hundreds of people at Apple. And once he knew the players, he would deal with them directly. He had total disregard for the hierarchical chain of command. He would remember what several hundred people did and call on whomever he needed, always bypassing their managers. It was as though everyone in the company reported directly to Steve himself. "Steve has the ability to buffer so much in his head," Jim Oliver explains. "He can remember the last conversation and the last e-mail exchange that he had with three hundred people."

250

The
Second
Coming
of
Steve
Jobs

He put especially intense pressure on the top executives. He tormented Heidi Roizen with constant calls to her office phone, home phone, cell phone, and pager, starting at 7 A.M. almost every day. She was so unnerved by his interrogations and his frequent tirades that she decided the only way to preserve her mental health was to ignore his calls. She tried to communicate with him only by e-mail, which enabled her to consider the issues calmly and rationally, unaffected by the irresistible force of his compelling live presence.

Heidi talked with Bill Campbell, whom Steve had named to Apple's board of directors. Bill was a bona fide tough guy, a former college football coach, but he confessed that he, too, was unnerved by Steve's constant phone calls.

"Do what I do," she advised him. "Don't answer the phone."

"That's what my wife said. I tried that. But then Steve would come over to my house. He lives only three blocks away."

"Don't answer the door."

"I tried that. But my dog sees him and goes berserk."

■   ■   ■

IN HIS FIRST MONTH as interim CEO, Steve began walking around the office carrying a sleekly curved piece of white foam.

It was the model for the size and shape of a computer, which would eventually become known as the iMac, for "internet Macintosh." It was the creation of Jonathan Ive, who was thirty and looked more like a scruffy bicycle messenger or skateboarder than the chief designer at a major manufacturer of consumer products.

While the physical look of the iMac had been conceived before Steve took over, everything else about the computer was still uncertain. Steve's thinking was strongly influenced by his friendship with Larry Ellison as well as their unspoken rivalry. Larry believed the future belonged to stripped-down machines, called network computers, or NCs, that would connect to the Internet and cost only half as much as PCs. He had even started his own company, Network Computer Inc., to try to cash in on the idea.

Steve decided that the iMac would be a network computer with a retail price of $799. "We're going to beat Ellison at his own game," he told his Apple colleagues, who were surprised to see Steve secretly delighting in the competition with his best friend.

■ ■ ■

In September, Steve began taking decisive action. Gil had cut the number of research and development projects from 350 to 50. Steve cut it from 50 to about 10. Instead of hoping for some stunning technical breakthrough that would save the company, Steve looked instead at improving Apple's advertising and restoring its cool hip image. He invited three ad agencies to pitch for Apple's business, including Chiat/Day, which had created the famous "1984" television commercial during Steve's first run at Apple.

Chiat/Day still had the same creative director from the

"1984" campaign, Lee Clough, who came to Cupertino and proposed a new slogan: "Think Different."

That's not grammatical, thought Jim Oliver as he sat there taking notes for Steve. But no one in the room had the guts to say so.

Lee Clough said that the comeback of Harley-Davidson motorcycles was a good model for Apple to emulate. Harley's advertising convinced people that they could feel its renegade spirit even if they were investment bankers rather than Hell's Angels. It rehabilitated a counterculture icon for the baby boomers who had grown up and sold out.

That's exactly what Apple needed to do.

252

The
Second
Coming
of
Steve
Jobs

■   ■   ■

APPLE'S NEW advertising campaign came together quickly.

Steve had always liked photos of cultural icons. At his first house in Los Gatos, near his mattress, he had kept pictures of Albert Einstein and an Eastern mystical guru. Steve also loved black-and-white photography. He hung Ansel Adams prints at the Palo Alto house. Those were the elements: the slogan, the icons, the monochrome tableaux.

The first outsider to see the new ads was *Newsweek*'s Katie Hafner. She arrived at Apple's headquarters at ten on a Friday morning for an interview with Steve. He kept her waiting a long time. Finally he emerged. His chin was covered by stubble. He was exhausted from having stayed up all night editing footage for the "Think Different" television spot. The creative directors at Chiat/Day would send him video clips over a satellite connection, and he would say yes or no. Now the montage was finally complete.

Steve sat with Katie and they watched the commercial.

Steve was crying.

"That's what I love about him," Katie recalls. "It wasn't trumped-up. Steve was genuinely moved by that stupid ad."

■   ■   ■

ON SEPTEMBER 30, 1997, Steve assembled Apple's employees for an outdoor party—with beer and strictly vegetarian cuisine—to celebrate the new campaign.

He explained that Apple's ads were going to convey an image and an attitude rather than simply describing a product. As a model, he talked about how Nike's ads projected a sense of athleticism and success without even showing its shoes.

"Apple spends a hundred million dollars a year on advertising," Steve said, "and it hasn't done us much good." They were going to continue spending $100 million a year, but now they were going to spend it better, he said, because now they realized that the Apple brand was one of the most valuable things they had going for them.

One of the employees in the audience was a young woman named Kate Adams. It was the first time she had seen Steve speak close up, and she was very excited. "It was a good—no, great—speech, delivered in a 'I might sound like I'm musing but I'm damned sure of what I'm saying' tone," she wrote in an e-mail message to a friend.

Her friend turned out to be a software entrepreneur, Dave Winer, who wrote DaveNet, a column that he e-mailed to hundreds of the most influential people in the industry, including CEOs like Bill Gates and Michael Dell. To Kate's surprise, Dave published her e-mail in its entirety: a long, detailed account of Steve's talk.

The next day, Kate received a voice-mail message.

"Hi, this is Steve Jobs. I'd like to get together and chat with you."

Steve's voice sounded cheerful. What did he want? Was this some management theory of his, calling random mid-level employees and picking their brains for a while? Or was he pissed off by the DaveNet column?

254

The
Second
Coming
of
Steve
Jobs

Kate called Steve's secretary and made an appointment. She didn't sleep well that night. The next morning at ten she entered Steve's office. He was in the corner, typing on his Next computer. Steve relied on three computers, and none of them was a Macintosh. He had black Next machines at his home and office and a Toshiba Tecra as his notebook.

With his back turned away from her, Steve waved and told her to sit down.

Kate eyed a pile of "Think Different" T-shirts as she waited for four minutes.

Steve turned to her.

"Hi, how ya doing?" he said amiably. Then he held up a printout of her message. "Can you tell me what this is?"

Steve had "sniffing" software that could screen and search his employees' e-mail.

"I was encouraged by your talk, and I just wanted to tell my friend Dave."

"You realize this is the kind of thing that can be published?" he asked.

"Well, it already has," she said.

"Do you realize this hundred-million-dollar figure is proprietary?" he continued. His tone was serious and confrontational but not outright hostile.

As she was walking out, he said:

"By the way, what do you do in the QuickTime group?"

"I'm on the engineering team," she said.

"OK."

She escaped. She knew that if she had said "marketing," she would have been fired. Steve still needed Apple's engineers, but he had no respect for its marketing people.

■   ■   ■

BEFORE STEVE'S TAKEOVER, Apple people loved to leak. They did so partly because the company really did have lackluster marketing. If you were proud of your work, the only way to let other people in the industry know about it was to leak it yourself. A number of websites, like Mac OS Rumors, were devoted exclusively to Apple gossip.

Steve insisted on his old "loose lips sink ships" policy. At first the employees were incensed. Before long, though, they began to trust Steve to do Apple's marketing for them.

Still, the Apple rank and file remained fearful of the Bad Steve persona. Word got around about Steve going into meetings, saying "this is shit" and firing people on the spot. People worried about getting trapped with him in an elevator for a few seconds, afraid that they might not have a job when the doors opened. The reality was that Steve's summary executions were rare, but a handful of victims is enough to terrorize a whole company.

For a while there was an elevator in Steve's building that had protective coverings on its walls because construction was going on, and someone said: "This must be Steve's elevator since it's padded." Another employee responded: "Is it for him or for us?"

Apple needed some kind of shake-up. It was filled with people who had virtually ignored and ultimately outlasted three CEOs as they did their own things. "I don't know if the previous CEOs at Apple had *any* effect on that company," says John Warnock of Adobe, which is Apple's biggest software provider. "We would have meetings with all those CEOs and *nothing* would happen, no traction, unless the group responsible went for the idea. The energy just dissipated into the organization, where the first person capable to make a decision is the one who makes it. But with Steve, he comes in with a very strong will and you sign up or get out of the way. You have to run Apple that way—very direct, very forceful. You can't do it casually. When Steve attacks a problem, he attacks it with a vengeance. I think he mellowed during the Next years and he's not so mellow anymore."

256
The
Second
Coming
of
Steve
Jobs

Before Steve's takeover, the campus had a leisurely atmosphere. Staffers loved to hang around smoking and chatting in the courtyard of the R&D complex, which always had ashtrays stocked at the outside and inside doors of all six of its buildings. Some employees seemed to spend most of their time throwing Frisbees to their dogs on the lawns.

Steve enforced new rules. He decreed that there would be no smoking anywhere on the Apple property. Then he banned dogs on campus, ostensibly because canines were messy and some people were allergic to them.

The employees were outraged: why didn't Steve understand them? Smoking in the courtyard was how they networked with their colleagues from other departments. It was a vital form of communication! Steve's prohibitionism forced them to take long walks to De Anza Boulevard so they would be off the Apple property. It wasted a lot of time.

And their dogs were essential to productivity, too. A lot of people worked very long hours at Apple, even nights and weekends. They were hardly ever home. If they couldn't care for and feed their dogs at the office, they would *never* get to see the pets.

It seemed as though Steve were pushing his own lifestyle on ten thousand others. At a company meeting, someone asked Steve what he thought was the worst thing about Apple.

"The cafeteria," Steve said.

Steve proceeded to replace the entire food-service staff. He hired the chef from Il Fornaio in Palo Alto. Before long, tofu was prominent in the menu offerings.

And yet, somehow, the reign of terror was beginning to work. Apple had long been like a civil-service bureaucracy, with thousands of entrenched employees who did pretty much whatever they wanted regardless of which political appointees were temporarily at the top. Now that was changing. People started to realize that Steve could assert his authority over seemingly any aspect of the company's life. Apple was going to follow the vision of a single person, from the no-smoking rules and the healthy cuisine to the editing of the TV advertisements. Steve was clearly in charge, and Steve was seemingly everywhere. He was trying to be something of a strict parent to Apple, which was like a bunch of bright teenagers who had gone for years without adult supervision.

■   ■   ■

STEVE'S MANIACAL FOCUS and micromanagement made it harder for him to devote time to his own family. His neighbors in Palo Alto would pass by his house on their nocturnal jogs, and almost every night they would glance at his window and see him staring at his computer, writing e-mail.

He was proud of his daughter Lisa, who had graduated from the public high school in Palo Alto. She sang well and she wrote folk songs, like the family's friend Joan Baez. She had been one of the editors of the superb school newspaper, where she worked closely with Ben Hewlett, the grandson of Bill Hewlett, the legendary cofounder of Hewlett-Packard and one of Steve's role models. The paper took on controversial topics, such as gay and lesbian issues, and it won a national award for an investigative piece questioning several hundred dollars of meal expenses charged by staffers of the school district.

258
The
Second
Coming
of
Steve
Jobs

In the summer of 1997, when she was between her first and second terms at Harvard, Lisa performed as a singer at a charity benefit for the Electronic Frontier Foundation (EFF), a libertarian activist group that lobbied to prevent censorship on the Internet. Since a good number of Silicon Valley's capitalists were aging liberal baby boomers who grew up with rock music and still played in garage bands, the EFF decided to put on its own amateur concert. It rented the Fillmore Auditorium in San Francisco, the famous venue where Jimi Hendrix, Janis Joplin, and the Grateful Dead had all performed.

Lisa took the stage. She bore a close resemblance to her father. She had his nose, his eyes, his mouth, his bone structure, his thin brown arched eyebrows, his hint of Middle Eastern ancestry. Her hair—straight and fine like his, but blond—fell to just below her shoulders, and she wore a sleeveless black top that accentuated her slenderness.

She leaned into the microphone and launched into Tracy Chapman's "Talkin' 'Bout a Revolution," a billionaire's daughter singing an anthem of working-class revolt.

The crowd broke into whispered conversations. Most of the people in the audience were around the same age as Steve Jobs, and only now were they starting their families. It was hard for them to accept that they were old enough for Steve to have a teenage daughter.

As Lisa sang, her father stood inconspicuously in the very

back of the auditorium, holding his baby Erin Sienna, who was turning two years old.

■   ■   ■

REED PAUL JOBS was six, and he was enrolled in Nueva, a remarkable private school. A who's who of Silicon Valley players sent their children there. Steve's involvement as a concerned parent put him in close contact with many of the people he had worked and fought with over the course of his career. Bud Tribble and Susan Barnes sent their kids to Nueva, and they would run into Steve at the school's science fairs. Andy Cunningham's daughter was in Reed's class, and Andy herself was on the school board. Bill Atkinson, one of the software wizards behind the Macintosh, was a Nueva parent as well. So was Jef Raskin, the visionary who started the Macintosh project and ran it for several years before Steve took it over and their egos inevitably clashed. Raskin's kids stood out because their names were palindromes, spelled the same backwards as forwards: Asa, Aviva.

Nueva appealed to wealthy, brilliant parents who wanted their children to have richly intellectual lives. The school was housed in a 1930s Italian Renaissance style mansion that had been built by the heir of a railroad tycoon. It was set atop Skyline Boulevard with panoramic views of San Francisco Bay and Silicon Valley. The enrollment was small, only three hundred students in grades one through eight, and the teachers and curriculum were exceptional. Steve Smuin, who ran the seventh and eighth grades, was considered by many students to be the best teacher they had ever encountered. He even taught Japanese to his thirteen-year-old pupils and took them on a field trip to Japan. But in 1997, he became the center of a controversy that bitterly divided the school's community and served as a test of the values and personalities of the Nueva parents, including especially Steve Jobs.

Soon after graduating from eighth grade, the last grade in the school, a former student sent an anonymous e-mail to all of the Nueva parents and teachers. The student accused Steve Smuin of pushing and shoving him and verbally abusing him.

The charges outraged many of the parents, but Steve Jobs defended the teacher, whom he had long admired. Their affinity wasn't surprising. Steve Smuin was like the Steve Jobs of teachers. Both men were undeniably brilliant but had a temperamental edge.

The school board moved to oust Smuin. Steve Jobs argued forcefully with the board members. He found himself joined in the cause by his old bitter rival, Jef Raskin. The two men enjoyed being on the same side, and they renewed their lost friendship.

When Smuin was ultimately ousted by Nueva, he founded his own middle school, Odyssey, in a nearby town. Steve Jobs provided funding for the new academy, and he removed Reed from Nueva and enrolled the second grader in public school in Palo Alto.

■   ■   ■

LAURENE JOBS began spending less time on her natural-foods business, and before long she and her partner would shut it down. She often worked out at the gym or took dance classes in the middle of the day, and she remained remarkably fit and attractive. She would prepare dinner for Steve, whose favorite dish was a salad of shredded raw carrots without dressing. Rupert Murdoch visited them in Palo Alto, and

260

The
Second
Coming
of
Steve
Jobs

he later joked to one of his lieutenants: "Having dinner at Steve Jobs's house is fine as long as you leave early enough so there are still restaurants open." President Clinton came over for dinner, too. Steve and Laurene slept in the Lincoln Bedroom and attended a state dinner for China's president Jiang Zemin at the White House, where they saw Clinton supporters such as Steven Spielberg, David Geffen, and Harvey Weinstein.

Steve enjoyed hobnobbing with celebrities and attending glamorous events and appearing once again on magazine covers, but he kept a sense of simplicity and tasteful restraint in his private life. He retained the spacious Woodside property as a place to hold Reed's birthday parties, but his family continued living in the relatively modest house in Palo Alto. Their neighborhood became fashionable and extraordinarily expensive as it was discovered by young multimillionaires from the Internet boom. And Steve Young, the famous quarterback from the San Francisco 49ers, lived two doors away from the Jobses.

Some of the neighbors refused to let their teenage daughters baby-sit for the Jobs children, since they thought that Steve's wealth and celebrity made the family a potential target for kidnappers or crazed fans. Still, Steve had no security and he almost always left the front door unlocked. What the neighbors did approve of was his beautiful garden, which they thought was the most beautiful in Old Palo Alto. He paid $1 million to buy the cottage next door and tear it down so he could expand his garden, where he grew some of his own vegetables and herbs.

Many of Steve's old friends, loyal or estranged, lived within a few blocks of the Jobs house: Andy Hertzfeld, the Macintosh's original software designer, lived next door to his best friend, Burrell Smith, the Mac's hardware designer, who lived next door to Tina Redse, who had married and had two children and separated from her husband.

Steve's relationship with Andy Hertzfeld was like a bizarre soap opera. Steve liked Andy and had great respect for his creative and technical abilities. In the late 1980s, Andy had started going out with a woman named Joyce. Steve didn't think that Joyce was good enough for Andy. He told Andy so, and he even tried to set up Andy with another woman.

262

The
Second
Coming
of
Steve
Jobs

Joyce was enraged by the episode. Andy felt so guilty that he continued supporting Joyce financially even after they broke up. He gave her around $250,000 worth of stock in his new company, General Magic.

In 1997, Andy became engaged to marry Linda Stone, a brilliant executive at Microsoft and a close friend of John Lasseter, who was trying to recruit her to Pixar.

Linda loved Andy, but she told him that he had to stop supporting his ex. Joyce wasn't the only one in Andy's care. Andy also provided financial support to two of *Steve's* ex-girlfriends, Tina and Chris-Ann. "It's Andy's 'Aid to Dependent Women' program, his harem of Steve's exes," says one of Andy's friends. "He feels powerful when he's supporting these women." Andy also served as a kind of big brother to Burrell Smith, who had become more lucid now that he was taking medication for his manic depression.

Linda broke off the engagement, and Andy married Joyce instead.

Now that Steve was interim CEO of Apple, he wanted to hire Andy again. Andy was fascinated by the drama around Steve. When they had worked together in the 1980s, Andy had felt a sense of exhilaration. He believed that Steve had inspired him to accomplish more than he otherwise could have, even though Steve sometimes humiliated him as well.

Now Steve was trying to lure Andy back to Apple, but Joyce wouldn't allow it.

Steve talked about the tangled situation when he ran into one of Andy's friends at a wedding. "It's too bad that Andy has fucked up," Steve said.

■   ■   ■

Apple

As the Christmas season arrived, Good Steve played Santa while Bad Steve acted like the Grinch. As a present to the staffers of Pixar, Good Steve wanted to throw a big party, but Pixar's earlier celebrations were hard to top, especially the Halloween bashes with killer costumes that the artists labored over. Steve announced his "Holiday Waltz," a formal dinner-dance with old-world élan. He held ballroom dancing lessons in the weeks before the event. He rented the main hall of the ornate Sheraton Palace Hotel in San Francisco. He hired musicians from the San Francisco Symphony Orchestra and provided a lavish spread of food.

Steve liked playing the role of Good Steve, but there was something about his best friend Larry Ellison that brought out the Bad Steve, as if they were mischievous boys trying to impress each other. As the two moguls were socializing on December 23, they came up with a practical joke to play on an utterly naive and innocent person, though the joke would ultimately make the newspapers and hurt their own reputations.

Their victim was Michael Murdock, a small-time computer consultant in the valley. Michael had worked for six years on Pixar's technical support staff, where he was the resident Mac expert and fix-it guy. He had never gone to college but he had loved Apple's computers since he was a teenager, and he knew *everything* about Macs. He lived in an apartment complex that looked like a motel and he still had posters of sports cars and pin up models on the walls even though he was in his mid-thirties. His living room was filled with stereo equipment and weight-lifting apparatus, and he kept an authentic *Star Wars* light saber prop on his shelf. He was the epitome of the loyal and passion-ate Apple customer.

Michael Murdock read that Apple was looking for a new CEO, since Steve Jobs was supposedly serving only as the in-terim CEO. So Michael sent e-mail to Steve saying that he was interested in the position. He sent messages to many of Apple's luminaries setting forth his ideas for saving the company. The *San Jose Mercury News* wrote about his quest, and famous peo-ple began offering him encouragement. While shopping at Fry's Electronics he ran into Jean-Louis Gassée, the former Apple executive, who said some kind words to him. He sent e-mail to Apple's cofounder Steve Wozniak, who invited him to lunch. They drove around Los Gatos in Woz's Hummer and went out for hamburgers.

Woz's support made Michael very happy. He didn't really believe that he would become Apple's CEO, but he thought that people were taking his ideas seriously.

On December 8, Steve Jobs sent him an e-mail:

"Mike, Please go away. Steve."

Michael respected Steve's wishes and stopped plying him with suggestions. But then, two weeks later, Michael received an e-mail from Apple board member Larry Ellison.

"OK. You can have the job. Larry."

A few minutes later he received an e-mail from Steve Jobs: "Yep, Mike, it's all yours. When can you start? Steve."

"Wow!! Really??? Cool!" Michael replied to the two men. He added: "I think we should announce this to the papers right away. That way, they will now [*sic*] that you are serious and not just trying to dampen somebody's Christmas spirit." He asked for an $80,000 salary and a high-speed T-3 Internet connection to his apartment, then concluded: "I can start on Monday . . . Merry Christmas to you and yours."

Steve responded: "Please do not come to Apple. You will be asked to leave, and if you don't, you will be arrested."

Michael sent copies of the messages to the media, which seized upon the story. "APPLE CHIEF EXECUTIVE JOB IS NO JOKING MATTER" ran the headline in the *San Francisco Chronicle*. "How do billionaires have fun?" the story began. "What does it say about two big shots like Jobs and Ellison that they would have wasted the time . . . plotting together like teenagers to torment a naive soul?"

Longtime Pixar executive Pam Kerwin had known Michael during his years there. She said that when she heard that Steve and Larry had played a prank on the poor guy, she thought: "it must have been a slow day on Mount Olympus. It was right out of Greek mythology. Steve and Larry couldn't find it in themselves to believe that this guy was sincere. No one could believe that someone could be that earnest and naive. But Michael is one hundred percent genuine. The sad thing is that he never got that the press was making fun of him. He was so innocent of that. It's unfortunate the Steve didn't react to him with greater sensitivity. Mike is the kind of Apple religious zealot who *made* the company. He was just totally passionate about it. Mike was emotionally committed to Apple, and it was only because Steve brought that same brand of dedication to Apple that people were able to trust him and let him advance his program. If people didn't love and blindly respect Apple and Steve Jobs, as Michael Murdock did, it wouldn't have happened. That's why Sculley and Amelio couldn't do it."

■   ■   ■

On January 6, 1998, Steve went to San Francisco for his keynote address at Macworld. He stalked onto the stage in a leather jacket and blue jeans, then he tore off the jacket and handed it to an assistant. It seemed as though he had just rode up on a motorcycle. Actually, the effect was calculated for theatrical value. Backstage before the speech, he had to take off the jacket to be wired for sound, then he had to put it on again.

266

The
Second
Coming
of
Steve
Jobs

Steve was the best showman in American business, and he worked hard at his art, preparing maniacally for weeks before an appearance. He got ready for a keynote much the way that the playwright Oscar Wilde had prepped for a dinner party: he spent countless hours rehearsing the succinct lines that he would throw off as if they were improvisations.

Steve delivered his ninety-minute address to the audience of four thousand Apple fans. Then he began to walk offstage, but after a few steps he suddenly stopped and turned to the crowd.

"I almost forgot," he said casually. "We're profitable."

Apple had made a $45 million profit in the previous quarter, thanks to Steve's cost cutting and the unexpectedly strong sales of its expensive new G3 computers.

It was big news, and he had saved it for the end, as though it were an afterthought.

■   ■   ■

While the Macworld appearance got Steve back in the newspapers, it called attention to the fact that he had immersed himself at Apple for six months but still refused to accept the title of CEO. He paid himself only $1 in salary as interim CEO, and he didn't own a single share of Apple stock.

The board of directors prodded Steve to commit formally to the company, which would be reassuring to Wall Street. The board tried to entice him with princely sums: first it offered him 5 percent of Apple's stock, then 8 percent, or about $270 million.

Steve simply wouldn't declare himself CEO. Even his old friends were puzzled by his motivation. Regardless of what he told the press, his obligations to Pixar took little time, and his family would have to cope with his renewed workaholism whether he was the supposedly interim chief or the admittedly permanent one.

Whatever his title, his leadership seemed to be working. On April 15 he announced a second consecutive quarterly profit, $55 million. Apple's stock had nearly doubled in 1998, from $15 a share to almost $30. The Apple board told the press that Steve could stay on as interim CEO for as long as he wanted. It wasn't looking for anyone else.

■   ■   ■

THE iMAC, Steve's biggest coup and the clincher to the turnaround, was still to come.

Steve had abandoned his original idea of the iMac as a stripped-down network computer when he saw that Larry Ellison, Sun, and IBM had all failed to popularize their own NCs. The Internet was booming, as people logged on from their offices and homes and popularized sites like Yahoo and Amazon.com. But even though a cheap stripped-down NC was all that people really needed to browse the Web, consumers still wanted full-fledged PCs, which had hard drives so they could access their files without always having to go online. And PC prices had fallen so dramatically—partially as a preemptive response to the perceived NC threat—that the NCs had failed.

As he shifted his plans, Steve nonetheless kept the concept of a relatively inexpensive sleekly shaped machine with the computer and monitor combined in a single casing, a so-called all-in-one design.

Steve acted purely on gut instincts with the iMac. All the research by other manufacturers said that consumers wouldn't buy all-in-one computers. "Steve said, 'I know what I want and I know what they want,'" recalls Steve's friend Mike Slade, the former Next marketing executive, who had become a consultant to Apple.

The *i* in iMac was shrewd but misleading. The machine wasn't an Internet computer any more or less than the Intel-Microsoft PCs (or other Macs, for that matter). The typical users of home computers had no trouble plugging phone lines into their modems, finding the America Online icons that popped up on the screens of their new PC monitors, and dialing in and signing up for Internet access. Steve was trying to capitalize on the buzz and the exploding popularity of the Net more through slick "positioning" than by product design.

Steve unveiled the iMac on May 6, 1998, in the auditorium of a junior college near Apple, the same site where he had held the Macintosh's premiere fourteen years earlier. The symbolism was clear: the iMac's one-piece design harkened back to the original 1984 Mac. The new machine, with its translucent curved plastic case and bright blue coloring, incited a frenzy of media coverage. Consumers put in 150,000 orders even before the computer went on sale on June 15. Apple sold 278,000 iMacs by the end of July. It was a breathtaking debut.

Steve's old Next colleague, Todd Rulon-Miller, telephoned and congratulated him.

268
The
Second
Coming
of
Steve
Jobs

Steve was silent on the other end of the line, which Todd took as a signal that Steve was enjoying the praise and wanted it to continue for a while.

"What's your goal?" Todd asked.

"To match Compaq's ship rate," Steve said. Compaq was the No. 1 manufacturer of personal computers, and it sold several times as many as Apple did.

Steve wasn't complacent with his saving a struggling company.

He wanted to be No. 1.

■   ■   ■

THAT MONTH, Laurene gave birth to Eve, Steve's fourth child.

When Steve's career was at a low only four years earlier, he spent more of his time at home with his family and he seemed to mellow somewhat and to become humbler and more mature. Now that he was at another professional high, even the arrival of a new baby couldn't temper his egomania at work and his profane, abusive treatment of his employees.

Jeff Cooke had a sense of excitement when Steve recruited him away from a fifteen-year career at Hewlett-Packard to become Apple's vice president of customer service and support. Jeff had used Apples since he was a college student in the late 1970s and had long admired Steve's accomplishments. When a headhunter called and promised an interview with Steve, Jeff thought that at the very least it was a chance to meet a legendary figure.

Steve showed up for the interview in shorts and sandals. He hadn't shaved in several days. Stains from a fruit smoothie were streaked over the belly of his black shirt. But no matter how slovenly he looked, Steve was charismatic and engaging as soon as he began describing his vision for the future of the personal computer. He said that the PC was only just at the beginning of the impact it could have on society, but to get the rest of the world to use it, the machines had to be cute and pleasant and as easy to use as a toaster.

Jeff was excited by Steve's talk and the idea of working together with the great man. He interviewed with the other members of Apple's executive team, who all seemed confident and enthusiastic. And Apple offered the chance to make a lot of money in a very short time, mainly from stock awards and bonuses tied to achieving certain milestones.

Jeff took the job.

From his first week at Apple, the shocks began. At HP, Jeff had been used to coming up with his own ideas and running with them. At Apple, he found that Steve had to approve every decision. Nothing could be done without Steve's green light. Steve wanted to be the one who came up with the plans, and he wanted the others to be implementers.

At Jeff's first meeting with his team, Steve walked into the room and said: "Everybody in service and support is fucking brain dead."

Jeff was taken aback but he thought to himself: this guy is a genius, he must know what he's doing, so just watch.

Steve went into a tirade about how Apple's service and support was the laughingstock of the industry. "It's up to you to prove me wrong," he said. Then he slammed the door and left.

"I don't know about you, but I found that highly motivating," said one of the managers with a tone of heavy irony.

Jeff had trouble reconciling Steve's bullying and intimidation on the job with the image of the charming "perfect gentleman" that Steve had presented in the job interview.

At another meeting of Jeff's department, Steve walked into

270

The
Second
Coming
of
Steve
Jobs

the room and danced around, waving his arms in the air pompously in an imitation of Gil Amelio.

"I have arrived, I am Gil, and I am fat!" Steve said.

It was a funny display, implying a lighthearted tone for the meeting, Jeff thought.

Then all of a sudden Steve went to the head of the table and said: "Service in this company is all fucked up and the people running it are all brain dead."

The managers in the room instantly became timid.

Jeff went ahead and outlined his three-month plan for change.

"Jeff, that might be the way you did it at HP," Steve said. "But I'm not a three-month guy, I'm an overnight guy."

Steve wanted to cut off abruptly Apple's relationship with one of its suppliers. Jeff was opposed to the idea, saying that it would risk a lawsuit and tie up Apple's inventory.

Steve wasn't afraid of a lawsuit.

"Call them and say fuck 'em," he instructed.

Jeff had fifteen years' experience in his field, and he wasn't afraid to argue his position with Steve. But Jeff's self-confidence only made Steve become more abusive and profane.

As Jeff left the room, he thought: Steve must have said "fuck" at least forty-seven times.

"Just fuck 'em" became one of Steve's favorite lines.

When he had taken over, he had inherited a program called SOS Apple, which let people sign a contract for unlimited customer support over the telephone for a lifetime. It was a bad financial move for Apple. Steve said to shut it down.

What about the customers who have a contractual obligation? Jeff asked.

"Just fuck 'em," Steve said.

The Federal Trade Commission sued Apple over the issue. Apple lost.

Jeff Cooke resigned in late October, after only four months on the job. He decided that he couldn't abide being entirely deferential to Steve and not being allowed to come up with his own ideas. Still, he believed that Steve was a "phenomenal leader," and that Apple's turnaround was due to Steve's vision and Steve's ability to rally people around a clear, focused set of objectives. "Steve can do that better than anyone I've ever seen," he says. The catch was that Steve's implementers needed to be selflessly subservient.

"I call it trading a little bit of your soul for a lot of money," Jeff Cooke says.

272
The
Second
Coming
of
Steve
Jobs

■   ■   ■

IN OCTOBER 1998, the Apple turnaround was clinched. Steve announced a third consecutive quarterly profit, $105 million. Apple's stock price had tripled since he took over. *Vanity Fair* promoted him from No. 32 to No. 14 on its annual "New Establishment" ranking of the fifty leaders of the information age, just behind the Hollywood power broker David Geffen. The two moguls were friends. David had recently been living in Steve's apartment in the San Remo on Central Park West while waiting for his own Fifth Avenue residence to be remodeled. Steve could empathize with David's plight: he had spent $15 million on the I. M. Pei redesign of his Manhattan co-op, and the construction phase had taken five years.

Steve's coziness with David Geffen came at a time when Steve was publicly at odds with David's business partner Jeffrey Katzenberg and their studio, DreamWorks. Pixar was slated to debut its second feature film, *A Bug's Life*, at Thanksgiving, but Jeffrey had rushed his production of *Antz* to get it into theaters a month earlier. Steve accused Jeffrey of copying Pixar's idea for an animated movie about ants, which Jeffrey might have been exposed to while he was still at Disney.

As he had with *Toy Story*, Steve held his own screening of *A Bug's Life* for his Silicon Valley friends and misleadingly called it a premiere. He threw the event at the Flint Center, the same place where he had unveiled the Macintosh and the iMac. The black-tie reception was held in a huge tent in the parking lot, with waiters serving sushi as well as vegetarian and Thai food. Pixar set up a velvet rope at the front and recruited people to pretend to be autograph hounds and fawn over the computer guys as if they were movie stars. Steve stood near the entrance, personally greeting his guests as they arrived. His old friend Bob Metcalfe pulled up in a limousine with Katrina Heron, the editor in chief of *Wired*. Alvy Ray Smith showed up. Since his long feud with Steve, Alvy had become a research fellow at Microsoft in Seattle. "When you're finished with that 'sabbatical' up there, come back to Pixar," Steve told him. Yeah, right, Alvy thought.

Louise Kehoe from the *Financial Times* spotted Larry Ellison. "Larry was looking miserable as sin because he wasn't the star of the evening," she recalls.

Larry finally latched on to Steve and Laurene and tried to remain in their little circle, but Steve managed to throw off Larry so he could continue to circulate among his guests.

■　　■　　■

A Bug's Life won the bug-movie wars. It earned $163 million in U.S. box-office receipts compared to $91 million for DreamWorks's *Antz*. By the summer of 1999, *Bug's* eclipsed even *Toy Story* as it became one of the five top-grossing animated films ever.

Business Week ran a cover story with the headline "Steve

Jobs, Movie Mogul," which elicited a few raised eyebrows in Hollywood. "Up in Silicon Valley or from Steve's point of view, he's a movie mogul," says a successful film producer who has worked in the technology business as well. "Down here, he's a guy who made a couple of movies."

The Hollywood types knew that while Steve's photo appeared on the magazine covers, John Lasseter was the overwhelming creative force at Pixar. "Everything that goes through Pixar has to have John's seal of approval," says Pam Kerwin. John signed off on every commercial, every THX trailer, even the details of the attraction at Disney's theme park in Florida, where the characters Flik and Hopper sing "It's Tough to Be a Bug."

"John *is* the Pixar asset," says Pam. "Everything there revolves on executing his creative vision."

Although John was as much of an autocrat at Pixar as Steve was at Apple, John's style of dictatorship was far more benevolent. John struggled with the extraordinary demands on his time, and he could lose his temper occasionally and be abrupt with people, but mostly he was a very nurturing and positive manager. He was very physically supportive of his people, giving them hugs and pats on the back to make them feel good. John was something of an overgrown boy, but he was also a sympathetic father figure. He was raising his five children, all boys, at his quirky house in the Sonoma wine country, which had an eight-foot-tall statue of Woody, the cowboy doll from *Toy Story*.

John realized that Pixar's future would ultimately be bigger than himself. He needed to cultivate other directors with their own creative visions and unique styles. He gave more autonomy to talented artists such as Andrew Stanton. He gave Jan Pinkava the freedom to direct *Geri's Game*, which won the Oscar for best animated short. But the ultimate responsibility for Pixar's artistic direction depended on John.

274
The
Second
Coming
of
Steve
Jobs

John was overweight, so Pixar hired a personal chef and a personal trainer for him at the office. He was too vital for the company to tolerate any risk to his health.

■　　■　　■

IN 1999 THE NEW YEAR began, as always, with Macworld. In his keynote speech, Steve Jobs unveiled the four new "fruit-flavored" colors for the iMac. He also showed off a new latch so it would be easier to open up the computer and get at the circuitry inside.

The crowd loved it. Steve was a rock star to them.

Bill Gates obtained a videotape of Steve's speech and watched it on his VCR. He was astonished by how Steve could excite an audience of thousands of people with such seemingly trivial pieces of news. What was such a big deal, Bill thought. Colors? A latch?

■　　■　　■

APPLE'S PUBLIC RELATIONS people kept tirelessly promoting the idea that middle age and family had made Steve nicer, mellower, and more mature. It was a shrewd effort to cover up that Steve was becoming more and more insufferable as he exulted in his renewed fame.

One time Steve called Ed Zander, the No. 2 executive at Sun Microsystems, who was taking over the day-to-day responsibilities for running the company.

"I want to see you right away," Steve said.

"I have stuff on my calendar," Ed said.

"No, it has to be right away," Steve insisted.

Steve walked into Ed's office and screamed at him for forty-five minutes about how Sun was "all fucked up."

"I see this is the new mellow Steve," Ed said.

Steve laughed and ended his tirade.

■   ■   ■

276

The
Second
Coming
of
Steve
Jobs

AS THE MEDIA renewed its hero-worshiping adulation of Steve, he responded by subjecting journalists to some of his worst abuse. *New York Times* reporter John Markoff waited for three hours in the Pixar conference room before someone informed him that Steve wasn't going to show up for their interview appointment.

In Steve's role as interim CEO of Apple, he would only give a fifteen-minute interview to each beat reporter every three months, usually right after one of his public speeches to thousands of people. Onstage Steve would be utterly charming and charismatic. But only moments later, backstage, Steve would usually be in a foul mood with the press.

Steve would see the reporters in the order of the perceived importance of their publications. Although the *Times* always got to go first, John Markoff chafed at being limited to fifteen minutes. *The Wall Street Journal* would come next, then down the line.

Steve treated the reporters as if they were his captive audience rather than his interrogators. He would spend the entire fifteen minutes pitching his latest product. The journalists were forewarned not to ask about anything else, or Steve might shut them off. Personal questions were strictly forbidden. When an MSNBC correspondent dared to ask why Steve persisted in calling himself the interim CEO, Steve stormed out of the room.

Jon Swartz, who covered Apple for the *San Francisco Chronicle*, felt that he would occasionally get a fleeting insight into Steve's mind, as if a venetian blind were opening for an instant and then closing shut. One of those moments came when Steve said his great passion was to make movies that would be loved for many decades, like Disney's *Fantasia*, rather than making a computer that would only be good for a year or two.

Mostly, though, the fifteen-minute interviews were incredibly frustrating. Once, Jon Swartz asked whether Pixar would limit itself to making G-rated films. Steve treated him to a sanctimonious diatribe. He even impugned Jon's own parenting skills. Would Jon let his kids see an R-rated movie?

"Steve is the most difficult of all the CEOs, the scariest and most intimidating to interview," Jon says. "You feel uneasy, as if you're transported into a Shakespearean scene but you don't know what your role is. A lot of us who cover him just want to break through once, or to say, 'I'm tired of your bullshit.' "

■   ■   ■

IN THE SUMMER OF 1999, TNT aired the debut of *Pirates of Silicon Valley*, a made-for-cable movie about the early careers of Steve Jobs and Bill Gates. Steve was played by Noah Wyle, who was well known for his role on NBC's *ER*.

Over the years, Steve's friends had speculated about who would play him in the movie version of his life. Ralph Guggenheim, the producer of *Toy Story*, had told Steve that he thought Tom Cruise would be perfect for the role. Steve was pleased with the notion, since he thought that Tom Cruise was very handsome. Ralph didn't say that another reason for casting Cruise was the star's talent for creating characters who were charismatic but dangerously narcissistic.

Cruise was too expensive for a TV movie, but Noah Wyle was perfect. The actor looked very much like the young Steve, and it was uncanny how he captured Steve's mannerisms.

Louise Kehoe from the *Financial Times* watched the movie along with her teenage daughter as *Pirates* portrayed scenes of Steve in his hippie mode from the 1970s.

"Why was Steve trying to be a hippie?" Louise's daughter asked her. "Wasn't he too late to be a hippie?"

She was right. Steve had been several years out of sync with the flower-child generation. By the time Steve was a teenager, his idol Bob Dylan was already old news. By the time Steve tried LSD, suburban housewives were reading *The Electric Kool-Aid Acid Test*. Steve lagged the zeitgeist because he was always trying to act as if he were older than he was. He emulated the tastes and interests of the kids who were a few years ahead of him.

Steve caught up quickly, and by the late 1970s he had become a cultural leader, a member of the vanguard, the creator of trends that would take off in the following years. He latched onto computers and made them cool. He latched onto business and helped make it cool. Steve's high-profile success in the late 1970s, a decade that wasn't known for entrepreneurship or business heroes, helped prepare the culture for the celebrity CEOs of the 1980s, like Lee Iacocca and Donald Trump and the Wall Street masters of the universe.

For about a decade, from 1985 to 1995, he fell out of sync again. As he grew accustomed to his wealth and developed the tastes of an elitist, he lost touch with the mass culture. He had little in common with the average consumer, other than his blue jeans. Everything in his house in Palo Alto was understated, muted, and austere: a few black-and-white photos,

278

The
Second
Coming
of
Steve
Jobs

some handmade wooden furniture in the Craftsman style, a $100,000 stereo, a Persian rug. Steve's old friends and colleagues had trouble envisioning a bright colorful plastic iMac along with the rest of his home.

But Steve *had* given the world the iMac. He had once again made a machine that the masses would love and could afford. He had sold two million iMacs in only twelve months. And he had quintupled Apple's stock price in two years.

In September 1999, Apple's stock reached an all-time high of $73 a share, eclipsing the previous high of $68 that was set during John Sculley's reign in 1991.

Steve Jobs had finally achieved his vindication.

6
being Steve

he proof was in the numbers: Apple's all-time-high stock price confirmed Steve's power in Silicon Valley, and then the extraordinary box-office results for Pixar's *Toy Story 2* showed undeniably that he had become a Hollywood impresario of the first rank.

284
The
Second
Coming
of
Steve
Jobs

Toy Story 2 was an astonishment: a sequel that many critics and fans thought was even better than the beloved original. It opened in November 1999, and it opened huge. It grossed $80.8 million in its first five days, breaking the Thanksgiving weekend record that had been set the year before by Pixar with *A Bug's Life*. It was the fourth-biggest opening weekend ever, surpassed only by the debuts of *Star Wars Episode I: The Phantom Menace* (at $105.6 million), *Jurassic Park* ($90.2 million), and *Independence Day* ($85 million). That put Steve Jobs in the rarefied company of George Lucas and Steven Spielberg, and it wasn't a fluke. He had delivered massive hits three times in a row. He was one of the very few movie producers who could be counted on for a huge score every year, a surefire blockbuster that would guarantee the success of the crucial summer or holiday seasons for a major studio.

Although Hollywood's insiders hadn't respected him after the first *Toy Story*, wary that he might be a one-time wonder, now his remarkable triple play forced them to recognize him as a powerful and lasting force in their clubby business. "The guy has made his bones," in the words of a studio executive. The prince of Silicon Valley had become one of the new princes of the San Fernando Valley. He had even showed up the old prince, Jeffrey Katzenberg, whose animated features for DreamWorks were being overshadowed by Pixar's productions. Jeffrey's *Prince of Egypt* earned less in its entire U.S. run than *Toy Story 2* took in during two weeks.

When Steve and Jeffrey first met a decade earlier, Jeffrey had asserted haughtily, "I own animation and nobody's going to get it," and he threatened to "blow the balls off" of anyone who dared to try. But Jeffrey didn't own it anymore. Steve had seized the lead in box-office clout, critical acclaim, creative artistry, and technological wizardry.

What were Steve's ultimate ambitions in Hollywood?

He hinted enticingly about his long-term strategy when he addressed Pixar's annual shareholders meeting in 1999. As he took the stage of the auditorium in San Francisco's Museum of Modern Art, he faced an audience that ranged from Wall Street stock analysts to small-time investors who had brought along their young children, hoping to get a sneak preview of the characters and scenes from future Pixar films. Steve wore a black mock turtleneck but even the dark color couldn't hide that he had a bit of a protruding tummy. His stubbly beard was graying, and his straight black hair was thinning noticeably. When he leaned forward to talk with someone in the front row, the audience could glimpse a small bald spot. At an Apple convention in front of thousands of people, he was Fidel Castro. At the Pixar meeting, in front of a couple of hundred, he was a legendary figure seen at life size.

But his ambitions were truly grand. He explained that Disney was his model, and that the "heart" of the entire Disney entertainment conglomerate was feature animation. Disney sold half the videos in the world, he said, and animation was the driver. Animation was vital to the success of Disney's theme parks, its Broadway musicals, its consumer products. It was the engine of the empire. And it was incredibly lucrative. An animated movie that did $200 million at the box office would bring in total revenues of $800 million with all the extras, and half of that sum, $400 million, was *profit*. Disney's feature animation operation was worth $10 billion, Steve said, maybe even more. That's what he wanted. He was going to create another money machine of that awesome scale and scope, another Disney. He told his shareholders: "We're trying to build a second one of these."

He left the explicit implications of his scenario largely unspoken. It was a between-the-lines message, but it was very clear: Disney was worth $10 billion. Pixar's market value had hovered for a long time around $2 billion. When Pixar became the next Disney, it too would be worth $10 billion. The shares were going to quintuple as Steve fulfilled his plan. That might mean Pixar theme parks, Pixar retail stores, Pixar live onstage. The movies were just the start, the foundation for a much larger empire, coming soon.

For some of Steve's fans, it wasn't soon enough. Gossip had spread on the Internet that Pixar and Apple were going to merge with Disney, and that Steve would take over as Michael Eisner's successor. At the Pixar shareholders meeting, someone asked Steve about this speculation, but Steve shrugged it off.

"There's no truth to the rumor that we're about to make a hostile takeover of Disney," he said with bemusement.

That much was true. Steve wasn't going to run the old Disney. He wanted Pixar to be the *new* Disney.

286
The
Second
Coming
of
Steve
Jobs

■   ■   ■

HIS PIXAR SHARES remained the sole source of Steve's wealth. By turning down the board's repeated offers of large blocks of Apple stock, Steve Jobs had forfeited a paper profit of upward of $1 billion. He still worked at Apple for $1 a year, saying that he only took that dollar so his family would qualify for the company's health plan. His old friends said that Steve was intent on making a statement, showing that he was saving Apple because of love, not money.

Steve had gone without a salary many times in the past. He hadn't taken one at Next for the first five years, until he married Laurene and bought the Palo Alto house and she insisted that they have more cash. His pay at Pixar had ranged from zero to $50 a year. He always made his money as an owner, not an employee. At Pixar and Next he had tried to keep as much stock as possible for himself. At Apple, he still didn't have more than a single share. He was one of the few megalomaniacal moguls who ever considered himself rich enough.

One billion was sufficient for him—or was it? In January 2000, when he finally accepted the title of Apple CEO, he also accepted two gifts from the board of directors: a Gulfstream V private jet, worth at least $40 million, and options on ten million shares of Apple stock, which were worth hundreds of millions of dollars. Why, after spending so much time making a symbolic gesture, did he ruin it all with such a reversal?

In other ways, too, he began to take on the trappings of corporate power and privilege. He fell back on an old bad habit from his first run at Apple, leaving his Mercedes in the handicap spots in the parking lot, which led one employee to put a sign on the car: PARK DIFFERENT. He moved from his conspicuously small office at Apple to a larger and more impressive executive office, which he had made fun of when it was built by Gil Amelio. He asked for approval from the city of Point Richmond to build a heliport near Pixar's headquarters. This way he could fly from Pixar to his hometown of Palo Alto in a few minutes. He could fly right over the Bay Bridge rather than having to fight the traffic on its surface. News of the heliport made the local newspapers, and many readers were appalled by Steve's baronial perk. When Steve went shopping for organic produce at the Whole Foods Market in Palo Alto, one of the checkout girls criticized him for the helipad, and he stood there, arguing with her while some of his old friends and neighbors watched.

From 1985 to 1995 he had felt alienated from the clubby atmosphere of the Silicon Valley establishment, but now he started to socialize more with the other techno-moguls. In 1998, Scott McNealy was talking about Steve with one of Steve's former executives. Scott said that he liked Steve and that "we're good friends but not get-drunk get-buck-naked friends." But Scott tried to get a little closer to Steve. The following year, he planned a camping trip with Steve and Steve's software executive, Avie Tevanian. The three men were all bringing along their young sons. Reed Paul Jobs could play with Maverick McNealy. Scott confessed privately that he wasn't much of a camper but he always liked the opportunity to drink a lot of beer with his male buddies.

288

The
Second
Coming
of
Steve
Jobs

Steve Jobs began socializing more with business leaders from outside of the valley, too. He attended investment banker Herb Allen's annual Fourth of July mogul-fest in Sun Valley, Idaho, where he hobnobbed with famous names like Oprah Winfrey, Paul Allen, Barry Diller, Jeff Bezos, Steve Case, Warren Buffett, and Katharine Graham. At the event he also rubbed shoulders with Michael Dell, who ate his words about how Steve should have closed down Apple. These days the rival mogul was saying publicly that Apple's iMac was a "wake-up" call to the rest of the industry about the value of design and ease of use.

In its October 1999 issue *Vanity Fair* promoted Steve from No. 14 on its "New Establishment" power list to a lofty No. 7, ranking him above many CEOs from companies that were much larger than Apple, such as Disney's Michael Eisner, IBM's Louis Gerstner, and Intel's Andy Grove. Steve had what *Vanity Fair*'s editor Graydon Carter liked to call the "X factor," a charisma and buzz and fascination that was an invaluable asset for a mogul. Despite the high ranking, Steve was outraged by one paragraph in the *Vanity Fair* article, which read: "Jobs, 44, who is well known for his intolerance of 'bozos' (i.e. people who aren't nearly as smart as he is), signaled his dismay at one meeting by pouring a glass of water over the head of an employee. And during a job interview with a young woman, he was wearing loose-fitting shorts and no underwear, which didn't stop him from uncrossing his legs and nonchalantly flashing the unsuspecting applicant."

Steve was incensed when he read the passage (which was written by the author of this book). It exacerbated his resentment of the media. Later that week in September 1999, his public relations people brought him into a conference room to meet with an accomplished journalist. Their deal was that the forty-five-minute interview would be taped and transcribed and then appear verbatim as the cover story for *Wired* magazine. The journalist was a rabid admirer of Apple, and he was trying to provide a friendly forum for Steve's ideas.

Steve stormed into the room and looked uncomfortable from the first minute.

The reporter began by asking an easy question that had been fed to him by the Apple p.r. people. Steve answered grudgingly, then began to berate the journalist.

"At forty-four, if you could go back and give advice to your twenty-five-year-old self, what would you say?" the reporter asked.

"Not to deal with stupid interviews," Steve said in a nasty tone. "I have no time for this philosophical bullshit. I'm a very busy person."

The reporter was shocked and intimidated. "My questions weren't even close to hostile," he recalls. "They were softball questions. But Steve was radiating complete hostility. He was completely rude and demeaning to someone who was trying to give him a platform so he could look brilliant. I was crying afterwards—not in front of him, thankfully. He's got some heavy magic. He can look at you in a way that's completely devastating and withering and totally steals away your self-confidence. Everything I said only made it worse. It was like looking at a python in a cage. I've interviewed junkie rock stars who were better interviews. Imagine what he'd be like if he hadn't studied Zen."

The magazine killed the story.

Apple had become a nearly ubiquitous advertiser in glossy

national magazines. Steve Jobs made the ad-buying decisions himself, and no one wanted to alienate him.

■   ■   ■

290
The
Second
Coming
of
Steve
Jobs

STEVE DIDN'T HESITATE to humiliate people, because he had gotten away with it for so long. One particularly awful episode came when the public relations firm that handled the Next account, Niehaus Ryan Wong, sent executives to pitch Steve for the Pixar account. Steve took an active role in Pixar's p.r., which often angered the people at Disney, who thought that Steve was more interested in promoting himself than promoting the movies.

Steve sat at the table, rocking back and forth, laying out his predictions for just how well *A Bug's Life* was going to do at the box office. Then, before letting the p.r. people make their pitch about their skills and expertise, he told them they didn't have a chance.

"I don't think you guys can do this," he said.

The senior people were cautious and remained silent, but the most junior member of the team, a woman who was just out of college, spoke up in their defense.

"Nothing you say means anything to me," Steve responded. "Why do you keep opening your mouth?"

Steve yelled at the young woman until she had tears running down her cheeks.

Afterward, he gave them the account.

■   ■   ■

STEVE'S EXECUTIVES knew that there were only two ways to deal with him: either submit entirely to his will or have the intelligence and courage to survive his brutal confrontations. "Steve tests you, challenges you, frightens you," explains Todd Rulon-Miller, who worked closely with Steve for six years. "He uses this as a tactic to get to the truth. Behind the profanity, it's his way of asking: 'Do you believe what you're saying?' If you wither or blather, you're lost. I thought those were character-building moments for me."

Even Steve's old friends could never be entirely comfortable around him. "Steve is Steve for these reasons," says Heidi Roizen. "You're never really 'in' with Steve. At any moment you can say something that he thinks is stupid and you'll be relegated to bozo status. He believes everyone is expendable. But very few people write off Steve forever. He's such an engaging person that no matter how much he steps on you, you'll come back. He's the most charismatic person I've ever met, and I've had the good fortune of knowing a number of famous people. He has *it*. I kind of feel the same way about Steve as I feel about chocolate. It's bad for me but I really like it so I try to keep it out of the house. I love being around Steve because he's the center of the universe—only it's *his* universe."

Heidi has maintained friendships with both Steve Jobs and Bill Gates since the early 1980s. Today, if the phone rings and it's Bill, she's not nervous at all. If Heidi has a problem, she knows that she can call Bill. If she's in Seattle, she'll visit Bill and his wife, Melinda. "Bill thinks of me as a friend, but with Steve you have this feeling that you are being judged," she says. "Steve is not a person you can be comfortable with. Steve can say things that make the hair stand on the back of my neck, things that make me shake, like 'Let me explain this to you very slowly.' If other people said that to me, I'd laugh."

Heidi believes that Steve's view of the world has a clear hierarchy. Steve himself is at the top. Then there's Larry Ellison, who's almost like Steve. Then there are Steve's top executives at Apple, Avie Tevanian for software and Jon Rubinstein for hardware, brilliant guys who have remained intensely loyal to Steve for more than a decade. Then there's a thin layer of reasonably smart people, such as Heidi herself. Then, at the bottom, there are great masses of bozos, who make up the vast majority of the population.

The irony about Steve Jobs is that he strives obsessively to make products for the masses but he is often mean-spirited when one of the little people dares to engage him in a conversation about his work or his products. Steve's handlers at his public appearances say that while Steve is masterful onstage in front of thousands of fans, he is uncomfortable face-to-face with single fans and he hates signing autographs. When a Next salesman tried to talk with Steve at a Next sales conference in Santa Cruz, Steve kept interrupting the man mid-sentence and repeating, "You don't know whereof you speak." Even as Next was struggling, Steve dared humiliate a loyal salesman in front of his peers.

No-name ordinary people never get much of a chance with Steve, but even the most brilliant and accomplished people have trouble getting along with him for more than a few years. "Quite honestly, no one is Steve's friend," says Guy Kawasaki, who did two stints as an Apple executive and has had careers as a successful author and entrepreneur. "Either you are useful to him or not. Steve isn't immoral, he's amoral. He doesn't know that what he's doing is wrong. He calls you a bozo but not because he wants to hurt you."

"It's hard being his friend," says Bob Metcalfe, who has done so for twenty-two years. "He's pissed off the rest of the world. He burns a lot of people and they can't understand. And when you're with him he's so opinionated and expressive. My rule is not to let myself be persuaded by Steve when we're together. Steve can win any argument, even when he's wrong, be-

292
The
Second
Coming
of
Steve
Jobs

cause you can't assemble the facts quickly enough. Steve pisses people off because he can bully them intellectually and he doesn't suffer fools gladly. He will not go along with the gang. He's not really a team player. He's persuasive even when it's not in his interest to be so."

Steve is oddly intolerant even with other powerful people. In the late 1990s, Steve and Laurene invited Bob Metcalfe to picnic with them at a Joan Baez benefit concert in a park. When Bob took out his roast-beef sandwich, Steve glared and lectured him about eating meat.

Steve is maddening and demanding as a friend, but he can be intensely loyal in certain cases. He kept up his support for old college friend Elizabeth Holmes even when she spent a few years in a Marin County commune that turned into a pernicious religious cult. When Elizabeth was matched with another cult member in an arranged marriage, Steve was the only one of her friends from the outside world who accepted the invitation and attended her wedding.

Steve expected his friends to be intensely loyal to him. When the Next cofounders began to quit on him in the early 1990s, it was like "breaking a covenant of trust," recalls Susan Barnes. Steve would only let them back into his world if he wanted or needed something from them. Not surprisingly, Steve came to the end of the 1990s with few longtime friends. He was still in contact occasionally with Bill Fernandez, his best buddy from his high school years, who had moved to Tucson and become a freelance website designer. Bill was touched when Steve said that Bill was the person who had known him the longest now that both of Steve's adoptive parents had died. Steve also said that Bill was his model for how to be a father. Bill was proud of his role as a parent, but he was surprised by the comment, since Steve never bothered to ask Bill for advice about parenting, except for one time when

Steve asked about protecting kids from the dangers of light sockets.

Steve's friends realized that much of his charm came from his flattery, but Steve was so deft that they usually fell for it anyway. In the late 1990s, when Steve was trying to renew his friendship with Jef Raskin following many years of estrangement, Steve knew the right strings to pull. He said that he always thought of Jef as an all-around smart guy, not just someone who was smart about computer interfaces. Jef was astonished. That was exactly how Jef liked to think of himself. Steve had sensed the perfect way to appeal to Jef's egotism.

"He's a supreme flatterer," says Jef.

The approach that Steve took with both Bill and Jef was what psychologists called "pacing and leading," and it was a well-known ploy that was taught to the people who needed to exert control or influence over others, from car salesmen to cult recruiters. Whether consciously or not, Steve Jobs had assimilated almost all of the classic psychological techniques for personal manipulation and coercion and used them to maintain his power. His *modus operandi* was almost out of a pysch textbook: First, you have to make the other people "regress" to a childlike state of helplessness. This can be done by berating, intimidating, disorienting, and confusing them. Then, once their self-confidence is destroyed and they become infantilized, they need a strong parent figure to provide guidance. Later they tend to attribute their achievements to the leadership of this parental authority.

Steve's approach had some intriguing similarities to the style of Werner Erhard, the guru who founded est (for Erhard Seminars Training), which was very popular in Erhard's home base of the Bay Area when Steve was coming of age in the 1970s. Erhard's lectures attracted well-educated, driven high-achievers who were also highly insecure. Erhard prom-

294

The
Second
Coming
of
Steve
Jobs

ised enlightenment, but as soon as his pupils were locked away for marathon sessions in a windowless hotel ballroom, he subjected them to intense verbal abuse, saying that they were all "assholes" and often making them cry and shake hysterically. When they emerged from the "training," they often claimed that it had greatly improved their self-confidence and gave them the determination to take control over their lives.

It's hardly an exaggeration to say that working at Steve Jobs's companies was like attending an est seminar. The brutally long hours that employees spent in windowless cubicles had the same effect as the time that Erhard's trainees spent in the windowless hotel ballrooms. It disoriented and physically exhausted them, inducing the state of childlike regression and making them more susceptible to their verbally abusive and domineering leader.

There's no evidence that Steve Jobs ever participated in est, but he did take part in kindred strands of the 1970s human-potential movement, such as primal scream therapy. Steve was a careful student of Zen, which Werner Erhard acknowledged as his greatest influence, and Steve had youthful experience as the follower of charismatic leaders, from his Zen guru Kobin Chino to the head of the All-One Farm commune, Robert Friedland. It wouldn't have been hard for him to learn the classic tools of manipulation and influence.

The cultlike aspects of Apple and Next were commonly discussed through the 1980s and 1990s. Steve's former employees would joke that "when you meet Steve Jobs, he'll make you drink the Kool-Aid," alluding to the massacre in Guyana of the People's Temple followers by the San Francisco demagogue Jim Jones.

Steve wasn't really a cult leader, but he did have a rare ability to influence. "Steve pulls strings I don't even know I have, like my *mother* does," says Heidi Roizen. "And he affects so many people this way—making you want to please him. It's very captivating."

■   ■   ■

296

The
Second
Coming
of
Steve
Jobs

WATCHING AND STUDYING Steve Jobs has been a favorite pastime in Silicon Valley for a quarter century, and there are many opinions and theories about what makes up this icon's mesmerizing, if frustrating, personality:

He alternates suddenly between being charming and horrible, like a child. One of the longest-running and most perceptive Steve-watchers in the media is Louise Kehoe from the *Financial Times.* Before she interviewed him for the first time, in the early 1980s, she heard of his reputation for being difficult to deal with. The tough reporter went into the meeting determined not to let him bully her around. But Steve seemed to sense her attitude and responded by acting like a courtly gentleman. He insisted on getting her drink himself, even though he had assistants waiting nearby. "He was totally disarming," she recalls. "He can read how you're feeling about him and he's very clever about countering it. He just read me like a book and it was so annoying."

Not long after, she watched as Steve berated one of his marketing executives right in front of her.

She believes that Steve's outbursts of verbal abuse are spontaneous rather than calculated. "I think it's infantile. A two-year-old can be utterly charming and utterly infantile. At ages two and thirteen, a child switches abruptly from being wonderful to being horrible, and Steve is like that. He has the same psychological development issues as a child. He does make you 'love' him and then he turns around and slaps you in the face."

He has an amazing ability to change his mind. Heidi Roizen wondered for a long time whether Steve was a pathological liar, someone who just couldn't prevent himself from dissembling. But then she determined that Steve wasn't really a liar at all. He could say X one day and Not-X the next day, and each time he would genuinely, passionately believe what he was saying. That's why he could always speak with such conviction. "Steve's brain has an amazing ability to recraft things and put a different spin on them," she says.

He's the ultimate product of a media culture. Christopher Escher, the former head of Apple public relations, says: "Steve becomes a bucket for peoples' worldview, and people project on him things that help them explain the world. An icon is like a mirror. I think that Steve is the consummate media figure. The tropes, the patterns, and the implicit language of his career— freshness, young star, banishment, recovery, and renewal—are the tropes of the media. It's not that Steve understands the mass media zeitgeist: he *is* it. Steve Jobs, like Bill Clinton, is the *product* of a media culture. He has an endless supply of rebirths."

He's a great man so the rules don't apply. Steve's numerous apologists say that his temperamental and abusive behavior is justified because he's a visionary who accomplishes extraordinary things. "If you're going to change the world, you don't do it through conventional means," says Todd Rulon-Miller. In the case of the Apple turnaround, many observers agreed that the company needed a forceful leader to guide it through the crisis.

Still, a number of Steve's ex-colleagues and friends argued

that it's possible to become a great business leader without becoming a monster of a human being. "As a culture we richly value corporate success," says Dan Kottke, Steve's college friend. "The question is: How much of an asshole do you have to be to be highly successful?"

His tenacity is what makes him great. Several years after leaving Steve's employ, Susan Barnes conducted a study about family-run businesses. She found that the key to success was "pure staying power, persistence, continually believing in something, dogged stubbornness to get things done, and continual optimism." That was a good description of Steve Jobs. Steve was beaten down many times but "he kept getting off the mat," she says.

He is still emotionally insecure. A while after Heidi Roizen quit her job at Apple to spend time with her family and become an investor and adviser to startup companies, she bought a new Apple G3 computer and flat-screen monitor. She was very pleased with the beautiful machines, so she sent an e-mail message to Steve, congratulating him. Even though Steve had incredible demands on his time, he was so hungry for the praise that he wrote back to her within the hour.

He sacrifices personal commitments for his own ends. In the late 1980s, Steve agreed to let Doug Menuez, a well-regarded photojournalist, have complete behind-the-scenes access at Next and document the daily life of the company for a story in *Life* magazine. Doug put in an extraordinary effort, taking thousands of shots over a period of several years. Then Steve killed the story, despite his personal commitment to the photographer. Steve said he felt "overexposed" at the time and that he thought *Life* magazine "sucked." He *was* overexposed, and *Life*'s reputation *had* diminished somewhat over the years, but

298
The
Second
Coming
of
Steve
Jobs

it was nonetheless dishonorable to go back on his word to a man who had committed so much effort. The situation was typical of the "just fuck 'em" attitude that Steve articulated later at Apple. Everything he did had to be "the best," "the coolest," and personal relationships or even contractual commitments wouldn't get in his way.

He works best with resilient youngsters. Andy Cunningham still runs the large firm she founded, but she says that now, at age forty-two, she would no longer have the energy, patience, or stamina to work for Steve. "When you're young, you can be led around by the nose," she says. "When you're in your twenties, it's like 'I'm changing the world and this guy is showing me the way.' You can afford to be squashed and get back up a thousand times." Now that she's in her forties and has a family of her own, "life is too short for this shit."

In the late 1990s, Susan Barnes talked with an Apple employee and compared notes about working for Steve. He told her it was like climbing a glacier every day just to take out the trash. Steve made everything very difficult, but his people did wind up doing exceptional work.

He's a great enigma. A high-level Hollywood executive who has worked closely with Steve compares him to the unhappy mogul in *Citizen Kane:* "I hope there's a sled called Rosebud."

He's the ultimate mirror of Silicon Valley. Roger McNamee, a well-known investor and pundit whose garage band has performed with Steve's daughter Lisa, says: "In my mind he is the *defining* personality of Silicon Valley. The career of Steve Jobs has paralleled perfectly that of Silicon Valley."

In the 1970s and early 1980s Steve and the valley were enfants terribles, thumbing their noses at giants. But they both lost their momentum in the late 1980s, when the new powerhouses emerged from elsewhere: Microsoft in Seattle, Dell and Compaq in Texas. Then, in the late 1990s, Steve had his great resurgence with Apple, and northern California became the red-hot center of the technology stock boom.

300
The
Second
Coming
of
Steve
Jobs

■   ■   ■

STEVE JOBS is the essence of Silicon Valley, the encapsulation of all the good and all the bad. He exemplifies its famous greed and its simultaneous ambivalence about its great wealth. He is a sophisticated elitist who nonetheless yearns for the patronage of the masses. He is torn between trying to change the world and trying to sell computers as though they were sugared water. He alternates between the desire to advance the state of the art in technology and the need to promote a brand that had more to do with slick image-making and advertising than technology. He is a control freak and an egomaniac, but his greatest wealth and success comes from supporting the creative achievements of others. At his professional nadirs, he can act with humility. At his professional peaks, he is a fearsome tyrant. He is loved and hated, and often by the very same people. He is not without his sycophantic admirers or his scathing critics, but most people who know him and have worked with him believe he is a man of great contrasts and contradictions. The Bad Steve can be loathsome, but the Good Steve can be one of the most creative, inspiring, and charismatic of figures. Paradoxically, failure brings out his humanity and success exacerbates his megalomania. But the two Steves can't be separated. They live in the mind and spirit of one person, and each is partly responsible for his successes and his failures. Over the course of three decades, the times have changed, the culture has shifted, but Steve has stayed largely the same, connecting and separating from the zeitgeist every few years. And as the century begins, they are in perfect sync.

Acknowl-
edgments

The people who work in Silicon Valley and Hollywood, whether they are celebrated moguls or unsung employees, share two very strong and contradictory emotions: First, they feel an overwhelming urge to get out the truth, as they see it,

about their strange realms. Second, they suffer from a constant state of anxiety about offending powerful players whom they might have to deal with in the future, given that both businesses are organized as if they were floating crap games.

Understandably, many sources were helpful to me but didn't want to be mentioned in any way. They have my private appreciation. I would like to thank the following people for sharing their recollections, whether in multiple interviews of marathon duration or in briefer conversations: Kate Adams, Al Alcorn, Herbert Allen Sr., Stewart Alsop, Gil Amelio, Susan Barnes, Barbara Barza, Emily Brower, David Chadwick, Jeff Cooke, Cate T. Corcoran, Robert X. Cringely, Andrea Cunningham, Christopher Escher, Bill Fernandez, Jean-Louis Gassée, Angela Grady, Ralph Guggenheim, Katie Hafner, Elizabeth Holmes, Justin Jed, Steve Jurvetson, Guy Kawasaki, Sky Keaton, Louise Kehoe, Pam Kerwin, Daniel Kottke, John Landwehr, Dan Lavin, Karen Logsdon, Lisa MacKenzie, Roger McNamee, Jamis MacNiven, John Markoff, Scott McNealy, Bob Metcalfe, Michael Murdock, Mike Murray, Jim Oliver, Simone Otus, Nicole deMeo Overson, Sylvia Paul, Tony Perkins, Lisa Picarelle, Julie Pitta, Dan Port, Terry Press, Kamini Ramini, Jef Raskin, Garrett Rice, Heidi Roizen, Gina Rabattino, Dan Ruby, Todd Rulon-Miller, Michael Rutman, Karen Sipprell, Mike Slade, Alvy Ray Smith, Wendy Smith, Karen Steele, Linda Stone, Jon Swarz, Tony Swei, Larry Tesler, Allison Thomas, Bud Tribble, Paul Vais, John Warnock, David Wertheimer, Ann Winblad, Dave Winer.

Also, thanks to the many people who graciously aided me with leads, referrals, recommendations, or ideas, including Pam Alexander, Maria Amundson, Kurt Andersen, Suzanna Andrews, John Atcheson, Josh Baran, Andrew Beebe, Marc Benioff, Paul Bergevin, Jim Calhoun, Marc Canter, Tricia Chan, Raines Cowan, Fred Davis, Nick Donatello, Owen

304
The
Second
Coming
of
Steve
Jobs

Edwards, Rebecca Eisenberg, Cynthia Fox, Terry Garnett, Steve Gibson, Heather Gold, Gaby Grekin, Melody Haller, Peter Heinecke, Laurence Hooper, Abigail Johnson, Karen Katz, Roger Katz, Michele Kraus, Marivi Lerdo de Tejada, Caryn Marooney, Julie McHenry, Kate McNichols, Doug Menuez, Anne Nelson, Chris Nolan, Megan Smith, Rick Smolan, Cheray Unman, Peter Wayner.

Thanks to Mary Nelson for her very able research assistance, and to Cate T. Corcoran and Emily Brower for sharing their personal collections. And gratitude to the members of the Syndicate: Eric Ransdell, Shyamala Reddy, Ilan Greenberg, Andy Nelson, and Katharine Mieszkowski.

My appreciation to Graydon Carter and Matt Tyrnauer at *Vanity Fair* and Martin Beiser at *GQ* for their support and encouragement during the course of this project.

Most crucially, I can't overstate my debt to my agent, Suzanne Gluck at ICM, whom I view as some kind of personal savior, and to my editor, Suzanne Oaks, who conceived of this book and improved it immeasurably with her close attention and her abundance of smart ideas.

Index